fic

This book is part of a series produced in association with The Open University. While each book in the series is self-contained, there are also references to the other books. Readers should note that references to other books in the series appear in bold type. The list of other books in the series is:

Asia-Pacific in the New World Order, edited by Anthony McGrew and Christopher Brook

Culture and Society in the Asia-Pacific, edited by Richard Maidment and Colin Mackerras

Governance in the Asia-Pacific, edited by Richard Maidment, David Goldblatt and Jeremy Mitchell

The Asia-Pacific Profile, edited by Bernard Eccleston, Michael Dawson and Deborah McNamara

The books form part of the Open University course DD302 *Pacific Studies*. Details of this and other Open University courses can be obtained from the Call Centre, PO Box 724, The Open University, Milton Keynes MK7 6ZS, United Kingdom: tel. +44 (0)1908 653231, e-mail ces-gen@open.ac.uk

Alternatively, you may visit the Open University website at http://www.open.ac.uk where you can learn more about the wide range of courses and packs offered at all levels by The Open University.

For availability of other course components, contact Open University Worldwide Ltd, The Berrill Building, Walton Hall, Milton Keynes MK7 6AA, United Kingdom: tel. +44 (0)1908 858785; fax +44 (0)1908 858787; e-mail ouwenq@open.ac.uk; website http://www.ouw.co.uk.

Economic Dynamism in the Asia-Pacific:
The Growth of Integration and Competitiveness

Edited by Grahame Thompson

Routledge
Taylor & Francis Group

LONDON AND NEW YORK

First published 1998 by Routledge
11 New Fetter Lane, London EC4P 4EE

Simultaneously published in the USA and Canada
by Routledge
29 West 35th Street, New York, NY 10001

Transferred to Digital Printing 2004

Routledge is an imprint of the Taylor & Francis Group

© The Open University 1998. Reprinted in 2000, 2003 (twice)

Edited, designed and typeset by The Open University

Printed in the United Kingdom by Biddles Ltd. King's Lynn, Norfolk

British Library Cataloguing in Publication Data
A catalogue record for this book is available from The British Library

Library of Congress Cataloging in Publication Data
A catalogue record for this book has been requested

ISBN 0-415-17273-X (hbk)
ISBN 0-415-17274-8 (pbk)

1.4

1004197120 T
1004656290 T

CONTENTS

Series preface

The five volumes in this series are part of a new Open University course, *Pacific Studies*, which has been produced within the Faculty of Social Sciences. The appearance of *Pacific Studies* is due to the generous and enthusiastic support the course has received from the University and in particular from colleagues within the Faculty of Social Sciences. The support has been especially remarkable given that this course has ventured into relatively uncharted scholarly waters. The potential risks were readily apparent but the commitment always remained firm. I am very grateful.

There are too many people to thank individually, both within and outside of the Open University, but I must record my appreciation for some of them. Within the University, I would like to acknowledge my colleagues Anthony McGrew and Grahame Thompson. *Pacific Studies* could not have been made without them. Their role was central. They were present when the course was conceived and they lived with it through to the final stages. They also made the experience of making this course both very enjoyable and intellectually stimulating. Christopher Brook and Bernard Eccleston made an enormous contribution to the course far beyond their editorial roles in two of the books in the series. They read the successive drafts of all chapters with great care and their perceptive comments helped to improve these volumes considerably. David Goldblatt and Jeremy Mitchell, because of their other commitments, may have joined the Course Team relatively late in the production process, but their contributions, especially to *Governance in the Asia-Pacific* have been much appreciated. Michael Dawson played an especially important role in the production of *The Asia-Pacific Profile* and his calm and genial presence was valued as always. Jeremy Cooper and Eleanor Morris of the BBC were responsible for the excellent audio-visual component of *Pacific Studies*. Anne Carson, the Course Manager of *Pacific Studies*, was consistently cheerful and helpful. All of the volumes in this series have been greatly improved by the editorial craftsmanship of Stephen Clift, Tom Hunter and Kate Hunter, who have been under great pressure throughout the production of this course, but nevertheless delivered work of real quality. The striking cover designs of Richard Hoyle and Jonathan Davies speak for themselves and the artwork of Ray Munns in all five volumes has been most impressive. Paul Smith, whose recent retirement from the University will leave a very real gap, made his usual remarkable contribution in providing unusual and interesting illustrations. Giles Clark of the Copublishing Department was a constant source of encouragement and in addition his advice was always acute. Our colleagues in Project Control, especially Deborah Bywater, and in the Operations Division of the University, were far more understanding and helpful than I had any right to expect. Anne Hunt and Mary Dicker, who have been responsible for so much of the work in this Faculty over the past several years, performed to their usual exacting standards by preparing the manuscripts in this series for publication with remarkable speed and accuracy. They were very ably assisted by Chris Meeks and Doreen Pendlebury.

Pacific Studies could not have been made without the help of academic colleagues based in the UK as well as in the Asia-Pacific region. This series of books has drawn on their scholarship and their expertise but above all on their generosity. I must record my appreciation to all of them for their participation in this project. The Course Team owes an especially large debt to Dr Gerry Segal, Senior Fellow at the International Institute of Strategic Studies, who was the External Assessor of *Pacific Studies*. He was both an enthusiastic supporter of this project as well as a very shrewd critic. His wise counsel and tough advice have greatly improved the volumes in this series. It has been a pleasure to work with Professor Colin Mackerras, Director of the Key Centre for Asian Studies and Languages at Griffith University in Australia. Griffith University and the Open University have collaborated over the production of *Pacific Studies*; an arrangement that has worked extremely well. The success of this collaboration has been due in no small part to Colin. Over the past three years I have come to appreciate his many qualities particularly his immense knowledge of the Asia-Pacific region as well as his patience and courtesy in dealing with those of us who know far less. I would also like to thank all of those colleagues at Griffith who have helped to make this collaboration so successful and worthwhile, especially Professor Tony Bennett, who played a key role during the initial discussions between the two universities. Frank Gibney, President of the Pacific Basin Institute, was always available with help, advice and encouragement. It was one of the real pleasures of this project to have met and worked with Frank and the PBI. This series has also benefited considerably from the enthusiasm and insight of Victoria Smith at Routledge.

The production of *Pacific Studies* was helped greatly through the assistance of several foundations. The Daiwa Anglo-Japanese Foundation awarded this project two grants and its Director General, Christopher Everett, was a model of generosity and support. He invited the Course Team to use the attractive facilities of the Foundation; an invitation which was accepted with enthusiasm. The grant from The Great Britain Sasakawa Foundation was also greatly appreciated as was the advice, encouragement and the shrewd counsel of Peter Hand, the Administrator of the Foundation. Mr Tomoyuki Sakurai the Director of the Japan Foundation in London was always interested in the development of *Pacific Studies* and I have no doubt that this resulted in a generous grant from the Foundation. Mr Haruhisa Takeuchi, formerly Director of the Japan Information and

Cultural Centre, was most supportive during the early stages of this project and his successor at the Centre, Mr Masatoshi Muto has been no less helpful. Finally, I must record my thanks to the British Council in Australia for their assistance which was much appreciated.

Richard Maidment
Chair, *Pacific Studies*
Milton Keynes, November 1997

Economic Dynamism in the Asia-Pacific: preface

Many individuals contributed to the production of this volume. In particular I would like to thank Jeffrey Henderson for his invaluable advice and assistance in structuring the book, suggesting chapter authors and commenting on the individual chapters. In addition Chris Brook, Bernie Eccleston, Tony McGrew, Richard Maidment and Gerald Segal offered their considerable advice on numerous drafts. The authors of individual chapters proved exceptionally efficient in working to a demanding schedule and taking into account the diverse comments from the Course Team and Editors. Without Doreen Pendlebury, Anne Hunt and Mary Dicker the final manuscript would not have been typed and presented so professionally. Tom Hunter and Kate Hunter did a marvellous job of editing individual chapters and to a very tight schedule.

Grahame Thompson
Walton Hall, January 1998

CHAPTER 1

Introduction: contours of economic development in the Asia-Pacific

Grahame Thompson

1.1   The regional record considered

Reports from international agencies on the future of East Asia published in the 1950s and 1960s were pessimistic about the growth and developmental potential for the region's economies. The general sentiment was that only Japan and the Philippines were likely to reach the status of advanced countries. How wrong this assessment has proved to be! Whilst Japan has presumably passed all expectations, the Philippines has been conspicuous by its relatively poor performance when compared to its East Asian neighbours (see Table 1.2 below). Even in the 1970s and 1980s, the UN development reports were cautious as to the prospects for these countries as a whole.

In fact their record has been outstanding, and has far eclipsed the growth rates of advanced countries and other developing areas alike. Figure 1.1 demonstrates the comparative record of the East Asian economies over the period 1965–90, particularly the eight so called 'high-performing economies' (HPAEs; Japan, the Republic of Korea (hereafter South Korea), Malaysia, Indonesia, Taiwan, China, Hong Kong and Singapore). This record is confirmed by the trends identified in Figure 1.2, which shows an index of income per head for various developing areas plotted between 1970–90, the period of the rapid growth of interest in the economies of the Asia-Pacific region.

The consequences of these growth rates were that in 1995 the GDP per head in Hong Kong and Singapore were US$ 23,900 and US$ 22,600 respectively, compared to an average of just US$ 19,400 for the rich industrial OECD economies as a whole. (Note that other countries were less well off at the time: Taiwan, US $13,200; South Korea, US$ 11,900; Malaysia, US$ 10,400; Thailand, US$ 8,000; Indonesia, US$ 3,800; China, US$ 3,100; Philippines, US$ 2,800 – all at 1995 purchasing power parity equivalents). By all accounts, these growth rates were as unanticipated by

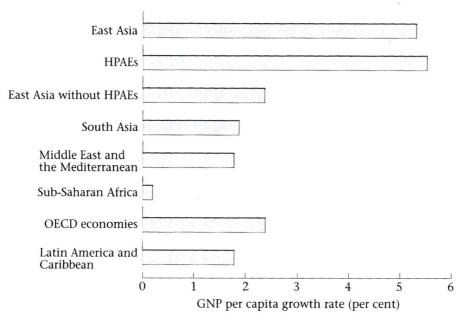

Figure 1.1 *Average growth of GNP per capita, 1965–90*
Source: World Bank (1993, p.2)

the countries involved as they were by the international organizations monitoring and analysing them. In retrospect, then, the period around the mid 1960s might be seen as one involving an unexpected *disjuncture* for the countries themselves, as well as for the international economic community beyond. It launched these countries onto a new and unanticipated growth trajectory.

These figures and trends provide the basic reason why the dynamic development of the countries in this region has become the object of so much analytical interest. Untangling the causes of this exceptional economic growth is the subject of a number of the chapters in this book, which examine the issue from different perspectives and approaches.

However, as soon as this is embarked upon another question immediately arises; How much should the countries in the region be considered as an integrating and interdependent regional grouping as a whole rather than as an isolated group of individual economies. Does it make up a genuine 'regional' economy? Broadly speaking, the chapters argue the positive case for this. The area at least demonstrates many of the main characteristics of a region as defined by **Buzan (1998)**. Considering it as a region, however – particularly as an economic region – means that three further interconnected issues also arise.

First is the relationship between the East Asian side of the Pacific Ocean and the North American side. As the chapters in the book demonstrate, it would be impossible to treat the East Asian countries independently of their North American counterparts, since one of the main reasons for the growth of the East Asian economies is the fact of their access to the North American markets, particularly that of the US economy (see Chapter 2).

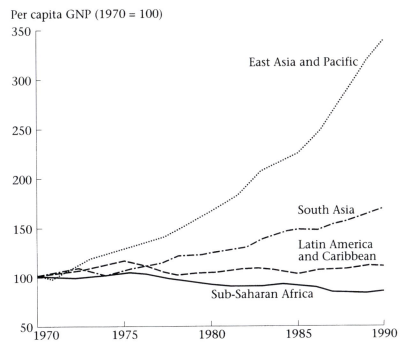

Per capita GNP (1970 = 100)

Figure 1.2 *Per capita GNP (1975 = 100)*
Source: World Bank (1997)

This provided the crucial demand for their products, and without it it is difficult to see how the economic advances they have made could have begun in the first place, let alone been sustained over the intermediate period. In addition there was the strategic and security relationships between the two sides of the Ocean that also fostered closer economic ties **(McGrew and Brook, 1998)**.

Second, the regionalization of these economies has involved a public 'institutional moment' as well as being driven by the private decisions made by market agents. This latter is generally agreed to have been the major reason why a regional economy as such is emerging. As the chapters testify, however, the precise nature of the institutional moment – described as an 'open regionalism' in Chapter 7 – is not one particularly familiar to a Western audience. The premier forum for this institutional moment in the construction of the Asia-Pacific as a region has been the APEC process, inaugurated in 1989. For reasons that are discussed in the book, this forum extended its embrace not only to the countries mentioned so far but also to the Anglo-American states to the South (Australia and New Zealand) and to Mexico in Central America, and to Chile in South America. The *diversity* of the economies linked together in this common purpose is the cause of both the strengths and the weaknesses of the integrative process, as later chapters demonstrate. But for reasons already mentioned it is still appropriate to treat the Asia-Pacific as a regional economy, as well as a set of individual ones.

Table 1.1 *East Asian trade as a share of total trade for different countries (exports plus imports as a percentage of total trade)*

	1913	1925	1938	1955	1990
China	65	46	70	43	59
Indonesia	32	38	26	32	60
Taiwan			99	50	42
Japan	41	47	70	22	29
South Korea			100	35	40
Malaysia	44	39	35	30	37
Philippines	18	15	11	17	43
Thailand	62	71	65	52	51
Simple average	42	43	59	35	45
Excluding South Korea, Taiwan	42	43	46	33	47
Excluding South Korea, Taiwan and Japan	42	42	41	35	50

Note: Higher percentages indicate greater trade intensity

Source: Petri (1994, p.111)

An interesting aside concerns the historical significance of the contemporary integrationist moves being made in the Asia-Pacific region. As is pointed out in Chapter 7, there were precursors of this in the 1960s and 1970s. But in many ways there was a similar (or even greater) level of integration amongst the East Asian group achieved earlier this century, particularly during the period of Japanese imperial expansion of 1931–45, than had been achieved by the early 1990s (Petri, 1994). Table 1.1 shows the levels of East Asian trade for a number of countries over the period 1913–90. Thus even in 1913 the level of East Asian trade integration was higher than it was in 1955, and nearly as high as in 1990. The imperial bloc established by the Japanese – known as the 'Japanese Co-prosperity Sphere' – involved enormous amounts of Japanese public and private investment in the countries it invaded as well as trade with them. Since 1938 the trade intensity of the East Asian economies between themselves has declined as they have become more 'international' in terms of the spread of their trading partners, even as Asia-Pacific integration developed after 1980. But the contemporary levels of specifically East Asian economic integration are not necessarily unprecedented.

However, there is a third aspect to the contemporary nature of regional development in the Asia-Pacific as a whole. It has also had something to do with the open nature of the global economy beyond the immediate shores of the Pacific Ocean. The growth of the region's economies has benefited from the liberal trade and overseas investment regimes adopted by the institutions set up to manage and govern the international economy after the ending of the Second World War. These organizations, particularly the World Bank and International Monetary Fund (IMF), the General Agreement on Tariffs and Trade (GATT), the World Trade Organization (WTO), and the Organization for Economic Co-operation (OECD), established the basic contours for a liberal open international trading system of the post-war years, one into which the economies of East Asia were adept at inserting themselves.

Thus there has been this further element involved in the overall picture of the development of this region and its economies; the structure of the international economy beyond the Pacific Rim itself. Of particular importance here is the engagement with the European economies and the integrative development of the European Union (EU) (see Chapters 2 and 13). One of the concerns expressed in this context has been the compatibility of the development of these regionalized economic blocks – considered in various permutations – with that open and liberal trading regime set up after the war (see Chapters 7 and 13). This regime came to be known as a 'multilateral' one in which all participants were treated as broadly on a par and formally at least negotiated and agreed amongst themselves on the nature of that trading system. The question this raises is whether the regionalism demonstrated by the EU, the North American Free Trade Agreement (NAFTA) and the APEC processes remain compatible with the continuation of a multilateral approach to international economic governance? This question is also explored in the chapters of this book where, broadly speaking, a positive answer to this is given, although with some qualification (see especially Chapter 14).

But herein lies another point of contention that figures in the chapters. What exactly has been the role of the World Bank and the GATT/WTO in the development of this region? Apart from these organizations emphasizing the maintenance of an open liberal international economy, they have also been instrumental in calling for policies of trade liberalization and internal de-regulation, directed at the East Asian economies in particular. Broadly speaking, this proposed policy package can be characterized as leading to a 'market friendly' approach to the economic policy pursued by the East Asian NIEs and ASEAN economies. The question is how far the actual practice of these economies followed this market-friendly advice, and what have been the implications for it emerging from the experience of their development strategies over the entire post-war period? Again this is the subject of considerable controversy, and it forms the core of one of the main themes for the book as a whole.

Whilst not an entirely new debate for the regional economies involved (see Chapter 4), the contemporary resonance of this controversy was stimulated by the World Bank's 1993 report, *The East Asian Miracle*. This report set many of the contours for the contemporary debate about the nature and form of the economic experiences in these countries. And the report has proved controversial, again as Chapters 3, 4, 6, 11 and 14 indicate. The story of how this particular report emerged and the intense diplomatic activity that went on around it is itself fascinating and revealing (Wade, 1996). The Japanese government financed the report since it wanted its particular development strategy properly assessed, and it thought that the other East Asian economies would demonstrate something novel and unique for the dominant Western interpretation of the experiences of these countries. That dominant interpretation was predicated on the intellectual line adopted by most Western economists and embodied in the World Bank's outlook and policy approach. The World Bank is often accused of being the bastion of a 'neo-classical' approach to the analysis of economic problems and to policy recommendations.

Box 1.1 Neo-classical economics

Neo-classical economics is the dominant approach within the economics profession. Its analytical structure begins with the decisions and behaviours of individual autonomous economic agents, and asks how their activities, initially considered separately, combine to produce the best outcome for society as a whole. Economic actors are presumed to act 'rationally' in terms of calculating their own best interests and advantages. It is the operation of the market and competition between agents that is the mechanism securing the co-ordination of their individual decisions. As far as possible this mechanism should be left to itself to establish the best possible allocation and distribution of resources, via the operation of the price system. Government intervention only serves to 'distort' this automatically functioning system, and leads to a misallocation of resources. The same is true of any other impediment to the proper functioning of markets and prices, like the activity of monopolies, trade unions, artificial restrictions on the entry to markets, rules and regulations that restrict business, etc. This approach to economics, then, offers both a powerful analytical endorsement of the benefits to be had from the operation of a free market, and a ready made set of policy prescriptions as to how to most appropriately achieve this objective.

The question raised in the context of the East Asian economies in particular is how far their own developmental experiences conform to this model, or can be used to further justify its policy recommendations. Herein lies a major thematic issue that characterizes a number of the chapters (Chapters, 2, 3, 4, 6, 7, 11 and 14) in this book. For many scholars who have studied the East Asian region, the image of a free market system operating to provide the dynamic growth indicated above just does not adequately describe the characteristics of those economies. Indeed, quite the reverse is the case. These economies, they would argue, developed precisely because they did not either conform to the neo-classical model just outlined, nor follow its policy prescriptions. In particular, the role that the state played in the economy was crucial to their success, and the state initially operated to 'protect' these economies from both the full operation of internal markets and, perhaps even more importantly, the international market beyond.

The precise nature of the arguments over this issue can be left to unfold as the chapters are considered in turn. Although this theme is traditionally characterized as the debate between an approach stressing the importance of the 'market' on the one hand, and that stressing the importance of the 'state' on the other – in the form of the state *versus* the market – it will soon become apparent that this image is too simple. To begin with there have been significant *differences* in the role that the state and the market have played even within the East Asian sub-region of the Asia-Pacific, let alone for the region as a whole. As is demonstrated in the chapters, it is more the delicate *balance between* governments and business interests, which typify *all* the countries in the region, that accounts for their *diverse* development trajectories. And this relationship is not a static one, but a dynamic changing one, reacting and evolving with changes in internal and external pressures and circumstances, in elite outlooks and in policy fashions.

1.2   Characterizing the economies as a whole

The issues of the relationships between governments and states (Chapter 6), the nature of the financial systems (Chapter 4), the organization of business interests (which are themselves differently specified – Chapters 7 and 9), the characteristics of labour (Chapter 5) and of policy elites (Chapter 7), all combine not only to illustrate diversity and differences, but to raise an issue about how we can best characterize as a whole the countries and economies being dealt with in this book. What is the specification of their socio-economic characteristics and formations? Can any sensible generalizations be made into which we can 'place' particular countries?

Clearly, at one level the differences between 'capitalist' economies and 'command' (or 'communist') economies forms one such categorization, and this difference is manifest within the region. China, North Korea and Vietnam were probably the best illustrative examples of the communist type in the mid 1990s, although they demonstrated their own peculiarities at the same time. However, supposing we were to classify all the other countries of the Asia-Pacific simply as 'capitalist' – which at one level is quite reasonable – then we will not have advanced very far. As the chapters demonstrate, the interesting nature of this region is the vast organizational differences between those economies that can be included under the category of 'capitalist'. The economic performance of these different economies varies enormously. So we would need some other level or criteria for distinguishing between the members of the 'capitalist' group. Quite what these levels and criteria are, or could be, is itself highly disputed within the social sciences, and we are not about to solve these problems here let alone embark upon a long discussion of what they might entail. Suffice it to say that the chapters very much develop their own categorizations and criteria as suits their purpose and analytical style. Without wishing to pre-empt any of this there are some ways in which these categorizations share common ground and terms, which it is worth drawing attention to at this stage.

The first level is in terms of the distinction referred to already: that between 'capitalist' economies, broadly conceived, and 'communist' or command ones. A capitalist economy is typified by the private ownership of resources, the central mechanism of resource allocation being the market, with the operation of a price system determined by the 'free' interaction between supply and demand, and typified by a freedom of contractual arrangements between dispersed economic agents. A command economy, by contrast, is typified by the collective ownership of resources, the setting of prices by administrative edict, the planning of resource allocation, and the hierarchical determination of contractual arrangements by bureaucratic means mainly between giant productive organizations owned by the state. The 'plan' allocates rather than the 'market'.

One complication with this simple dichotomy is that forms of collective or public activity are operative within what are clearly capitalist economies, so the activity of the state is sometimes a crucial component in the overall operation of the capitalist economy, to varying degrees – the East Asian NIEs being obvious examples. On the other hand, in command economies, there has usually been at least some role and space for market transactions and operations, even if only a small one. For instance, some of the economic activity carried out in contemporary China could be argued to conform to a market system, with 'relatively' free price formation, whilst the ownership of resources remains more or less completely collective (in various forms and degrees – see below).

Thus we need a second level, which would be structured in terms of broad socio-economic or socio-cultural differences between types of *capitalist* economies. Here a range of characterizations is possible.

An obvious sub-category is what are often described as Anglo-American type economies. Examples of these in the Asia-Pacific are the USA, Canada, Australia and New Zealand (even Chile might be included within this category). These economies often include strong commitments to a *laissez faire* ideology and practice, but historically combined with mixed-economy (public and private enterprise) elements. They rely upon a 'liberal' market economy, with free and open contractual arrangements, strong and independent industrial sectors and financial systems, an emphasis on macroeconomic management instead of 'industrial policy', and only moderate state intervention organized under a basic 'hands-off' philosophy.

In contrast to this would be the 'authoritarian capitalist' form, perhaps best exemplified by South Korea, Indonesia, Singapore, Burma/Myanmar, and perhaps Malaysia in the Asia-Pacific. This type of economy is typified by strong involvement of the state either directly in organizing economic activity and regulating it, or in setting the framework of encompassing rules and regulations for the operation of business and commerce. The 'guiding hand' of the state would be important here, often taking a paternalistic and even benign dictatorial form. Dissenting and autonomous sources of economic power are looked upon with great suspicion, and often overtly suppressed (e.g. organized labour). The economic elites are often small cliques involving extended families, ethnic groups and wealthy corporate interests.

A third discernible category could be classified as a 'negotiated economy'. This type of capitalist economy operates in a manner which stresses compromise between the various social strata, interest groups and corporate partners, negotiating to establish and maintain social order and peace. The form of the economic mechanism is to allow and encourage a formal autonomy in the operation of commercial life, though this may in fact be highly organized in terms of oligopolistic, cartel-like and conglomerate business groupings. But within this arrangement the emphasis is on the cautious formation of compromises to establish a consensus between the parties involved in key economic decisions about the allocation and the distribution of resources. Often this is done 'informally', through bargained negotiation (involving business and government agencies, which implicitly co-opt labour into the process). Any overt 'direction' in economic matters is avoided. State ownership of resources is minimal and often frowned upon. The classic example of this type of economy in the Asia-Pacific is represented by Japan, but there are strong elements of it to be found in Taiwan as well (though Taiwan also traditionally has higher levels of public ownership).

A final form of economy that can be considered at this intermediate level might be classified as 'manic' or 'chaotic' capitalism. There are two possible consequences of this form; a very successful variant and a very unsuccessful one. The main features of it are a relatively 'unorganized' form of economic order, which gives it a certain instability and 'transitional' nature. The 'manicness' is instilled into the economy by an emphasis on short-term entrepreneurialism, profiteering and marketeering (which are sometimes combined with corruption). All this can either act to prevent the stabilization of the economy for long-term prosperity or, perversely, produce quite the opposite and lead to a particularly dynamic outcome. The economy is typified by an extreme form of *laissez-faire* ('hands-off') approach, both in terms of ideology and in the actual practice of the market system. Examples of this in the region would be Hong Kong for the 'dynamic' outcome, and the Philippines for the 'blocked' version. This type may also be emerging in other areas like Thailand, parts of mainland China and Papua New Guinea (PNG). Mexico also demonstrates some of its characteristics.

The point about these classifications is not necessarily to slot any single economy totally into any one or other of them, but to present them as typical forms of socio-economic organization made 'available' to economic analysis. It may be that a particular country demonstrates predominant features that allow it to be classified accordingly, but very often (and perhaps most frequently) countries will demonstrate a mix or combination of features. They will thus be characterized by hybrid forms. The allocation of countries to examples given above is meant for illustrative purposes only, though it does give something of the flavour of each. Different analysts would no doubt allocate countries differently, or indeed challenge the broad classifications themselves (see Chapter 14 for a somewhat different way of presenting such a typology). Alternatively, they might not find these particular divisions useful and ignore them.

Indeed, to some extent that is what is done in the chapters that follow in the book. There is a variable use made of these kinds of categorizations.

In addition, there is yet another level at which some of the chapters conduct their analyses. Chapters 9 and 10, for instance, also discuss specific *national systems* of business and innovation respectively. Whilst using some of the same analytical architecture as just sketched out, these cut across it in various ways according to their own particular objects of interest and analysis. Other chapters concentrate upon specific country examples not mentioned here which add additional, but different empirical weight to the categorizations made above (Chapter 12). Furthermore, Chapter 6 concentrates upon the very specific nature of *business-state* relations in some of the countries already mentioned, which its authors think better illustrates the diverse and perhaps unique pattern in each country. What is more, Chapter 7 argues that a key difference in the outlooks of the 'Asian' and the 'Western' members of APEC in their attitudes towards the process of regional economic integration may have something to do with broad socio-*cultural* differences and 'Asian values'.

But why should we be overly concerned with these issues? What difference does it make if there are very different socio-economic characteristics typifying particular countries? The response is to stress once again that differences matter. They matter to our understanding of the differential performance of the economies in the region, they matter to our understanding of the internal dynamics of its integration, and they matter for an understanding of what is happening to the economies contemporarily and what might happen to them in the future.

In some ways what Japan, the NIEs, the ASEAN countries and China have experienced, and indeed are continuing to experience, can be described as 'pathways from the periphery' (Haggard, 1990). Just as the advanced industrial economies of Europe and North America had done before, these economies – beginning with Japan in the 1950s – have been moving from a position of underdevelopment to one of advanced development. They have been moving from the 'periphery' of the industrial system towards its 'centre', or perhaps more accurately towards its 'centres'. Indeed this dynamic movement has been creating often very new centres. What we have then is a dynamic evolution – involving different 'pathways' – but a movement not without its disjunctures and interruptions, as we have seen. The key point is that these different pathways are themselves importantly dependent upon the development and evolution of the different socio-economic formations already outlined, and these pathways and their socio-economic form are different ones. There is no single evolutionary path or model – a set of stages – through which all the countries have mechanically passed, or will pass, irrespective of their particular and potentially unique development strategy. Although, as the chapters demonstrate, it is possible to generalize about their experiences at a number of levels and in respect to a number of policy features, every country has 'played' those features or policy moves in a specific way according to their own history and circumstances. Thus whether it is the 'flying geese' model (Chapters 2, 10 and 14), the move from import substitution to export led growth (Chapters, 2, 3 and 6), the common emphasis on the equitable distribution of income (Chapter 11), the general role of the state and the market (Chapters 3, 4, 6 and 14), the growth of population and migration (Chapters, 3, 5 and 12), the commitment to 'open regionalism' (Chapters 7 and 13), all these have been inflected through the specific circumstances of each of the societies and their economies.

But neither should the emphasis placed upon the continued salience of the different and often unique socio-economic formations be exaggerated. These may themselves be undermined and change. Of particular pertinence here is the contemporary dramatic increase in a neo-liberal emphasis on de-regulation, liberalization and privatization which seems to be affecting the economies of East Asia just as it has those of the Anglo-American type. Although this is not a completely new development, the present wave of fresh policy moves being adopted in these countries – which is even affecting the remaining communist states as well – is so sustained and widespread that it marks a potential radical turning point. To a large extent this policy shift is driven by a reinvigorated sense of the need for all economies to become 'internationally competitive' under a globalizing economic trend, not just an APEC regionalizing one. Quite how the different economies will react to this trend in the long term remains an open question, but it will undoubtedly affect them all in one way or another (Chapters, 4, 8 and 9). Although this is unlikely to result in a single common socio-economic formation being generated for all the countries in question – a kind of hybrid Anglo-American *laissez faire* capitalism – could it work to seriously undermine the pertinence of the above classifications? Here another issue arises.

1.3 What of the future for the region?

Figures 1.1 and 1.2 above provided evidence of the growth and significance of the economies in the Asia-Pacific region up to 1990, particularly those in East Asia. The period between the mid 1960s to 1990 may perhaps prove to be the high point for those economies involved. Since 1990, something of a reaction against viewing them as necessarily being able to unproblem-atically maintain their dynamic growth rates has set in. This can be judged against the data presented in Table 1.2 and Figure 1.3. The historical record on growth rates is compared in Table 1.2, confirming the picture already presented up to 1990. Since then, over the period between 1990 and 1996, growth has faltered a little in some of the leading economies of the region. This is particularly true of the four 'little dragons' – Hong Kong, Singapore, Taiwan and South Korea. Of course, there still remains a continued growth potential in the following group of ASEAN countries and China (but see below), though they may also eventually experience the loss of dynamic being seen in the first group of industrializers. The possible reasons for this slowdown in growth rates are explored in a number of chapters, particularly Chapter 3 (though this chapter is confident of a continued growth dynamic for the economies).

Table 1.2 GDP annual average percentage growth rates

	1970–79	1980–89	1990–96
Hong Kong	9.2	7.5	5.0
Singapore	9.4	7.2	8.3
Taiwan	10.2	8.1	6.3
South Korea	9.3	8.0	7.7
Malaysia	8.0	5.7	8.8
Thailand	7.3	7.2	8.6
Indonesia	7.8	5.7	7.2
China	7.5	9.3	10.1
Philippines	6.1	1.8	2.8
Rich industrial countries	3.4	2.6	2.0

Source: *The Economist*, 1 March 1997, p.23

Another indicator of a possible change in dynamic for these economies can be seen from Figure 1.3, where the growth of merchandise export trade is given for 1995 and 1996. This slowed dramatically for the six main 'tiger' East Asian trading nations, from 14.5 per cent in 1995 to 3.5 per cent in 1996 (their average annual growth in trade between 1990 and 1996 was 10 per cent). This slowdown was one of the reasons behind the serious

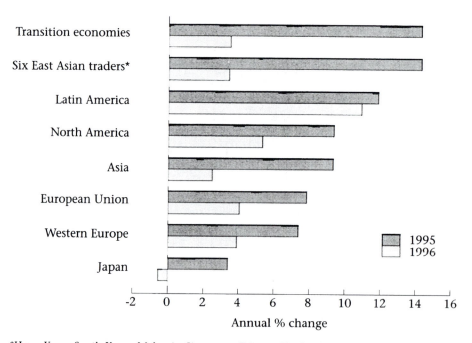

*Hong Kong, South Korea, Malaysia, Singapore, Taiwan, Thailand

Figure 1.3 *World merchandise export trade volume*
Source: WTO (1997)

financial crisis that hit the East Asian economies in the second half of 1997 (see Chapter 4). This financial crisis threatened to seriously undermine the growth of some of the following ASEAN economies, and even the region as a whole. North American trade also slowed, though not so dramatically, and Japan experienced a negative growth in merchandise export volume in 1996. Note also how Latin American export trade remained relatively buoyant, perhaps indicating a new dynamic emerging from these countries, many of which also abut the Pacific Ocean. In general there was a world-wide slowdown in merchandise trade growth from the unusually high rate in 1995 of 8.5 per cent to a more normal 4 per cent in 1996.

Clearly, we should be very careful not to read too much into just a single year's figures or even those for a run of a few years. But the trends shown for the mid 1990s should make us cautious in expecting the dynamic identified from the 1960s to 1990 to necessarily continue into the future. It is possible that the early 1990s will be looked back upon as a period of another *disjuncture* – another turning point – for some of these 'early starter' economies. This is all further explored in the chapters below.

Of course, the dynamic of the region as a whole is hardly called into question or exhausted when there are a series of 'second-comer' economies moving up behind the 'early starters', and where the US economy itself seems at last to be emerging from a long period of adjustment and poor economic performances (Chapter 3). The 'optimistic' outcome here concerns the leading role that the Chinese economy may play in the future. Estimates of the world's leading economies in 2020 are shown in Figure 1.4.

It is mainland China that presents the most intriguing case study for the future of the region, as discussed in Chapters 2, 3 and 14. Will China become the largest and most important economy in the world by 2020 as the data in Figure 1.4 suggest? This clearly remains an open question, but the analyses contained in the chapters will undoubtedly contribute to a better understanding of the processes involved in China's growth prospects, as well as the obstacles that stand in the way of such a course (Chapter 14). An interesting feature here is the characterization of the Chinese economy itself, particularly in the context of the categorizations already discussed above. Has it now for all intents and purposes effectively become 'capitalist' or is it still a centrally planned command economy at heart? Both the 'commanding heights' of its economy and its newly emerging manufacturing sectors remain in either public ownership or collectively owned in one way or another (Chapter 14) – though large-scale privatization has increasingly become official policy there as well. Prices are still centrally set or heavily controlled. So how can such an 'administered' economy as that of the Chinese one achieve the startling growth results of the past and those predicted for it in the future? (See Table 1.2 for the historical record of Chinese growth rates.)

One thing that has clearly happened in China is a massive decentralization of economic administration: to regional governments, to municipal administrations and to local urban and rural collectives (Chapter 3). This is particularly so of the very dynamic rural and agricultural

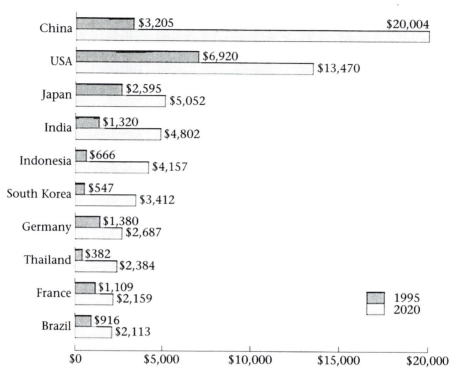

Figure 1.4 *Estimates of the world's largest economies 1995–2020 (in US$billions)*
Source: Central Intelligence Agency (1995)

sector in China. With this enormous variety of arenas and levels of economic governance, the precise nature of the property rights regime in China remains unclear and obscure, but it is certainly not a classical capitalist one, at least as that has come to be understood in the West.

This Chinese experience clearly provides an uncomfortable one for those international organizations and analysts that have insisted on the operation of clear cut capitalist free markets for the successful economic growth in the region (e.g. the World Bank mentioned above). This is again an indicator of the *diversity* of economic organization seen within the region. Part of the fascination with this region thus rests with the possible lessons that can be learned from the variety and diversity of its experiences: for the way we approach not only economic analysis but also for the actual manner in which economic organization has evolved in such a richly varied part of the world. This is something explicitly returned to in the final chapter of this volume.

1.4 The chapters in outline

It remains now to outline the rationale and pattern of material covered by the rest of the chapters.

Chapter 2 begins by looking at the broad pattern of economic flows that characterize the relationships between the countries of the region. In

The capitalist free market system at work in rural China?
A street scene in Kunming

addition it provides a preliminary classification of the countries according to their developmental status and resource availability. This serves to establish the grounds for understanding the dynamic of the region's economies and the key interlinkages between them. At the same time the chapter opens up the analysis of the large themes that have typified debate about these economies, some of which were noted above, and it indicates the different development trajectories of the major players in the region. The key economic linkage identified in the chapter is that between the USA and the East Asian economies, the nature and dynamics of which are explored in the chapter.

Chapter 3 follows the preliminary analysis of growth offered in Chapter 2 with a thorough review of the whole debate about why growth happened in this region and what the prospects are for its future. The chapter looks at the basic relationship between savings and investment, and then proceeds to examine how different economic models and approaches have handled the analysis of the growth process in this region.

The chapter is optimistic about the continued growth potential in the region despite some approaches which stress the potential slow down in the region's growth as the possibility of generating further factor inputs shrink in the main economies.

Chapters 4 and 5 build directly on Chapter 3. Chapter 4 examines the sources of one of the main building blocks for growth, that of capital investment. The chapter traces the developments of the individual country financial systems, to see how financial capital was generated during the development process. It looks at the important role that the public authorities played in both generating capital and deploying it in the East Asian economies, and how the state acted as a directing and regulatory body. The differences between financial and productive investment is highlighted and the role of macroeconomic management is examined. There is thus a discussion of monetary policy and exchange rate policy. Finally the chapter asks whether the financial markets in the region are integrating just as the real goods markets seem to be.

Chapter 5 turns to the other key building block for growth, namely labour, but the chapter does this in a particular way by concentrating on the gendered nature of the growth dynamic of the region. What has been the nature of the relationship between male and female workers in the East Asian miracle? Here it is the inequalities in the labour market that are highlighted, and the subordinate, and often unrecognized role that females have played in economic growth that is focused upon.

Chapter 6 examines one of the most controversial aspects of the debate about the rise of the Asia-Pacific economies. What has been the role of the state in their development? The chapter explores this feature via a very close analysis of the different roles the state has played in the region, emphasizing the key relationships between the world of business and the public authorities. The basic argument is that the traditional state versus market formulations, however sophisticated these may be, are unable to capture the carefully crafted and often uniquely balanced modalities of the role ascribed to the state activity in these economies.

Chapter 7 inaugurates a change of direction for the book by looking at the process of integration within the Asia-Pacific region. This chapter represents a very personal view on the formation and success of the APEC process, written by one of its foremost advocates. The author is the Japanese representative on the 'eminent persons' group of policy advisers who operate to influence the APEC agendas and who guide the process through its negotiating phases (so called 'policy sherpas'). The analysis emphasizes a 'top down' approach to integration, where it is the role of government leaders to propose initiatives and negotiate between themselves over a strongly liberalizing agenda. The APEC process is termed an 'open regionalism', and its similarities and differences to the EU, NAFTA and genuine 'multilateralism' are highlighted.

The next chapter takes up the issue of the integration process driven by private decision-making processes, in particular that of overseas investment. But Chapter 8 is also something of a personal viewpoint. It looks at the role of multinational corporations (MNCs) in the development of the region, but in a very particular light. Other chapters emphasize the importance of foreign direct investment (FDI) in the process of integration and growing interdependence (Chapters 2, 4, 9, 10 and 14). This chapter questions the centrality given to 'overseas investment' in the Asia-Pacific region. Through a close and detailed analysis of the actual flows of foreign investment and foreign production, the chapter questions whether the process of integration has actually developed very far in the region. It is sceptical about the appropriateness of using FDI as a measure of overseas production, and proposes a series of other measures which, it is suggested, demonstrate the so far limited and very uneven extent of internationalized production in the region.

Chapter 9 is more straightforward, though equally challenging. Here it is the nature of the differential forms of business organization that is focused upon. A series of national systems of business are built up as explanatory devices. Contrasting the Anglo-American model of a 'business system' with that of the Japanese, South Korean and the Taiwanese 'Chinese family business', brings out the differences in the organization of production in these economies. The analysis also has important implications for our understanding of how these business systems are adapting and changing as the processes of international and regional integration gather pace.

Chapter 10 compliments Chapter 9 with an investigation into the specific role that technology plays in the process of economic development and regional integration. Rather like Chapter 9, it constructs the notion of a definite national system, but this time of innovation, and contrasts the different national and regional systems of innovation that are current in the Asia-Pacific. The chapter also compliments the analysis of Chapter 3, since the growth process is one centrally involving technological advance. For Chapter 10 the MNC represents an important and influential conduit through which technological innovation is conducted and spread throughout the region, though the patterns of its operation are themselves dependent upon the 'efficiency' of the national and regional systems into which that technological innovation is placed or from where it arises.

Chapter 11 represents another move in the trajectory of the book, this time to look at the consequences of the growth and integration processes. Who have been the winners and who the losers from these processes? Although the East Asian countries have been marked by their relatively egalitarian policies and outcomes, there are always those who suffer and those who benefit from any process of development. This chapter analyses the nature of the equalities and inequalities to be found in the region, but concentrating on the losers. Other than in Chapter 5, the main focus and sentiment of the book has been to stress the positive nature of the growth and integration processes. The objective here is to rebalance this with an emphasis on the 'downside' of these, though still recognizing the relative equality within which these economies have progressed.

Chapter 12 follows this up with a look at the experience of the smaller territories and states in the region, in particular the Pacific Islands. These are often ignored in taking the wider picture of growth and development, but the pressures they display – population growth, the transformation of traditional production, the pressures on and reorganization of local resources, the migration of labour – all reverberate in the other larger countries as well. It is the impact of all this on the environment that is highlighted in this chapter.

Chapter 13 opens out the Asia-Pacific to beyond its own regional boundaries. It connects up with Chapter 7's analysis, but takes a different approach. The chapter is more sceptical as to the future prospects and past successes of the APEC process, but at the same time is sympathetic to the attempt to generate an adequate governance mechanism for the region as well as for the global economy beyond. The key relationships between the APEC process, the EU and the role of the USA is stressed.

Chapter 14 concludes the book with a review of some of its main themes, but also does some new things and brings new insights to bear on old themes. It stresses the opportunities and dangers inherent in the emergence of a new and potentially unstable regional economy. The chapter looks to the lessons to be learned from the experiences of this regional growth and integration, both analytical lessons and practical organizational ones; and stresses the integrative scope of the regional economy in a rapidly globalizing world.

References

Buzan, B. (1998) 'The Asia-Pacific: what sort of region in what sort of world?' in McGrew, T. and Brook, C. (eds).

Central Intelligence Agency (1995) *Factbook*, Washington DC, Central Intelligence Agency.

Haggard, S. (1990) *Pathways from the Periphery: The Politics of Growth in Newly Industrializing Countries*, Ithaca, Cornell University Press.

McGrew, A. and Brook C. (eds) (1998) *Asia-Pacific in the New World Order*, London, Routledge in association with The Open University.

Petri, P.A. (1994) 'The East Asian trading bloc: an analytical history' in Garnaut, R. and Drysdale, P. (eds) *Asia Pacific Regionalism*, Australia, Harper Educational.

Wade, R. (1996) 'Japan, the World Bank, and the art of paradigm maintenance: *The East Asian Miracle* in political perspective', *New Left Review*, no.217 May/June, pp. 3–36.

World Bank (1993) *The Asian Miracle: Economic Growth and Public Policy*, Oxford, Oxford University Press.

World Bank (1997) *World Development Indicators*, Oxford, Oxford University Press

WTO (1997) *Overseas Trade Statistics*, Geneva, World Trade Organization Secretariat.

PART 1

Economic Dynamism Considered

Patterns of trade, investment and migration in the Asia-Pacific region

Partha Gangopadhyay

2.1 Introduction

During the last two decades the Asia-Pacific region has outpaced all other regions in terms of economic growth and also assumed paramount importance in the new global economic order. This region registered significant increases in both intra-regional and inter-regional trade and investment flows: more than half of all the world's merchandise exports reach the regional markets. Significant changes have also taken place in the labour markets that have important ramifications in terms of migration. The Asia-Pacific region is also characterized by a great diversity: the region has major industrial giants like the USA and Japan. This region is also the home for rising economic powers like Taiwan and Korea and vibrant developing nations like Indonesia, Thailand, Mexico and Malaysia. Thus, it is important to categorize the nations of this region on the basis of some acceptable criteria. Traditionally there have been three criteria commonly used: level of economic development, rate of economic growth and the trade and payments position. Based on these three criteria we arrive at five groups of nations:

1   The industrial giants such as the USA and Japan.

2   The land-rich nations such as Australia, Canada and New Zealand.

3   The rapidly growing newly industrialized economies such as Hong Kong, South Korea, Singapore and Taiwan (NIEs).

4   The near-newly industrialized nations such as China, Thailand, Malaysia and Indonesia.

5   The traditional developing nations such as Burma/Myanmar, Vietnam, Cambodia, and Laos.

Different groups have confronted different economic problems during the last twenty years and have diverse resource bases. Thus their trade, investment and growth prospects differ considerably. It is critical to note that the trade, investment and growth prospects are heavily influenced by the present stage of development, the resource bases of a nation and also by national economic policies.

The plan of the chapter is as follows: Section 2 provides a brief summary of the above groups of nations. Section 3 introduces the trade strategies of some of these nations and analyses their government's successes and failures in this context. This will mean reclassifying the nations a little. Section 4 provides a detailed analysis of the major problems of the Asia-Pacific trade: the persistence, spread and consequences of trade imbalance between Japan and the USA, the impacts of such imbalances on external stability and the impacts of Japanese and American patterns of trade on the Asia-Pacific region. Broadly speaking, this analysis underlies the main structural feature of the whole Asia-Pacific economy – the way Japanese trade surpluses are matched by US trade deficits, and whether this pattern can continue into the future. Section 5 examines the causes behind the recent changes in trade-flows in this region. It highlights three issues to explain such changes: the creation of strong trade intensity, in the emerging 'flying-geese' pattern of industrialization in the region, and the existing economic complementarity between nations. Section 6 provides the general model of development that most of these nations have been emulating: the statist development with an outward-oriented policy. The resultant trading structure and its sustainability is then analysed. A critical element of development in this region is the flow and distribution of investment. A detailed analysis of the sources and distribution of foreign direct investment (FDI) is presented. The impact of economic growth on the labour markets of the region is also examined. Finally, Section 7 concludes the chapter.

2.2 A brief summary of the groups

Group 1: The USA and Japan are the dominant economies and their economic performance, trade, investment and growth will be a critical factor in determining the overall economic progress of this region. Both these nations have almost exhausted the usual sources of economic growth: shifting resources from agriculture to industry, increasing labour force participation and increasing capital formation through increased domestic savings. At this juncture the major determinants of their economic performance are two-fold. First, a sound short-term macro-economic management is needed to boost the confidence of investors. Such macro-management calls for low interest rates, low inflation and small budget deficits. Secondly, a long term set of policies are needed to reduce structural rigidity and improve factor productivity. For the USA, such macro-economic management entails:

1   Change in the domestic savings-investment balance by boosting domestic savings.

2 Reduced fiscal deficit – a fiscal deficit is the (negative) gap between government revenue and expenditure.

3 Reduction in the demand for increased protectionism.

For Japan the key problems are to reduce structural rigidity in home goods industries and to rationalize the domestic capital market. (The structural rigidities imply restrictions on the flow of resources between industries that inhibit a smooth adjustment in production. Suppose the demand for motor cars goes up while the demand for rice goes down. If labour and capital cannot be easily transferred from the rice sector to the motor car sector, then the current increase in demand for motor cars cannot be met domestically despite the availability of labour and capital. Thus structural rigidity embodies inefficiency in allocating resources across industries.)

Group 2: Australia, New Zealand and Canada are industrialized nations but the size of their industrial sectors are smaller than that of Japan, or the USA. More importantly, these nations rely on their abundant natural resources for overall economic performance – they remain mainly primary producers of minerals and agricultural products. All these nations have embarked on deregulation and liberalization of their key sectors to attain efficiency. These nations also have critical dependence on the international markets on which they trade their primary products, and thus growth of the international economy and openness of the international markets play a key role in affecting their economic performance.

Group 3: The third group of countries achieved unprecedented growth of their national incomes during the last three decades. Until the 1960s all these nations were labelled as the backward economies of the Asia-Pacific region. They had very low per capita incomes and low standards of living with a small industrial base. In the 1960s none were regarded as having a high growth potential. But quite contrary to expectations, these nations registered growth rates for nearly three decades in excess of growth in any other nations (see the relevant country profiles in **Eccleston et al., 1998**). It is this group of nations whose development path has been quite unique in recent history. These nations have not only questioned the existing models of growth but also provided important lessons for other parts of the world.

By 1990 these countries had per capita incomes higher than the average of the World's middle-income countries. As a result, they are often labelled as the 'newly industrialized economies'. The important thing to note is that all these four countries – Hong Kong, South Korea, Singapore and Taiwan, have had an outward-looking development strategy: export growth exceeded the growth of national income in each nation for more than three decades (**Eccleston et al., 1998**). Except for Singapore, the growth in exports was double that of national incomes. Also the export growths exceeded the growth in investment. In contrast, middle-income nations of other regions experienced a slower growth of exports until 1980, but since then their export growth exceeded the growth in their national incomes.

The growth of the NIEs has been so rapid that their consumption growth also exceeded the average consumption growth in the global economy as a whole. Since their population growth rates declined, all these economic changes led to a substantial improvement in the standard of living and quality of life in the NIEs. Gradually, non-agricultural employment rose, which lifted the wage rate. For example, in South Korea, the income distribution became more equal after the 1970s (see Chapter 11). In addition, the growth of imports was as rapid as the growth of exports. Thus an outward orientation contributed to the unprecedented performance of these economies. It is important to note, however, that there are significant differences in these four economies: Singapore and Hong Kong have a very small agrarian sector while the other two have a vibrant agriculture sector. Secondly, private foreign investment was encouraged in Taiwan and Singapore whereas Hong Kong displayed a more neutral attitude towards it. In South Korea, there was an explicit bias against foreign investment until 1980. The bias in South Korea was in favour of the *Chaebol*, their domestic large business firms (see Chapters 6 and 9). The size of the firm in Taiwan and Hong Kong has been of a smaller scale, while Singapore's average firm size lies somewhere in between.

Group 4: This group of nations achieved and sustained above-average growth rates for three decades. Yet their achievement failed to reach the outstanding performance of the third group (though China has been expanding particularly rapidly since the mid 1980s). One may call this group a 'follower group' as they try to emulate the economic policy and development strategies of the Group 3 nations. In the mid 1990s these nations accelerated their pace of economic growth. They have now achieved the status of 'almost NIEs'.

Group 5: This group of nations still maintain a crucial dependence on agriculture and the industrial sector has yet to reach maturity. Growth rates of per capita incomes are close to the average of the developing world at large, though they could be the major sources of future growth and economic progress for the Asia-Pacific region. So far they have failed to achieve above-average growth rates.

2.3   Trade and national economic strategy

Government and development

In the 1960s the developing economies of the Asia-Pacific region were caught in the vicious cycle of poverty: they had low per capita income because of low labour productivity. Labour productivity was low due to a very small capital stock per head. Why was the capital stock so small? Because they had little savings to produce investment. Why were savings low? Because they had little income to save. Thus, the vicious cycle of poverty emerges. It was argued that market forces alone could not lift these nations from this vicious cycle of poverty. The 'visible hand' of government intervention was thought to be necessary to beat this cycle (Alam, 1989).

The second crucial idea in the literature on development economics was that agriculture is a backward sector and not capable of improving productivity and providing a surplus output. The industrial sector was given a primacy since it was believed to be an advanced sector. Consequently, the allocation of investment was drawn under the control of the government, and emphasis was placed on the allocation of capital in favour of the industrial sector. The notion was that industrial development, with stagnant agriculture, could bring about economic progress. In most of the developing nations such a bias against agriculture existed, except in the East Asian nations. Agriculture assumed a critical role in these nations (Balassa, 1988).

The third crucial idea of development economics was import-substituting industrialization: growth of domestic industry was encouraged to take place behind protective walls, far from the influence of competitive international markets. Imports were consciously curtailed and most of the developing nations adopted restrictive trade regimes. The East-Asian fast growing economies gradually departed from this inward-looking strategy and adopted an open economy model with critical dependence on both exports and imports (Balassa, 1988; Bhagwati, 1988).

The important point is that economic systems of all nations lie within a spectrum that ranges from pure bureaucratic command systems to atomistic market based competition. The Asia-Pacific nations are no exception. In this region the state wields different degrees of control over the economy. There are three levels of state involvement (Perkins and Roemer, 1991):

1   The state played a major role in capital formation – as in Taiwan and Japan – mainly to provide the infrastructure investments (Chapter 4).

2   The government also intervened in the production and distribution of certain key commodities and services.

3   Governments wielded significant control over the private sectors through:
    (a) Central bank control over commercial bank interest rates (see Chapter 4).
    (b) Quota restrictions on the import of key inputs.
    (c) Some controls existed on the sales and purchase of foreign exchange.
    (d) Discretionary taxes and administered prices were widely prevalent.

For example, in the socialist states of China, North Korea and Vietnam private enterprises enjoy very little autonomy from the visible hand of the government. It might be said that private enterprises are merely a component of the state bureaucracy in these nations. The degree of autonomy of large private enterprises is also low in South Korea, the Philippines, Taiwan and Indonesia. In some of these nations foreign exchange regulations and import restrictions were widely used. In South Korea, for example, in the 1970s, private banks were given directives to carry out investments deemed socially desirable. The government relied on the control of investments to induce private enterprises to take risks that would accelerate the growth of the economy (see Chapter 6).

The economic success of a nation in this kind of system depends on the nature and degree of controls and also on the extent that market forces are distorted by such interventions. In such countries well functioning markets did not already exist in many areas – they had to be stimulated or created, and many markets were regulated. These regulations included price regulation, quantity restrictions and input controls, which led markets to 'fail' in their task of allocating resources. This 'market failure' registered itself in the inability of sellers to supply the goods at internationally competitive, or justifiable, prices. Since the prices did not reflect the true costs, the allocation of resources based on these prices was also distorted. These endemic market failures caused a static mis-allocation of resources due to badly functioning price mechanisms, for example, in China, Vietnam, North Korea, the Philippines, and Mexico. Pessimism over the ability to export and market failures led to import-substituting industrialization in which the state tried to act as a benevolent allocator of resources to rectify the market failures. Similar economic strategies were chosen by Indonesia, Malaysia, Thailand and the Philippines to protect domestic industries from the forces of international competition (Higgott *et al.*, 1993).

But in the recent years a serious concern has emerged about the interventionist nature of the state in economic matters, which has now been blamed for 'government failure'. Such government failure has been widespread amongst developing nations.

Box 2.1 Government failure

Government failure occurs mainly because of *rent seeking, predatory behaviour* by the state itself and the emergence of *distributional coalitions*. Controls and regulations that accompany state intervention create monopoly profits and rents as entry to such industries is restricted. If there are interventions in markets then there are artificial impediments placed in the way of firms who want to enter these markets. The lack of competition in such markets would restrict outputs and increase prices, which will create the 'monopoly rent', or excess profits. Rent seeking activities embody the efforts of firms to capture these excess profits, or monopoly rent. Rent seeking activities thus entail direct and indirect use of resources by firms to gain entry into such markets. Adverse economic effects of rent seeking behaviour can be explained in the following way: suppose theft is a profitable opportunity which attracts many otherwise law-abiding people into this activity. As the incidence of theft goes up the government is forced to spend more resources employing more police to combat it. Such resources come from other economic activities which lower the outputs of these activities. First, the main economic effect of rent seeking is, therefore, the reduction in outputs in other sectors. Second, control and regulations also create predatory behaviour by the state: the level of government intervention is more than the optimum level from the standpoint of the society since the state bureaucrats may get financial gains from restrictions on markets and consequent rent seeking activities among competing firms. Third, economic agents form 'distributional coalitions' to enhance their shares in the national income. Such distributional coalitions adopt pressure tactics and lobbying activities to influence government policy in their favour. All these activities lead to government failure.

Yet the success of the East Asia NIEs was mainly driven by state-led industrialization. Thus a basic question is: Why have governments not failed in the East Asia NIEs? The possible answer lies in the following.

- The economies of the NIEs were also characterized by sector-specific interventions.
- The states adopted export-oriented industrialization.
- The states maintained the importance of the public sector.
- The states avoided succumbing to the pressures of rent-seeking due to institutional arrangements. In North-East Asia the state enjoys relative freedom from predatory activities and coalitional pressures from interest groups.
- A dynamic and centrally controlled elite bureaucratic system manned by well-trained management talent came into existence.
- An authoritarian political system with the political exclusion of the labour movement has been in power.
- A close link between government and business was established.

Relations between business and government and development

In some of the ASEAN nations and in much of Latin America the state machinery was fragile in the sense that it has been easily exposed to the ravages of rent-seeking, and was beset by an incompetent bureaucracy. But in a shift from the import-substituting industrialization to export-oriented development in the 1960s and 1970s Taiwan, Singapore and South Korea formulated policies without falling prey to rent-seeking activities. The corporate sector formed an alliance with the bureaucracy in which the 'state elites' had a leading role. Distributional coalitions were effectively controlled by authoritarian elite governments. In Taiwan the state intervened through direct investment and by establishing a network of state-owned enterprise. South Korea's approach was built on the Japanese model: planning officials sought to harness the energies of private corporations by guiding them into 'prioritized industries'. Among the incentive schemes were the provision of credit on favourable terms and the provision of infrastructural support (Chapter 4). This strategy has been called 'industrial targeting strategy'. The states did not succumb to the pressure of interest groups while formulating the targets and operating the strategy (Dornbusch and Park, 1987). Rather the state 'disciplined' the private enterprises to make productive use of the subsidies and to use them for enhancing export performance (see Chapters 3, 4 and 6).

The role of foreign capital in North-East Asia was also restricted, and the emphasis placed upon encouraging domestic enterprises. Multinational companies were not allowed to enter in large numbers to set up direct operations. The multinationals were only granted entry on the condition that their activity would be in harmony with the national priorities. In Latin America and South-East Asia foreign direct investment played a dominant role while the national states exercised little control over them. In contrast, the corporate sector in North-East Asia was dominated by national firms who were under the influence of an elite bureaucracy (Chapter 6).

Government and outward-orientation in East Asia

An outward-oriented strategy creates a competitive environment that enhances the incentive to perform. The world economy is also a large market and thus the economies of East Asia could benefit from economies of scale. A typical firm of an East Asian nation can now produce a larger output for the world market and, thereby, reduces the unit cost of production. The forces of international competition also induced the private enterprises to reduce costs and thereby made domestic enterprises more internationally competitive.

While exports played a critical role in these nations, how central was the role of government in their economies? The 'governmental guidance' in Japan and South Korea had been instrumental in allocating resources and managing production decisions. On the other hand, Hong Kong has been more of a *laissez faire* economy where government took a 'hands-off' approach. In Singapore significant interventions were applied in the labour and capital markets. In South Korea, however, the government had a very active role. Taiwan was less interventionist than South Korea.

Although in South Korea the government intervention was the greatest, the incentives for exports were uniform and did not lead to inefficiencies or too many sectoral distortions (Dornbusch and Park, 1987). The role of the public sector in overall investment was also limited; public expenditure as a percentage of national income was around 20 per cent, which was one of the lowest among the developing nations. During the 1960s a regulatory environment was introduced into South Korean industry and an active government hand was seen in promoting certain industries. In the early 1970s, the government promoted and guided investment into the heavy industries. But very soon the attempt was considered to be a failure and was reversed. It is necessary to understand, then, that the South Korean government has been quite flexible and since the 1980s liberalization has played an important role for the South Korean economy. Import liberalization started as early as 1960. During the subsequent years tariff rates were lowered and quantitative restrictions on trade were gradually removed. In the 1960s budgetary and financial reforms were introduced and in the early 1980s structural adjustments were undertaken. Thus, the South Korean economy displayed a continual process of liberalization even though the role of government expenditure was quite limited in comparison with other developing nations.

Many have argued that the major lesson from the East-Asian economies is the contribution of on-going liberalization and removal of controls to their economic progress (Krause and Kim, 1991). At the outset, an agrarian transition was initiated by investing funds to raise agricultural productivity. As industrial growth starts to pick up, it was found essential to gradually lift controls over the industrial sector and expose it to the forces of international competition. Labour markets were largely left unregulated and the exchange rate was kept competitive to give a decisive boost to exports.

Similar patterns have been observed in the USA and Japan in the late 1980s. In Japan tax reforms and financial liberalization took place roughly at the same time. In the USA tax reforms and deregulation also gathered momentum in the 1980s. In the South-East Asian nations – such as Malaysia, Indonesia, Philippines, Thailand – natural resources played a significant role in promoting growth. But other than in Indonesia, these nations rely less and less on primary products and natural resources and more and more on the international economy.

The common theme of economic changes in the Asia-Pacific region is to identify and remove the constraints on efficient resource allocation and growth. Before examining that we look at the major features of trade in the Asia-Pacific region.

2.4   Asia-Pacific trade in the current economic conjuncture

Major features of the Asia-Pacific trade

One of the most crucial aspects of the Pacific trade flows has been the persistent commercial imbalance between the USA and Japan (Higgott *et al.*, 1993; Kojima, 1973). For nearly two decades Japan has been the major *creditor* in the international economy. Japan consistently maintains a trade surplus with the USA and the world economy while the USA has had a huge trade deficit.

Second, the Asia-Pacific developing economies have traditionally 'looked East' towards Japan to emulate its economic strategy (Ariff, 1991). The key to this strategy was to maintain a trade surplus and there has been a lateral spread of the commercial imbalance in the region as more and more Asia-Pacific nations ran a trade surplus, especially against the US current account. In the late 1980s and early 1990s most of these economies undertook currency realignments and revaluations to create pronounced movements in their relative prices in favour of positive balances, but despite this the ASEAN countries in particular developed persistent trade

Japan ties up the Asian market

deficits in the mid 1990s (see Chapter 4). However, the USA became increasingly indebted, which has led to economic conflict with Japan. This is because Japan is the 'immature creditor', with large trade surplus along with a capital surplus, and is also the world's second largest economy. One of the consequences of such huge imbalances is the emergence of an era of potential protectionism.

The GATT/WTO-based political regime for the governance of international trade relations is intended to ensure that domestic interventions by individual economies do not lead to any mutually destructive consequences. The major danger in this context is the fast-emerging 'new protectionism' which takes the form of administered and negotiated non-tariff restrictions to trade (Schott, 1989). For example, since the 1950s the USA and other industrial nations have been utilizing voluntary exports restrictions (VER hereafter) for curtailing flows of exports of textiles, steel, and electronic products mainly from Japan and South Korea. Under this scheme an importing country encourages another country to reduce its exports voluntarily under the threat of higher all-round trade restrictions. Such growth of protectionism has been widespread which prompted the following comment: 'The growth of protectionism appears significant but its consequences do not' (Bhagwati, 1988, p.56). One possible explanation of this conundrum is the gradual emergence and establishment of 'managed trade': the new protectionism seeks to fix bilateral or overall market shares, and to slow down the increase in imports to give the domestic economy time and space to adjust to the changes in international markets. Under 'managed trade', governments aggressively bargain to establish market shares. In this context, VERs and anti-dumping moves have been part and parcel of the regime of 'managed trade'. What are the implications of these features of trade? One of the major implications is in terms of the external stability of a nation. We address this issue in the next section.

External stability and growth in the region

It is a common observation that economies that are insolvent do not grow (Ariff, 1991). Thus, a cautious macroeconomic management is an essential component of the 'East Asian growth model'. Conversely, economies that are experiencing high levels of growth on a sustained basis find it easier to achieve external stability. In other words, these nations find it easier to repay international debts since they have high economic growth. Thus, the key to maintain external stability is to maintain economic growth.

To put this into perspective let us examine the South Korean experience: changes began in 1958 and gathered momentum by 1964. The exchange rate was rationalized and the won was depreciated in real terms. In 1964 the exchange rate was floated in an attempt to maintain its constant real value. The government achieved significant macroeconomic stability in 1965: inflation came under control and interest rate reforms were carried out. By the end of the 1960s quantitative restrictions on imports were withdrawn as exporters were allowed to import any amount of intermediate inputs. From 1967 the government gradually reduced tariffs and also liberalized imports (Krause and Sekiguchi, 1980). However, financial liberalization was slow, but it is continuing in the 1990s. These early measures of liberalization were targeting the trade and payments regime to dismantle the bias against international trade. South Korea's exceptional performance in terms of growth was mainly driven by the growth of exports. Yet in 1975 South Korea retreated back to a controlled environment and adopted the strategy of import-substituting industrialization. The purpose was to establish 'upstream' industries which produce inputs for other industries, such as heavy industry and chemicals. This led to a considerable slow-down in the growth of the economy. By 1981–82 the government reverted back to the outward-looking strategy and the growth rate accelerated. Thus liberalization in South Korea was not a 'once for all policy action'. It has been a disjointed but on-going process that encountered difficulties at times (Dornbusch and Park, 1987).

The second point is that the high ratios of exports to national incomes helped the Asia-Pacific nations avoid a debt crisis even though debt/output ratios for most of these nations were high in the 1990s. For example, South Korea and Indonesia had very high debt-output ratios, yet their debt-servicing records are good (Sachs, 1985): most of these nations make regular payments of interests on debts and also pay back parts of the principal on borrowed capital. The relevant question therefore is: what determines the external stability of a nation?

There are three critical factors affecting their external stability (Ariff, 1991). First, manufactured export growth contributes to the diversification of exports away from the primary products, such as agricultural products and other natural resources. Such diversifications enhance external stability. Second, in almost all the nations external-orientation has reduced their domestic distortions progressively since the distorted domestic prices have been replaced by international prices. Such a progressive removal of distortions has a positive impact on external stability since the nation becomes more efficient in the use of its resources. Third, macroeconomic instability forces a nation to adopt short-run stabilizing measures which inhibit market forces. Such impediments to market forces create distortions which adversely affect economic performance, as happened in the USA. Thus the macroeconomic stability and indirect intervention also helped these economies stabilize their external sector.

What is external stability? To put it simply, this can be seen as the gap between domestic savings and domestic investment of a nation such that the nation finds it easy to make necessary repayments without major distortions in resource allocation (see Chapters 3 and 4). To put it differently *imbalance* exists when the balance between the current account and long run capital flows can only be restored with an exchange rate adjustment. The primary question is whether such imbalances exist in this region. There are two possible sources of these: first, the role of Japan may cause such imbalances in this region. We take up this issue in the next section. Second, the USA–Japan trade imbalance may permeate the stability of the region. We examine this further below.

The Japan problem in the trans-Pacific trade

Japan may pose a serious problem for Pacific trade. In order to examine this let us look at some of the critical features of the trans-Pacific trade.

Between 1970 and 1990 the Pacific share of world trade went up from 42 per cent to 53 per cent. In the same period intra-regional trade went up from 17 per cent to 26 per cent of the world trade. It is also noteworthy that the APEC markets absorb nearly two-thirds of all exports of the region. The USA and Canada absorb one-third of all exports of the thirteen other APEC nations. The acceleration of economic integration of the region has been impressive, yet there are significant impediments such as restrictions on trade in agricultural products, voluntary export restraints and 'managed trade' by dominant players of the region (see Chapters 7 and 13). In the North-East Asian nations (Japan and South Korea) there exist significant barriers that protect domestically influential groups. Yet the major problem in the Pacific trade is Japan's unusual trading pattern (Higgott *et al.*, 1993).

Is Japan a problem? Trading conflicts such as the ban of American-made aluminium baseball bats from the Japanese markets often hit the headlines. It is unequivocally true that there are significant trade barriers to accessing markets in Japan. The Japanese government also admits to these restrictive barriers and attributes them to the Japanese social customs and the labyrinth of internal administrative controls. The major problem is that the

Japanese trade pattern has created a massive bilateral trade imbalance *since Japan has more exports than imports*: Japan is the major creditor of the Asia-Pacific region as well as in the global economy.

A major source of this feature is its very low import volume: it is estimated that Japan would import 40 per cent *more* manufactures if its markets were as open as other OECD economies. On the other hand, the USA's low savings ratio and high budget deficits have made the USA highly indebted – it has had to borrow to finance its trade and budget deficits. Thus the trade imbalance between these two super powers has created a significant problem for overall pan-Pacific trade. We return to these issues below. But despite some of its adverse impact on the Asia-Pacific region, Japan plays a positive role in shaping the economic future of this region, and this is addressed in the next section.

The positive contribution of Japan to the region

By the end of the 1980s, Japan turned out to be the world's largest source of foreign direct investment (FDI). Japan has further increased its FDI since the Plaza Agreement in 1985.

> Box 2.2 The Plaza Accord
>
> During the first half of the 1980s the Reagan Administration tightened fiscal expansion in the USA which resulted in high interest rates and consequent strengthening of the US dollar. This strengthening of the US dollar coincided with the build up of huge deficits in the USA's current account. By 1985 the USA became the largest debtor nation which created the possibility and fear of a dollar crisis. This fear induced the top five industrial nations to co-ordinate the devaluation of the US dollar against their currencies. The Ministers of Finance and the central bankers of these five nations met in the Plaza Hotel in New York in September 1985. It is interesting to note that the yen had been appreciating against the dollar since February 1985. The Plaza Accord in September 1985 further accelerated the pace of this appreciation of the yen. Such developments led to the emergence of Japan as the major creditor in the international economy. The appreciation of the yen reduced the competitiveness of Japanese exporters, and it put pressure on domestic producers to locate their activity abroad where production costs were lower. Thus began the large scale increase in Japanese FDI (Kwan, 1994). FDI represents capital for productive activity rather than for financial investment purposes – which is termed portfolio investment.

It is important to look at who are the beneficiaries of the Japanese FDI. The major destination for Japanese FDI has been North America, which takes a 40 per cent share. On the other hand, less than 20 per cent on average has gone to the developing nations of the Asia-Pacific. However, it is noteworthy that 80 per cent of all Japanese FDI to the developing world goes to the developing nations of the region. Two recent changes can be observed: (1) Japan has increasingly sent FDI to the ASEAN nations and to

China; (2) Japan is still the most significant investor in South Korea, Thailand and Indonesia. In Taiwan, Hong Kong and the Philippines it is second to the USA, in Malaysia it is second to Singapore. In order to get a clear picture see Table 2.1.

Table 2.1 *Japanese FDI in the Asia-Pacific (in US$m)*

Period	Hong Kong	Singapore	South Korea	Taiwan	China	Thailand	Malaysia	Indonesia	Philippines
1973–76	64	146	292	111	0	71	154	550	78
1977–80	85	467	295	134	1	120	251	843	143
1981–82	30	323	59	96	8	99	77	476	55
1983–84	19	342	69	130	22	118	227	268	20
1985–86	66	198	178	385	46	112	97	93	57
1987	108	268	247	339	30	210	148	295	na
1988	85	179	254	303	203	625	346	298	na
1989	116	678	257	360	206	784	471	167	na
1990	114	270	147	513	161	714	592	536	na
1991	92	240	130	405	251	807	880	576	100
1992	73	210	105	292	500	657	704	610	60

Source: Japanese Ministry of Finance (1992)

The major upsurge in FDI from Japan after 1985 is clear. But the distribution of the FDI provides interesting contrasts: the FDI to Singapore rose significantly until 1983–84, then it declined until 1988. FDI to South Korea and Hong Kong also fluctuated during the 1970s and 1980s but stabilized at a lower level in the late 1980s and early 1990s. The FDI to Taiwan remained quite stable after 1985, while the FDI to China has expanded rapidly. The major recipients of FDI were Thailand and Malaysia, during the early 1990s.

Regional implications of the USA's trade imbalance

In the 1980s the US economy emerged as the largest debtor nation. The US trade deficit reflects the inability of US products to compete in the global economy. It also reflects the massive imbalance between savings and investment in the USA – domestic savings being much lower than investment, leading to a potentially unsustainable current account deficit. Thus, the trade deficit has been a symptom of the ailing US economy. In part, this experience of a trade deficit by the USA is caused by restrictions on US products in the global economy.

What is the immediate implication of the USA's trade imbalance? A large US current account deficit allows other nations in the global economy, and particularly those in the Asia-Pacific region, to follow a strategy of export-led growth and, thereby, export to US markets. The US trade deficit also allows other nations to reduce their own budget deficits since it provides them with buoyant economies. Thus the USA's plight is to the advantage of the other nations of the region. In recent years, however, most of the Asia-Pacific nations have started shifting away from US markets. Table 2.2 documents this shift. The crucial feature is that the trade imbalance between Japan and the NIEs has more than doubled during 1987–92 while the Japan–USA trade imbalance was reduced by 10 per cent in the same period. In addition, between 1987–92 the NIEs–USA trade imbalance declined by a massive 60 per cent.

Table 2.2 *Trade volume and imbalances in the Asia-Pacific region (US$bn)*

	Trade volume	Trade imbalance
Japan–NIEs		
1980	26.6	11.8
1987	58.3	20.3
1992	98.8	46.5
Japan–USA		
1980	55.8	6.9
1987	115.1	52.1
1992	148.0	43.7
NIEs–USA		
1980	32.5	3.0
1987	81.2	34.1
1992	110.9	13.9

Source: Kwan (1994, p.109)

The linkage between Japan and the USA has weakened, mainly due to the growth in importance of Japan's trade balance with NIEs. The NIEs reduced their dependence on the USA for their export markets and increased their dependence on Japan for the supply of capital goods. Figure 2.1 indicates the shift in importance from the USA to the NIEs for Japan's trade balances.

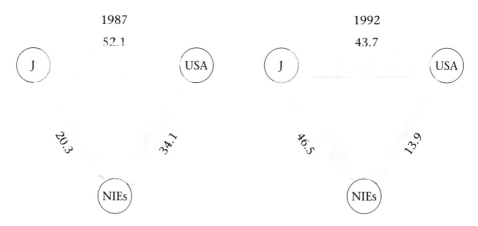

Key: J = Japan   NIEs = newly industrialized economies
    = indicates the direction of trade surpluses and their relative size

Figure 2.1 *Trade imbalances ($USbn)*
Source: Table 2.2

2.5 Recent changes and future prospects of the Asia-Pacific trade

Changes in trade flows among the Asia-Pacific nations

During the 1980s world exports increased by 35 per cent while the export from the Asia-Pacific region went up by nearly 60 per cent. The centre of this growth included Japan, the NIEs, Thailand and the USA. South Korea, Taiwan and Hong Kong displayed high growth *rates* in trade with most of their partners. Thailand also recorded a good export performance which was very close to that of the NIEs in the late 1980s. There was also an impressive performance by Singapore and Malaysia. The less successful in the growth league were Indonesia and the Philippines, at least until the early 1990s.

Japan and the USA displayed contrasting growth rates: Japan experienced massive growth rates in exports while the USA did so in imports. Japan's exports more than doubled with most of its partners. But its imports were contained within a 7 per cent growth rate. The major sources of imports were from the NIEs, and Thailand. Australia and New Zealand had a more balanced growth in comparison with the USA. Very strong trade intensity indexes (the ratio of trade between partners and overall world trade) were recorded between the following partners: Australia-New Zealand; USA–Canada; Singapore–other ASEAN members; Malaysia–Thailand; Malaysia–Philippines; Singapore–Hong Kong; Hong Kong–Taiwan; Hong Kong–Philippines.

Such a strong trade intensity is mainly driven by the following factors: traditional trade ties, geographical proximity and entrepôt trade relations. In entrepôt trade one nation exports raw materials to another nation which exports back the finished products and may thereby benefit from the cheap labour of the second nation. Japan, South Korea and Taiwan also displayed very high trade intensity as a group. The ASEAN nations, Australia and New Zealand showed strong trade intensity. Canada has high trade intensity with the USA, yet has very low trade intensity with the rest of the Asia-Pacific. South Korea and Taiwan increased their import intensity from Australia and New Zealand and increased their export intensity with the USA and Japan in the early 1990s. Interestingly, Japan reduced its trade intensity with all the Asia-Pacific nations, except the USA (see Chapter 4).

Evolving patterns of comparative advantage

There are two critical factors behind the changes in trade flows in the Asia-Pacific region. First, the trade flows were affected by changes in the comparative advantages of individual economies in this region. Second, the rapid economic growth driven by a sudden industrialization also changed the pattern of trade in this region.

Box 2.3 Comparative advantage

Consider two trading partners: Japonica and Ameritas. Both could produce two commodities, say plastic chopsticks and wooden toothpicks, which they trade between themselves. But Japonica has a *comparative advantage* in the production of plastic chopsticks while Ameritas has a *comparative advantage* in the production of wooden toothpicks. What does this mean? Basically it costs Japonica less to produce chopsticks *relative* to their cost of production in Ameritas, while it costs less to produce toothpicks in Ameritas *relative* to the cost of production of these in Japonica (costs are measured here in terms of the best alternative opportunity for production *foregone* by the decision to produce either of the commodities in the two economies).

Now, it may be that in *absolute* terms Japonica has a cost advantage over Ameritas in the production of *both* chopsticks and toothpicks, but the relative advantage is with Japonica in chopsticks and with Ameritas in toothpicks, so they specialize in that commodity for which they have the relative or comparative advantage. Thus every country has a relative advantage in some commodity or other, in which it would specialize and trade on the international market. This is the basis for the *mutual advantage* to both nations in trading. It is productivity levels that lie behind the relative differences in the costs of production in the two countries, and this is determined by different types of resources they have available ('factor endowments'), and technological differences between nations.

In simple trade theories, the comparative advantage of a nation is determined by its 'factor endowments'. The availability of cheap inputs determine, among other things, the comparative advantage. The specific stage of industrialization of the particular country also affects the comparative advantage by influencing the available technology. In the process of industrialization, the structure of comparative advantage shifts from simple, labour-intensive products to sophisticated capital and technology-intensive products. Japan has a clear structure of specialization with high comparative advantage of exports in a limited range of industrial products, for example, electronics, metal products, machinery and miscellaneous manufacturered products. The specialization of the USA is much more diversified. The structure of comparative advantage of Canada, Australia and New Zealand is centred on fewer products which are mainly foodstuffs and resource-based goods. ASEAN nations have a structure of comparative advantages which is similar to the structure of the resource-rich developed nations of the region. South Korea and Taiwan have high comparative advantages in industrial products and low advantage in primary products.

The 'flying geese' model has sometimes been employed to analyse the changes in comparative advantage of different industries in the East Asia countries during the process of their economic development. Initially the model captured the development of specific industries in a single country. In recent years the model has been extended to incorporate shifts of industries from one nation to another.

Box 2.4 The 'flying geese' model

The development of a modern industry in 'latecomer industrialization' typically begins with the import of a product from the advanced nations followed by its import substitution. This subsequently leads to export initiatives, which forms the core of the 'catch up industrialization'. The idea is that each industry passes through five stages – introduction, import substitution, export, mature and reverse-import stages. These stages are represented by the humped shaped pattern for each industry shown in Figure 2.2(a). In the introduction stage domestic production starts with an imitation, or transfer of technology, yet the domestic market is mainly flooded with imports. In the second stage domestic production expands faster than increases in domestic consumption and imports start declining. The industry moves to the next stage when an export surplus is created. In the mature stage, production and exports start declining. Finally, the industry becomes a net importer again when the domestic costs increase. This accounts for change in the comparative advantage for each of the industries.

This pattern of first a low comparative advantage followed by an increase in the comparative advantage, and then a decline in the comparative advantage, is reproduced for each industry in turn (A, B, C, D, etc.) as the process of development progresses, hence the 'flying geese' analogy – each industrial profile looks like the flight formation of a flock of geese. The industries in which a country specializes are progressively more technically advanced and sophisticated, pointing to the nature of the developmental process.

The second part of the Figure, 2.2(b) shows what happens when this model is transferred from a single country to a sequence of countries who are thought to go through much the same cycle as just sketched above for each industry in turn. Another 'flying geese' pattern arises, this time pointing to the way different countries, or groups of countries, follow one another in a sequence of development (1, 2, 3, 4, etc.). This happens for each industry in turn.

Until the mid 1960s Japan's leading export sector was manufacturing industries of high labour intensity, like textiles, and Japan had the status of an almost NIE. Since then Japan's capital intensive machinery sector has been in steady ascendancy. By 1980 Japan reached the industrialized country stage. Starting from a developing country stage, Taiwan and South Korea both reached young NIE status by the late 1960s. In the early 1970s Taiwan reached the mature NIE stage and reached the industrialized country stage in the 1990s, but Hong Kong lagged behind. The ASEAN nations still have a trade structure similar to that of developing nations – though this is rapidly changing. The 1980s increase of Japanese FDI was concentrated on the manufacturing sectors of the ASEAN nations, which could change Malaysia and the Philippines into young NIEs by the turn of the century. It is expected that by the turn of the century Thailand will reach the mature NIE stage.

(This 'flying geese' model is further discussed (and criticized) in Chapter 10.)

Indicator of comparative advantage

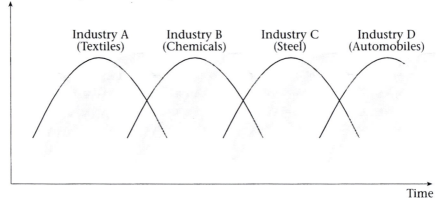

Industry A (Textiles)   Industry B (Chemicals)   Industry C (Steel)   Industry D (Automobiles)

Time

(a) For a particular country

Indicator of comparative advantage

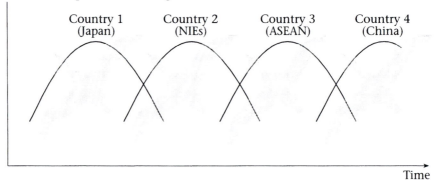

Country 1 (Japan)   Country 2 (NIEs)   Country 3 (ASEAN)   Country 4 (China)

Time

(b) For a particular country

Figure 2.2 *Stages of trade structure*

What is the rationale behind the flying geese model? It is due to a shifting competitiveness of an industry over time which is itself caused by changes in factor endowments of nations in the course of economic development. This process is further assisted by technology transfer from more developed to less developed nations.

A second feature of the regional trade patterns is the growing importance of intra-industry trade in the region. Intra-industry trade involves an interchange of products belonging to the same industry, for example cars are being exchanged between Japan and South Korea. Intra-industry trade between two nations is mainly driven by income levels (positively) and income gap (negatively). The index is very high between Japan and the NIEs, and ASEAN and the NIEs. An exception is the index between Hong Kong and Taiwan mainly because the trade here was driven by re-exports to and from China. Since the mid 1980s intra-industry trade between Japan and the East Asian nations has increased mainly due to the rapid industrialization of the East Asian nations.

In search of complementarity among the Asia-Pacific economies

Inter-industry trade between nations is driven by comparative advantage which is determined by the differences in technologies and resources or endowments. The more dissimilar nations are in terms of resources and technologies the more profitable will trade be between them. Thus if two nations have significant differences in terms of technologies and resources, the nations are said to have high complementarity. Thus we focus on the historical interdependencies, and not on the strategic ones (Higgott, Leaver and Ravenhill, 1993). High complimentarity has been observed in the following cases:

> Japan *vis-à-vis* Australia, Canada, Indonesia and Malaysia
> South Korea and Taiwan *vis-à-vis* Australia and Malaysia
> Malaysia *and* Singapore
> South Korea and Taiwan *and* Hong Kong

Low complementarity has been observed between:

> ASEAN *and* Canada, Australia and New Zealand
> *Among* the ASEAN countries
> Canada *and* Australia and New Zealand

Reductions in complementarities took place in the 1980s between Japan, and South Korea and Taiwan; and between South Korea and Taiwan themselves; and between Canada and Australia. A marked decline in complementarity has also been observed in the trade between Indonesia and Thailand, due mainly to Indonesia's self-sufficiency in rice cultivation.

2.6   Trade, development and investment flows

The model of economic development in the region

The NIEs and nearly NIEs of Asia have tried to emulate the best features of the Japanese experience (Alam, 1989). The key elements of their development strategy were two-fold: first, all these nations adopted outward-oriented trade strategies. Secondly, in many of the East Asian nations the state was actively involved in guiding the process of industrialization by channelling resources into particular sectors. The state protected domestic and newly-emergent industries and also provided subsidies and assistance to leading firms. Thus in Japan, followed by South Korea and Taiwan, the state provided a disciplined form of administrative guidance to pave the way for industrial development (White, 1989). Similar state intervention is also seen in South-East Asia, yet there the intervention lacked rigorous discipline. The intervention in Thailand has been much less pronounced. In Indonesia the state has been actively and extensively involved in the process of industrialization through regulations and direct investment. One crucial thing to note is that the quality of bureaucratic agency differed across nations. The quality and independence of the bureaucracy was high in North-East Asia, but was substantially less so in the South-East Asian nations.

The critical trading-structure of the Asia-Pacific region

As mentioned above, the key trading feature of the region is that Japan is the major supplier while the USA is the major absorber of commodity, and other flows. In turn, Japan supplies capital, intermediate products and technology to the NIEs and the ASEAN nations. These Japanese investments strengthen the supply side of their economies and also make them internationally competitive. The products these nations produce with Japanese capital and technology are then exported primarily to the USA.

As a result, Asia-Pacific developing economies achieved a strong export-led growth due to the supply side boost coming from Japanese export and due to the strong demand from the US market. In recent years the US demand has been declining mainly due to decline in its trade deficit. The US trade deficit is still very large, however, nearly US$120 billion per year in the mid 1990s, which still provided a large market. In the coming years in order to stabilize the world capital market the US government will need to take measures to cut its budget deficit, increase domestic savings, adjust its exchange rates, and strengthen the supply sides of its economy (Haggard and Kaufman, 1992). This could result in the steady decline of international demand by the USA. In order to maintain the economic tempo of development in the region, Japan would have to absorb the products from the Asia-Pacific region.

Already there are some signs that Japanese imports of finished goods have been steadily rising due mainly to an upward revaluation of the yen, which makes imports cheaper relative to home production. The key issue is whether Japan can effectively replace the USA as the major absorber of exports from this region. The role of Japan as an export absorber of the region will depend on the following factors:

- Whether Japanese fiscal measures are expansionary.
- Whether the budget deficits can be expanded.
- Whether there is a strong growth in private investment to boost Japanese demand for imports.
- Whether its consumption patterns include more imports.
- The extent to which barriers to imports are reduced.

The critical questions are two-fold. First, how quickly will Japanese demand grow? Second, how much of this increased demand will be met from the Asia-Pacific region? Part of the answer will be found in the dismantling of non-tariff barriers to trade, government regulations, the introduction of domestic reforms and the adjustment of domestic price movements.

Another critical feature of the region is the persistent trade surplus of the NIEs: during the last ten years these nations have amassed more than

US$120 billion a year as trade surplus. This massive trade surplus from the region accounts for 50 per cent of the USA's trade deficit.

What are the sources of this trade surplus? First, the massive increase in export earnings by these NIEs. Second, these nations made significant gains due to terms of trade movement: their export prices registered larger increases than the increases in import prices. Third, the appreciation of their real exchange rates also boosted the surplus since the value of their surplus went up measured in terms of their domestic currency. The overall picture for this Asia-Pacific region can be summed up in terms of Figure 2.3.

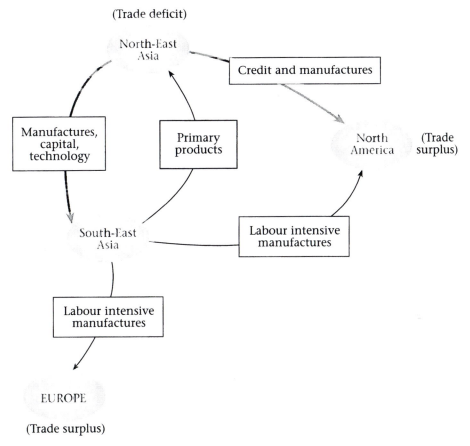

Figure 2.3 *Trade patterns and payment surpluses*

Notes: Deficits on surpluses are measured as SEA against other nations. Arrows show major flows of goods and services.

Japan has maintained a consistent current account surplus even in the face of a strong yen. But it is expected that in the future Japanese exports will decrease and imports increase to reduce the current account surplus. In fact, Japan has managed to maintain a steady current account surplus, which implies that the demand for Japanese goods in the world economy remains strong. One possible explanation for this is the large and increasing US federal budget deficit which could have boosted domestic demand in the USA and thus demand for Japanese exports as well. One notable feature is that aggregate spending has been rising faster in Japan than in the USA. The emerging basic structure of trade is thus the following: The North-East Asian nations, due to their poor resource base, rely heavily on oil and raw material imports. In order to pay for these items these nations need to maintain a surplus on their trade in manufactures with other nations. So far the South-East Asian nations have proved to be complementary to the North-East Asian nations: the South-East Asian nations export resource-based primary goods and maintain a negative balance of trade in manufactures with the North-East Asian nations. In recent years, however, these South-East Asian nations have captured some of the labour-intensive manufactures and begun to balance their overall trade in manufactures. This implies that in the long run this region must find a market for its manufactures outside this region to maintain a trade surplus in these items.

In order to catch up with the NIEs the South-East Asian nations have consistently imported capital, technology and components from Japan and thus maintained a chronic deficit with Japan. This dependence means that these South-East Asian nations have to earn a surplus from other nations. So far they have sent their products to the USA and Europe and used their surpluses earned there to finance their deficits with Japan. The durability of this pattern depends on the maintenance of their ability to export in the USA and European markets (see also Chapter 4).

Two other interesting cases are South Korea and Taiwan. From the early 1980s South Korea's current trade account began to improve. By 1986 the trade surplus reached 8.4 per cent of the South Korean national income. Exports grew at a rate of 18 per cent per annum, mainly driven by a strong US demand, while imports grew on an average 7.5 per cent per annum. During the 1980s the real exchange (nominal exchange rate minus the inflation rate) also depreciated by 5.6 per cent, while Japan's exchange rate had a massive appreciation of nearly 29 per cent in the 1980s. On the other hand, Taiwan failed to depreciate its exchange rate. As a result, South Korea was steadily gaining ground in the international economy at the expense of Japan and Taiwan. The slow growth of South Korean imports was mainly due to low oil prices in the 1980s. The savings-investment gap considerably improved due to a steep rise in savings, from 23 per cent of GDP in 1980 to 37.3 per cent in 1988, while investment remained stable at 29 per cent of GDP. Taiwan had been running a trade surplus for nearly two decades (over the 1970s and 80s). In 1986 this surplus rose to 22 per cent of the national income. In the mid 1980s its net exports declined while the domestic demand picked up. By 1987 the strong US demand led to a buoyant export market for Taiwan. Taiwan also managed to reduce its savings-investment gap, mainly due to a decline in its investment boom.

Thus, at the beginning of the 1990s the overall picture was as follows: For the East Asian NIEs and Japan, the USA had been the largest market for their exports. In the late 1980s–early 1990s, Japan, Taiwan and South Korea as a group accounted for more than 30 per cent of the USA's imports. It seems that the USA will continue to be the dominant partner of the NIEs and Japan. Yet the budgetary changes in the USA may pose serious challenges for these economies. But there are a number of ways in which the Asia-Pacific region could cope with the deflationary effect of any US budget cuts. First, these nations could enhance their economic integration, and the diversity between them will make increased integration a possibility. Second, intra-industry trade amongst the NIEs will be an important contributor to their future growth. Third, Japan may act as the absorber of demand for this region. We see some signs of this as Japan increases its imports and consumer spending increases at a high rate.

The rise in regionalism is evident in the Asia-Pacific: intra-regional trade rose from 30.9 per cent in 1986 to 43.1 per cent in 1992 while the US market dropped from 34 per cent to 24 per cent over the same period. Intra-regional share of exports of NIEs increased from 31.9 per cent to 43.5 per cent while that of the USA slipped from 37 per cent to 24 per cent. Asia has also emerged as the major market for Japan. For the USA also the Asia-Pacific region has become a major export market. Thus there are signs of the necessary readjustments in regional trade flows. The USA is becoming less important as a destination for exports compared to Japan, the NIEs and the near NIEs.

What are the major determinants of trade flows? There are mainly three sources:

- The partner country's share of world imports which is mainly driven by the competitiveness of its exchange rate.
- The complementarity between nations.
- Bilateral trade barriers.

Trade and regional economic linkages in the Asia-Pacific Rim

In order to place the discussion on economic linkages in the proper perspective consider the data contained in Tables 2.3 and 2.4:

Table 2.3 *Foreign direct investment in South-East Asia (US$m) 1983–94*

Country	1983	1984	1985	1986	1987	1988	1989	1990	1991	1992	1993	1994
Indonesia	292	222	310	259	385	576	682	964	1482	1774	2004	2109
Thailand	348	400	162	261	182	1082	1650	1700	1847	1969	1493	640
Malaysia	1261	791	695	489	423	719	1846	2958	3998	5183	5206	4348
Philippines	105	9	12	127	307	936	563	530	544	228	763	1126

Source: IMF, International Financial Statistics, Various Issues

Indonesia, Malaysia and Thailand in particular have been profoundly affected by the FDI from Japan and the NIEs of the Asia-Pacific region. On the other hand, the Philippines received a very small share of FDI.

The data in Table 2.4 clearly shows that the surge in FDI has come from the East-Asian region, where Japan took the leading role. Yet there is a clear

Table 2.4 *Foreign direct investment by country of origin (as % of total of receiving countries) in the near NIEs: 1986–89*

Country making investment	Countries receiving investment			
	Indonesia	Thailand	Malaysia	Philippines
Japan	17	44	31	20
Hong Kong	9	7	4	17
South Korea	10	2	2	2
Singapore	4	5	11	3
Taiwan	3	11	25	19
NIEs	25	25	42	40
Japan+NIEs	42	69	73	60

Source: Asian Development Bank (1991)

picture of uneven investment flow: between 1986–89 44 per cent of Japanese FDI in South-East Asia went to Thailand, while Indonesia received only 17 per cent. During the same period Thailand received 2 per cent of the South Korean FDI in South-East Asia while Indonesia received 10 per cent. The obvious question that follows concerns the reasons behind such a surge: first and foremost, all these South-East Asian nations had low labour costs and hence high profit margins. These high profit margins attracted capital. Secondly, all these economies undertook attractive and serious reforms that granted special deals to foreign investors. After the Plaza Accord, the Japanese Yen appreciated and exports from Japan became less attractive and Japanese investors looked for offshore markets to avoid the high export prices of Japanese goods. The investors of the Asia-Pacific region were also faced with rising protectionism in Europe and in the USA. Thus, all these factors meshed together to create a surge in FDI in the South-East Asian nations, which mainly came from North-East Asia. Box 2.5 indicates the Japanese firm Toyota's strategy of investment in SEA.

Box 2.5 Integrated international production in the automobile industry: Toyota's network for auto parts in South-East Asia

Exports of motor vehicles from Japan amounted to nearly four million vehicles in 1995. About 32 per cent of these were made by the Toyota Motor Company, whose exports amounted to almost 38 per cent of total Japanese car production. In addition, Toyota's overseas production increased from 152,000 vehicles in 1985 to 1,253,300 in 1995 – more than one-third of its total automobile production. In 1995, the number of vehicles produced overseas by Toyota exceeded, for the first time, its exports from Japan. At the end of 1995, Toyota had some 143,000 employees, more than 70,000 outside Japan.

Toyota has established integrated manufacturing systems in all three of its main markets – North America, Europe and Asia. At the end of 1995, Toyota had 35 overseas manufacturing affiliates in 25 countries, more than one-third of which were in Asia. Plants in China, Indonesia, Malaysia,

Philippines, Taiwan Province of China and Thailand produced 370,962 vehicles, nearly one-third of the company's overseas production in 1995.

Although Toyota's vehicle production in the region, as elsewhere, partly results from Asian countries' restrictions on imports of automobiles, the company has responded to the regional industrial co-operation policies of the ASEAN countries by establishing (in consultation with individual governments) a network of affiliates for parts supply to local and regional markets (including Japan). Toyota's intra-firm trade of parts and components in the region is co-ordinated by the Toyota Motor Management Company in Singapore (see Figure 2.4). Toyota exports diesel engines from Thailand, transmissions from the Philippines, steering gears from Malaysia and engines from Indonesia. In 1995, intra-firm exports among these affiliates accounted for about 20 per cent of exports of parts and components of the company's manufacturing affiliates worldwide. Exports of these affiliates geared to other destinations outside the ASEAN market accounted for another 5 per cent.

Toyota also plans to undertake specialized production of various models in its Asian affiliates, both for local sales and exports within and/or outside the region. These include Toyota's all-purpose vehicle (the Kijang) in Indonesia and a compact car in Thailand for possible exports in Asia but also to destinations in South America and the Middle East.

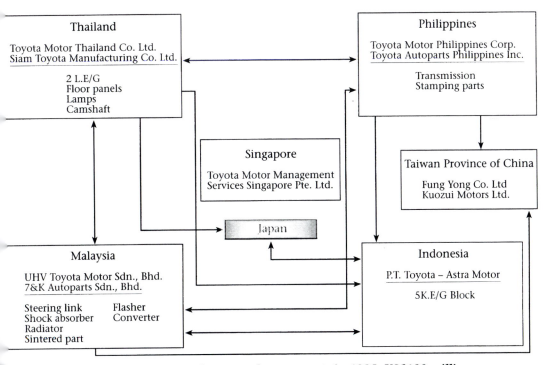

Figure 2.4 *Transaction amount of parts and components in 1995: US$100 million*
Source: UNCTAD (1996, p.100)

Lessons from the ASEAN trade

All the ASEAN economies had fluctuating fortunes during the 1980s. In the late 1980s, all these economies experienced an economic upturn. They witnessed an improvement in their current account and fiscal deficits, rationalization of their exchange rate regimes, falling debt service ratios, diversification and growth of exports and diversification of export markets, and an improving investment climate.

It is critical to note that the economic performance of these small open economies is driven mainly by external changes. Since most of them face common changes in the global economy, domestic policy plays a critical role in coping with these changes. Due to delayed responses of Indonesia and Thailand in reforming their real domestic economic sectors, their growth rates declined (MacIntyre and Jayasuriya, 1992). In the long run the policy makers must concentrate on investment and growth to pay back any debts they incur in the short run. In recent years, the ASEAN nations boosted short run growth by adopting counter cyclical policy: during the global recession these nations maintained domestic demand by creating budget deficits. Such budget deficits were mainly financed by borrowing from overseas (except Singapore) which led to a high debt burden for these nations in the early 1990s. Only when the domestic growth declined did these nations adopt short-run demand management policies to tackle the problem. Thus counter cyclical policies may turn out to be costly unless investment and growth pick up in the long run..

Resource gaps and investment flow in the Asia-Pacific region

In the 1980s when most of the ASEAN nations faced significant debt problems, the Asian NIEs became net international creditors (lenders). The developing nations of the Asia-Pacific region, by contrast, saw an increase in capital inflow (they became borrowers). Perhaps paradoxically, the developed countries of the region – the USA, Canada, Australia, New Zealand – also became net importers of capital, from Japan and the NIEs. In 1983–90 42 per cent of the Japanese FDI went to the USA and 17 per cent to Europe, 8 per cent to the NIEs, 4 per cent to ASEAN and 3 per cent to Australia.

A major strength for the Asia-Pacific economies has been the flow of FDI from within the region. The FDI involves the direct purchase of the assets of the private sector of a foreign nation by overseas firms who thereby stimulate the foreign economy. By contrast portfolio foreign investment takes place through the stock market of the recipient nation. The overseas investors allocate their capital across different sectors of different nations according to the indicators of the domestic stock markets (Chapter 4). The Japanese have also been major net portfolio investors. The USA was an important direct FDI and portfolio recipient, absorbing US$50 billion in direct investment and US$207 billion in portfolio investment between 1985–88. Over the same period the ASEAN nations received a total of US$6.8 billion in FDI, while China received US$6.5 billion. South Korea

The USA's FDI in China has been through private companies such as Pizza Hut

became an important investing country, especially in the South-East Asian region. The upshot is that some of the Asia-Pacific nations have become increasingly indebted relative to their national income, yet they have been successful in avoiding any serious debt crisis (Ariff, 1991). The secret is that the Asia-Pacific nations exhibited higher investment ratios over a longer period of time than other debtors – so they have generated enough growth and exports to finance their debt burden. Long term trends in the balance of payments are shown in Table 2.5.

The six stages are the usual pattern for nations to traverse. A country in the young debtor stage relies heavily on overseas funds to finance investment. All the accounts at this stage are negative. A country becomes

Table 2.5 *Six stages of balance of payments cycle*

Stage	Balance on Trade Account	Current Account	Capital Account	Countries
1 Young debtor	–	–	–	Thailand, Malaysia, Philippines
2 Mature debtor	+	–	–	Indonesia
3 Debt reducer	+	+	–	China
4 Young creditor	+	+	+	Japan, Taiwan
5 Mature creditor	–	+	+	Singapore
6 Asset liquidation	–	–	+	USA

Note: – means deficit on this account.
+ means surplus on this account.

Source: Kwan (1994, p.19)

a mature debtor mainly driven by the export boom which leads to a surplus in trade. In the next stage further expansion of exports pushes the current account into surplus. A country enters the next stage when it invests significantly in offshore markets. In the next stage the nation becomes a mature creditor when the trade balance turns negative driven by expanding imports. The final stage embodies a huge trade deficit that calls for some asset liquidation (selling of assets). Thus most of East Asian nations borrowed to build the production side of their economies, which positively impacted on their export performance.

2.7 Labour markets and migration

Economic growth in the region has created a relative labour scarcity and consequent improvement in standards of living of workers in some nations. Workers from less advanced nations now tend to migrate to the richer ones. Policy makers have also turned to limited migration as a means to overcome the labour shortage. Thus labour movement between nations has become an important issue. Labour movements, or migration, are mainly driven by two factors: push and pull factors. The push factor exists when migrants make a decision to migrate to avoid poverty and a poor standard of living at home. The pull factor works when the migrants make a move abroad to achieve an improvement in their quality of life. In any migration decision both these factors are present. The crucial message is that the relative standards of living and labour market conditions are the major determinants of the labour flows. In order to examine migration we focus on these twin issues here (see also Chapter 5).

Relative poverty and underdevelopment

Despite their experience of massive economic growth many of the Asia-Pacific nations are still beset with poverty and relative deprivation. Japan, the NIEs and two of the ASEAN countries (Thailand and Malaysia) have experienced a sharp reduction in poverty mainly through the indirect 'trickle down effect' of growth and also through the direct programmes of poverty alleviation (see Chapter 11). For example, in the NIEs the incidence of poverty declined by half during the 1970s and today less than 10 per cent of the population are affected by poverty. In the ASEAN nations the incidence of poverty also declined by half between 1960 and 1990, and in the late 1990s less than 20 per cent of the population are affected by poverty. In Indonesia, for example, in 1975 40 per cent of people lived in abject poverty, while this was less than 17 per cent in 1990. With the reduction in the incidence of poverty the standards of living in these nations have significantly gone up. Against this backdrop we still see endemic poverty in the Philippines, Vietnam, Laos, some parts of Indonesia, and in many parts of Latin America. In these nations on average 30 per cent of the people still suffer from poverty and destitution. Thus, in the Asia-Pacific region there is an economic dualism: there are nations with high to medium standards of living such as the USA, Canada, Australia, New Zealand, Japan, the NIEs, Malaysia and Thailand. On the other hand, there are a large number of nations beset with the problem of low standards of living. Naturally, then, there is a tendency among workers of some of these nations to move internationally in search of a higher standard of living. Thus, there is a large supply of migrant workers in the region. In recent years the labour market conditions have tightened in many of the fast track economies leading to a massive increase in demand for migrant workers. The twin forces of demand and supply have resulted in limited migration in the region. In order to shed light on the actual flows and their ramifications, it is important to consider the labour markets of these nations. How important is this issue? The Asian Development Bank (ADB) recently reported, 'Some expatriate Philippino domestic servants are trained teachers. They earn more in Hong Kong than doctors in Manila' (ADB, 1994). Thus there is a great incentive for people to move across nations for better opportunities in the labour markets. What has caused such changes in the labour markets of the Asia-Pacific nations? We examine this now.

The labour markets

There are two polar cases. First, there are nations which have experienced significant tightening of their labour markets: that is, availability of labour relative to demands in such nations is low. Second, there are nations where there is still a surplus of labour. Thus, the migration pattern is from the second group of nations to the first group. Hong Kong's labour force increased in the 1990s at an annual rate of 2.5 per cent, yet unemployment remained low at 1.5 per cent per annum due to high economic growth and historically low women's participation rate. In Hong Kong the participation rate in the labour market has been steadily declining due to increased affluence. In South Korea due to an economic down turn in the mid 1990s, unemployment has climbed to 3 per cent. In Singapore the shortage of labour has become a major concern. The labour market has been tight with less that 3 per cent unemployment. In 1993 the retirement age was increased from 55 to 60 to ease the pressure on the labour market in Singapore. The financial sector and the construction sector have been under enormous pressure from labour shortages. In order to plug the gap, Singapore relies heavily on foreign workers: on average, foreign workers constitute 20 per cent of the total labour force. In Taiwan the unemployment rate was less than 2 per cent during 1990–96, but there is a severe shortage of labour in low paid jobs. In Malaysia the unemployment rate was around 3 per cent despite a healthy growth in the labour force. In order to cope with increased demand for labour Malaysia critically relies on foreign workers. At least half a million out of the 8 million workers are from overseas. In 1993 Malaysia lifted a ban on the entry of foreign workers: the manufacturing sector is free to recruit skilled workers and to hire unskilled workers from the pool of foreign workers already in Malaysia. Despite such a relaxation of immigration rules, there is a large body of illegal immigrants, mainly from Indonesia and Philippines, in Malaysia, which forced Malaysia and Indonesia to come to an agreement in 1993 to control such labour flow. In Thailand unemployment was about 3.2 per cent in the early 1990s which made the labour market very tight. The Labour force growth there has significantly slowed down due to demographic trends and extension of compulsory education. Despite high unemployment rates in Australia, Canada, New Zealand and the USA, these nations still attract migrants who move there in search of a better quality of life.

By contrast, in Indonesia the unemployment rate is 10 per cent while the incidence of poverty is 17 per cent. The official unemployment rate in China is 5 per cent, yet there is a serious disguised unemployment rate in the state owned enterprises where productivity and wage rates are low. Cambodia is plagued by unemployment and poverty. For Vietnam there is not much published information. There is a significant growth in labour intensive services and small scale and medium scale industries that expand job opportunities. But such an expansion has been offset by shedding of jobs in the civil service and the military. Every year there are about one million new entrants in the labour market. The conservative estimate puts the unemployment rate in excess of 10 per cent in Vietnam. Similar situations can be seen in the Latin American nations. Despite a lot of inertia in the movement, there is a large scale, often illegal, flow of labour from the second group of nations into the first group of scarce labour economies of the Asia-Pacific region.

Rationale behind labour shortage

We have already highlighted that NIEs and near NIEs of the Asia-Pacific region experienced tightening of their labour markets. The factors responsible are two-fold:

1   Sound labour market policies.

2   Spectacular economic growth.

Sound labour market policies
The major policy was to restrain the real wage growth rate and allow growth in employment until full employment is reached. Once the economy reached full employment, real wages were allowed to grow. In 1960 the unemployment rate fell to 1.7 per cent in Hong Kong due to restraint on real wages: since real wages were held down, an increase in the inflation rate increased profitability, and hence investment, which boosted the economy and created employment. Due to similar policies, Taiwan's unemployment rate fell to 4.3 per cent in 1963. Until then real wages were sluggish as they grew by only 0.5 per cent per annum. Once full employment was almost achieved, real wages started soaring: in Hong

Kong the real wages were increased four-fold within 30 years, seven times in South Korea, eight times in Taiwan, ten times in Japan. The labour market tightening was policy-induced which led to massive increases in real wages and consequent improvements in earning opportunities and higher standards of living. This prompted Bhagwati to write:

> These countries appear to have used authoritarian methods to keep trade-union wage demand under control and to build on this base a successful macro policy of low inflation without which they would likely lapse into repeated over-valuation, or occasional exchange controls, and the attendant inefficiencies of implied import substitution.

(Bhagwati, 1987, p.100)

The other type of migration derives from the flows of Japanese FDI. The Japanese multinationals have spread quickly in Asia and their primary goal is to transplant Japanese production organization onto Asian soil, mainly by fostering Japanese labour management regimes. The top management comprises mostly Japanese ex-patriots. Thus, there is a spread of migration of high profile managerial talents from Japan to the rest of the Asia-Pacific region (see also Chapter 10).

What is the implication?

The major role of migration is to achieve a better mix of labour and capital which normally improves the general welfare of a country. But such migration comes at a potential cost: the most obvious cost is that migration is upsetting the ethnic homogeneity of these nations. This has created unfortunate tensions. Second, in most of these countries the migrants are forced into segmented labour markets, which are characterized by wage discrimination. Finally, migration of professionals has led to a better spread of human capital, albeit with a resentment from many locals.

2.8   Conclusion

Conventional wisdom places a high emphasis on trade and investment policies to improve the standards of living in the Asia-Pacific region. The perception is that the complementarity of resources, highly skilled labour markets and outward looking commercial sectors would act as an engine of economic progress in this region. Most of the East Asian economies have been heavily reliant on the external sector.

The further notable feature of their economies has been the rising degree of economic interdependence during the last few decades. There are two possible explanations. First, the formation and growth of trading blocks, such as ASEAN, APEC, NAFTA and AFTA, have provided the formal effort in integrating these economies (see Chapters 7 and 13). Second, and possibly more importantly, the 'flying geese' paradigm argues that the neighbouring nations are at different levels of economic development and hence have diverse comparative advantages. The diversity of comparative advantages has enhanced the trade and investment flows among them.

In this light, the issues concerning trade and investment have four distinct foci. First, we examined the trade patterns among these nations and unravelled the strengths and weaknesses of the trans-Pacific trade. Second, we addressed the question of sustainability of the trade patterns. Third, we examined the flows of investment to highlight how the comparative advantages are created and exploited by the investment flows in this region. Fourth, we examined the labour flows.

The crux of the trading issues is that both Japan and the NIEs have traditionally maintained a trade surplus with the USA to finance their deficits with the primary commodity exporting nations. These nations in turn rely on Japan and the NIEs to maintain the investment boom and growth, and to export their marketable surplus to the USA and the Western European nations. Such a trading pattern has been characterized as the triangular pattern of trade in which Japan acts as the 'supplier' and the USA acts as the 'absorber', while the NIEs maintain a positive trade surplus with the USA. The persistence of growth and progress of the region depends on the sustainability of such a trading pattern. This in turn depends on the external stability of these economies: whether the USA will continue its large trade deficits which are a product of domestic imbalance between savings and investment. If the USA reduces its budget deficit, most of the economies of the region will face external instability and will need to diversify their export markets. Since the 1985 Plaza Accord, these economies have shown signs of dynamic changes and the ability to diversify: the growth rates of the Asian nations no longer follow that of the USA, while inter-regional trade and investment have assumed critical importance. Exchange rate fluctuations and induced changes in trade and FDI have been the major determinants of growth (see Kwan, 1994). A shift has appeared in East Asian exports from the US market to the other Asia-Pacific markets: the share of intra-regional trade rose from 30.9 per cent in 1986 to 43.1 per cent in 1992. In contrast, the share of exports to the US market declined from 34.1 per cent to 24 per cent in the same period. The FDI from the East Asian nations also played a key role in fostering growth in this region: for example, the FDI from Japan has become the most important determinant of the growth rate in the ASEAN countries.

Thus a critical question is: can the USA continue to act as the major absorber of the region until the other economies can take up the slack? There are signs that the USA is reducing its external deficits, which will have severe repercussions on the growth prospects of the region. Unless Japan, the NIEs and the near-NIEs expand their imports and thereby expand their demands, the region could face a marked slow down in growth.

Quite naturally, there is a significant flow of labour from the less developed nations to more developed nations of the Asia-Pacific region. Such migration is mainly driven by the tightening of the labour markets in the more developed countries in contrast to a surplus of labour in less developed ones. Though such migration is welfare improving, it has caused ethnic tension. Migration in some of the Asia-Pacific nations has also led to segmented labour markets in which foreign workers are consistently discriminated against. The upshot is that the potential of the Asia-Pacific nations is yet to be fully realized, due mainly to expanding opportunities through increased interdependence. Capital is quite mobile in this region leading to increased economic growth for most. The critical problem is that of movement of labour across borders. For capitalists the Asia-Pacific region is a borderless economy, while labour still faces social and ethnic divisions. The success of the region will thus also critically depend on how fast the labour markets will integrate. This remains at best an open question.

References

Alam, M. (1989) *Governments and Markets in Economic Development Strategies: Lessons from Korea, Taiwan and Japan*, New York, Prager.

Ariff, M. (1991) *The Pacific Economy: Growth and External Stability*, London, Allen and Unwin.

Asian Development Bank (1991) *Asian Development Outlook*, Manila, ADB.

Asian Development Bank (1994) *Asian Outlook*, Report, Manila, ADB.

Balassa, B. (1988) 'The lessons of East Asian development: an overview', *Economic Development and Cultural Change*.

Bhagwati, J. (1987) 'Protectionism: old wine in new bottles' in Salvatore, D. (ed.) *The New Protectionist Threat to World Welfare*, New York, North Holland.

Bhagwati, J. (1988) 'Export-promoting trade strategy: issues and evidence', *World Bank Research Observer*, vol.3, no.1.

Dornbusch, R. and Park, Y.C. (1987) 'Korean growth policy', *Brookings Papers on Economic Activity*, Washington DC, Brookings Institute.

Ecclestone, B., Dawson, M. and McNamara, D. (eds) (1998) *The Asia-Pacific Profile*, London, Routledge in association with The Open University.

Haggard, S. and Kaufman, R. (1992) *The Politics of Economic Adjustment*, Princeton, Princeton University Press.

Higgott, R., Leaver, R. and Ravenhill, J. (1993) *Pacific Economic Relations in the 1990s, Cooperation or Conflict?*, London, Allen and Unwin.

Japanese Ministry of Finance (1992) *Exes Cain Take Gepps*, Tokyo, Japanese Government.

Kojima, K. (1973) 'Reorganisation of North-South trade: Japan's foreign economic policy for the 1970s', *Hitotsubashi Journal of Economics*, vol.13, no.2, pp.1–28.

Krause, L. and Sekiguchi, S. (1980) *Economic Interactions in the Pacific*, Washington DC, Brookings Institute.

Krause, L. and Kim, K. (1991) *Liberalization in the Process of Economic Development*, Berkeley CA, University of California Press.

Kwan, C.H. (1994) *Economic Interdependence in the Asia-Pacific Region*, London, Routledge.

MacIntyre, A. and Jayasuriya, K. (1992) *The Dynamics of Economic Policy Reform in South-East Asia and the Southwest Pacific*, Singapore, Oxford University Press.

McKibbin, W. and Sachs, J. (1989) 'Implications of policy rules for the world economy' in Bryant, R. *et al.* (eds) *Macroeconomic Policy in an Interdependent World*, Washington DC, Brookings Institute.

Perkins, D. and Roemer, M. (1991) *Economic Systems Reforms in Developing Countries*, HIID Press.

Sachs, J.D. (1985) 'External debt and macroeconomic management in Latin America and East Asia', *Brookings Paper on Economic Activity, no.2*, pp.523–64, Washington DC, Brookings Institute.

Schott, J. (ed.) (1989) *Free Trade Areas and US Trade Policy*, Washington DC, Institute for International Economics.

UNCTAD (1996) *World Investment Report 1996: Investment, Trade and International Policy Arrangements*, New York, United Nations.

White, G. (1989) *Development States in East Asia*, London, Macmillan.

CHAPTER 3

Growth: its sources and consequences

Ajit Singh

3.1   Introduction

This chapter, which is in three parts, reviews economic growth, its causes and consequences in the Asia-Pacific countries. The first part (Sections 3.2–3.7) is concerned with the question of fast economic growth in a group of East Asian developing countries. It reviews the extraordinary economic progress of these nations during the last three or four decades and examines alternative explanations for this phenomenon. This analysis is based on my previously published papers (Singh, 1994, 1995a, and 1997b) to which the reader is referred for a further discussion of the issues and for the sources of the data presented.

In reflecting on East Asian economic expansion, the Chinese economy, because of the size of the country's population, deserves special consideration. The second part of this chapter (Section 3.8) is therefore concerned with the fast economic growth in China over the last fifteen years. The Chinese economy expanded at a rate of nearly 10 per cent per annum in the 1980s, a shade above the pace of South Korea. In the 1990s, the Chinese average annual growth rate has been even faster, nearly 2.5 percentage points greater than South Korea's. The important point is that when South Korea grew at nearly 8 per cent a year for fifteen years, it was an extraordinary achievement of which the world took note. But when China, with a billion people, achieved an even faster growth rate, it was not just extraordinary, but a potentially epoch-making event.

The third part of this chapter (Section 3.9) is concerned with a rather different kind of economy on the other side of the Pacific, i.e. that of the world's most advanced industrial country, the USA. During the last two decades, relative to other industrial countries, the US economy has, as we shall see, performed quite well in certain important dimensions. Specifically, its employment record is much better than that of Western Europe – the average annual unemployment rate in the USA in the 1990s has been roughly a third less than that of the European Union countries. On the other hand, productivity growth, and hence growth of real wages,

The new economic zones like Shenzen, close to Hong Kong, have helped fuel China's rapid economic growth

in the USA has been much slower, both with respect to that country's own previous record and in relation to Western Europe and Japan. Real wages of manual workers have not increased in the US economy for the last twenty years. This part of the chapter will briefly examine some of the analytical issues raised by these strengths and weaknesses of the USA's economic record.

For reasons which will become clear in the following discussion, the bulk of this chapter is concerned with the extraordinary drama of East Asian economic growth. The story of the USA, although important in its own right, is not of such historic significance as is the East Asian drama and therefore gets less attention here.

3.2 Fast economic growth in East Asia: an international perspective

It is no exaggeration to say that the economic expansion of a number of countries in East Asia over the last three or four decades is the most successful story of sustained industrialization and economic development in the history of mankind, at least in the narrow sense of rising per capita incomes.

Japan set the example. Recall that Japan in 1950 produced less than 5 million tonnes of crude steel per annum and a little over 30 thousand motor vehicles of all types. The USA's output of steel at that time was nearly 90 million tonnes and it produced about 7 million automobiles per year. By the mid 1970s the Japanese had caught up with the USA in the production of steel and replaced West Germany as the world's largest exporter of cars. By 1980 Japan overtook the USA to become the largest producer of automobiles in the world.

The Japanese experience has by no means been unique. It was self-consciously emulated by countries like South Korea and Taiwan, with results that are perhaps even more spectacular. In 1955, South Korea was unequivocally industrially backward. Its net value of manufacturing output per head was US$8 compared with US$7 in India and US$60 in Mexico. Since then, South Korea has managed to transform itself from being largely an agricultural society to the point where it is the second most important country in the world in electronic memory chip (DRAM) technology (through its firm Samsung). By the year 2000, the country is expected to become the fourth largest car producer in the world. Nothing could be more symptomatic of the changing map of world industry when, reversing historic roles, a hitherto developing country like South Korea becomes a chief foreign direct investor in the heart of the industrial West, i.e., the UK. In 1996 the South Korean giant LG Group decided to install a factory in Wales and invest US$2.6 billion. This was said to be the largest single investment in the European Union from outside the member states.

To put East Asian economic development in a comparative inter-national perspective, Table 3.1 provides information on overall economic growth over the last three decades for different regions of the world economy, as well as for selected developing and developed countries. In this table the World Bank's definition of 'developing countries' is used, i.e.. it is: 'all low and middle income economies'.

The following points which emerge from Table 3.1 deserve particular attention:

1   Over the fifteen years 1980–94, East Asia has been by far the most dynamic region in the world economy. Although the East Asian economies were growing very fast even in the previous fifteen years (1965–80), the gap between their growth rates and those of other developing regions, for example Latin America, was relatively small (7.3 per cent *vs* 6 per cent for Latin America). However, in the 1980s, economic growth collapsed in Latin America (from 6 per cent per annum to 1.7 per cent per annum) while there was an increase in East Asian economic growth to 7.9 per cent per annum.

2   The regional data in Table 3.1 is at a high level of aggregation. For example, the East Asia region of the Pacific comprises many countries, including large countries like China and Indonesia as well as small Pacific island countries such as the Solomon Islands and Tonga. There are, however, only a small number of these countries (but including some of the most populous ones), which have recorded sustained fast growth over the last three to four decades. These are the countries which have captured the world's imagination by virtue of their extraordinary economic success and are, therefore, the main object of analysis of this chapter. Table 3.2 reports the basic data on economic

Table 3.1 *Trends in GDP growth: selected developing regions, China and India, selected industrial countries and the world: 1965–94 (average annual percentage growth)*

	1965–80	*1980–89*	*1990–94*
Low income economies (excluding China and India)	4.8	2.9	1.4
China	**6.8**	**10.2**	**12.9**
India	3.6	5.8	3.8
Middle income economies	6.3	2.2	0.2
Latin America	6.0	1.7	3.6
Sub-Saharan Africa	4.2	1.7	0.9
South Asia	3.6	5.7	3.9
East Asia and Pacific	**7.3**	**7.9**	**9.4**
All low and middle income economies	5.9	3.1	1.9
High income economies	3.8	3.2	1.7
USA	**2.7**	**3.0**	**2.5**
Japan	**6.6**	**4.1**	**1.2**
Germany	3.3	2.2	1.1
World	4.1	3.1	1.8

Note: The World Bank defined income groups according to GNP per capita in 1994 as follows:

1 Low income US$725 or less.

2 Middle income US$726–US$8,955.

3 High income US$8,956 or more.

Source: World Bank (1992, 1996); IMF (1996).

growth for these high performance economies – Hong Kong, Singapore, South Korea, Malaysia, Thailand, Indonesia, and China.

3 It is customary and analytically useful to distinguish between two groups of countries within East Asia – specifically between North-East Asia (Japan, China, North Korea, South Korea, Hong Kong and Taiwan) and South-East Asia (Brunei, Burma/Myanmar, Cambodia, Indonesia, Laos, Malaysia, Philippines, Singapore, Thailand and Vietnam). South Korea and Taiwan, together with Singapore and Hong Kong, are also referred to as the first-tier 'newly industrializing economies' (NIEs). Malaysia, Thailand and Indonesia, where fast economic growth began a little later, are referred to as the second-tier NIEs; in the terminology of Chapter 2, the 'almost NIEs'. As we shall see below, in the discussion in the following sections, the second-tier NIEs have followed different economic policies in some important respects from those of the first-tier countries. It is significant, as may be observed from Table 3.2, that despite this, during the period 1990–96, the second-tier countries have been just as successful as the first-tier ones (though see Chapter 1).

However, it is also important to note that although the recent economic record of these two groups is indeed similar, detailed data compiled over a longer period reveals that there is an appreciable performance gap between the groups. The exact result will depend on which periods and which countries have been considered, but over the last three decades or so the annual per capita GDP growth rates of Japan and the first-tier NIEs have, on average, been roughly 2 percentage points higher than those of the second-tier NIEs. The cumulative impact of this growth gap over 30 years is significant. For example, Malaysia's per capita income in 1961 was almost three times that of South Korea and almost twice that of Taiwan (Malaysia then included Singapore, so purely 'Malaysian' income would have been somewhat lower). It remained higher than South Korea's per capita income until 1981, but in 1993 was less than half that of South Korea, and about one-third that of Taiwan (UNCTAD, 1996).

4   The North-East and the South-East Asian NIEs have not only had an excellent record of long-term economic growth, but have also had much lower inflation rates than countries in other developing regions, particularly Latin America. World Bank (1996) statistics show that the average annual inflation rate of Asian-Pacific countries during 1980–93 was 7.1 per cent compared with the developing country average of 72.8 per cent, and 245 per cent for Latin American and Caribbean countries.

Table 3.2 *Fast growing East Asian NIEs. GDP growth: annual average percentage, 1970–96*

	1970–79	*1980–89*	*1990–96*
Hong Kong	9.2	7.5	5.0
Singapore	9.4	7.2	8.3
Taiwan	10.2	8.1	6.3
South Korea	9.3	8.0	7.7
Malaysia	8.0	5.7	8.8
Thailand	7.3	7.2	8.6
Indonesia	7.8	5.7	7.2
China	7.5	9.3	10.1

Source: *The Economist* (1 March 1997, p.23)

The East Asian countries' excellent record of economic growth and relative price stability has certainly translated into impressive increases in the average standards of living, reductions in poverty, increasing real wages and rising employment:

● The International Labour Organisation (ILO) provides evidence that during the 1980s, in fast-growing East Asia, the former labour surplus economies such as Taiwan, South Korea, Singapore and Malaysia found themselves confronted with labour shortages. As a result, there was a significant immigration of labour into these countries from neighbouring low-income nations. In these dynamic economies manufacturing employment rose at a rate of over 6 per cent per annum during this decade whilst, at the same time, real earnings increased at an average rate of 5 per cent per annum.

● With respect to poverty, available evidence for the 1980s for individual fast-growing NIEs suggests sizeable reductions in its incidence. Thus in

China the incidence of absolute poverty fell from 28 per cent of the population in 1980 to 10 per cent in 1990; in Indonesia the corresponding reduction was from 29 per cent to 15 per cent; in the Republic of South Korea from 10 per cent to 5 per cent, and in Malaysia from 9 per cent to 2 per cent (see Chapter 11).

- A remarkable feature of the development of the East Asian NIEs during the relevant period has been that not only has the rate of growth been very high, but income distribution has become more – rather than less – equal. However, this conclusion that inequality has declined may hold in relation to incomes, but not necessarily for wealth (see Chapter 11).

The above highly positive record of the East Asian NIEs stands in striking contrast to that of Latin America and Sub-Saharan Africa in recent years. For example, with regard to Latin America, the ILO reports that during the 1980s, there was a steady fall in modern sector employment, with paid employment falling at a rate of 0.1 per cent per annum. This reversed the trend of the previous three decades when steady economic growth had led to a significant expansion of modern-sector employment. In most Latin American countries, the average real wage fell during the 1980s, recovering in only a few countries towards the end of the decade. Minimum wages fell on average by 24 per cent in real terms across the region, while average earnings in the informal sector declined by 42 per cent.

3.3 Why did North-East Asian NIEs grow so fast?

The central analytical and policy question raised by the East Asian NIEs economic experience is of course, what are the causes of the fast economic growth in these countries?

There is no agreement on this question. Indeed, there is a continuing controversy in which the main protagonists are the World Bank with some orthodox economists on one side, and a number of academic economists, not all of whom are heterodox, on the other. This debate is important for two reasons. First, the World Bank professes to base its policy recommendations for countries around the globe on what it regards as the lessons to be drawn from the experience of these highly successful East Asian countries. Second, from an analytical point of view, the debate is clearly of central importance, precisely because of the fast growth of these economies over a sustained period. Thus, the resolution of this debate would inevitably have an important bearing on the economists' general ideas on growth and development.

With the publication of the World Bank's important study, *The East Asian Miracle*, in 1993 there has been some useful narrowing of differences between the two sides. However, there remains a wide gulf on a range of significant issues as will become clear from Box 3.1.

Box 3.1 Two seminal World Bank studies:

'The Challenge of Development' and 'The East Asian Miracle'
The World Bank's studies, *The Challenge of Development* (1991) and *The East Asian Miracle* (1993) are seminal works which provide a comprehensive account of the bank's economists' thinking on development problems and their conclusions on public policy. *The Challenge of Development* is important because, in the words of the then President of the World Bank, Barber Conable, it 'synthesizes and interprets the lessons of 40 years of development experience' by the bank's economists. The significance of the 1993 study, *The East Asian Miracle*, lies in the fact that the Bank economists invariably justify their policy advice to developing countries around the world by reference to the experience of the sustained fast growth of the East Asian economies. However, the two studies complement each other and need to be studied together. The first provides the Bank's general analytical framework and its broad market-oriented approach to development issues. The second, whilst acknowledging heavy government intervention in East Asia, argues nevertheless that the experience of these countries is still compatible with the 1991 Report's recommendation of a market-friendly approach, and therefore does not necessitate any significant departures in the Bank's policy advice. This argument is, however, highly controversial as will become evident in the course of this chapter.

The total factor productivity (TFP) approach to economic growth

In view of the fact, as suggested above, that the World Bank's views on the subject have wide practical policy significance for developing countries, it will be useful to start this discussion with a careful examination of the bank's economists' analyses of East Asian economic growth. The theoretical foundation of these analyses is the so-called TFP approach to economic growth. In this approach, which is based on the growth accounting framework of conventional economics, economic growth is decomposed into three components: the first due to the growth of labour input, the second due to the growth of capital input, and the third due to an increase in the productivity of both capital and labour. The latter is referred to as the growth in the TFP of labour and capital. This can, in theory, arise from a variety of factors, including, importantly, technical progress, economies of scale, and an improvement in the quality of the inputs.

This framework was initially used by economists for estimating empirically the sources of economic growth for advanced economies. It was typically found that only a small part of a country's economic growth can be explained in terms of increases in the supply of labour or capital inputs, and that most of the remainder (for example, as much as 80 per cent for the US economy) is due to an improvement in the productivity per unit of labour and capital. It is, however, important to note for our later discussion that in such empirical exercises, the total factor productivity of capital and labour is not measured directly. It is instead estimated indirectly as the 'residual' growth; it is the difference between the actual growth rate, and that due to the expansion of the labour and the capital inputs separately. This residual is then broadly attributed (often by qualitative analysis) to the factors of the kind mentioned earlier. Since it is difficult to measure technical progress, economists have great difficulty in saying precisely, in quantitative terms, what proportion of TFP growth is, for example, due to technical progress, and what proportion is due to an improvement in the quality of labour and capital. In view of this, the TFP or the 'residual' growth rate is sometimes referred to as a 'coefficient of ignorance', in that economists have not yet found a way of ascribing it exactly to the various factors which may be involved. The precise way the TFP approach works in a technical sense is shown in Box 3.2.

Box 3.2 Sources of economic growth, the production function approach

The production function links production (Y) to inputs of capital (K), labour (L) and technical progress (A).

Thus

$$Y = A f (K,L) \tag{1}$$

This specific production function, called the Cobb-Douglas production function after the names of Professors Cobb and Douglas who widely used it in the 1930s, takes the following form:

$$Y = AK^{\alpha} - L^{(1-\alpha)} \tag{2}$$

where, the exponent α lies between 0 and 1.

The Cobb-Douglas production function has the property of constant returns to scale, that is, a given proportionate increase in capital and labour respectively leads to the same proportionate increase in output. From the point of view of economic theory, this function also has the property that if the factors K and L are paid their marginal products as they would be under perfect competition, α will be the share of capital in total output and $(1-\alpha)$ that of labour. Moreover, the payment of factors according to this scheme will be equal to the total product. This result follows from manipulation of the production function as (2).

Further manipulation of equation (2) involves taking logs on both sides and deriving the following expression;

$$\text{Log } Y = \text{Log } A + \alpha \text{ Log } K + (1-\alpha) \text{ Log } L \tag{3}$$

differentiating with respect to time, (denoted by t) we obtain,

$$1/Y \bullet dY/dt = 1/A \bullet dA/dt + \alpha \bullet 1/K \bullet dK/dt + (1-\alpha) 1/L \bullet dL/dt \tag{4}$$

This may be expressed as;

$$\dot{Y} = \dot{A} + \alpha\dot{K} + (1-\alpha)\dot{L} \tag{5}$$

Where, $\dot{Y}, \dot{A}, \dot{K}, \dot{L}$ denote the instantaneous proportionate growth rates of the respective variables.

Equation (5) is the basis of the decomposition of the growth of output into that of the growth of capital, that due to the growth of the labour force and that due to technical progress, given here by,

$$\dot{A} = dA/A \bullet 1/dt \tag{6}$$

The equation implies that output will increase, on account of technical progress even if there is no increase in the inputs K and L.

The total factor productivity of growth is given by,

$$\dot{A} = \dot{Y} - \alpha\dot{K} - (1-\alpha)\dot{L} \qquad (7)$$

i.e. it is a measure of the total growth of output which cannot be accounted for by growth due to the combined effect of the growth of either the labour input or the capital input. The combined effect is measured as a weighted average of the inputs of labour and capital together where the weight (α) of the capital input is the share of capital in total output, and the corresponding weight of labour $(1-\alpha)$ is the share of labour in total output.

This approach to sources of economic growth has serious limitations. Briefly, first, it is an entirely 'supply side' analysis of economic growth – it does not take any account of 'demand'. Second, it assumes full employment and full utilization of resources, so that, equation (5) suggests that output will increase if there is an increase in labour cost. The proposition is however only realistic if the increased labour force were all able to find jobs and were not unemployed, hence the demand side is important. This theory also ignores the fact that capital and labour may not contribute to economic growth in the simple additive fashion employed by equation (5). There may be interactions between capital, labour and technical progress which may suggest, for example, that employment can only increase if there is an increase in the labour force, or that technical progress can only take place if there is an increase in the supply of capital goods. The TFP approach ignores all such interactions. For a lucid discussion of the subject, the reader should consult Nelson (1981).

Be that as it may, the World Bank economists' basic thesis is that economic growth is determined essentially by the growth of TFP. Those countries which have a higher TFP growth will also have a higher overall economic growth and vice versa. Bank economists further assert that changes in TFP are determined mainly by economic policy – the degree of openness of an economy, the extent of competition in the domestic product and factor markets, and investment in physical and human capital (education), particularly the latter. The underlying chain of causation is that competition and education promote technical progress, and therefore TFP growth, and hence economic expansion. 'Free mobility of people, capital, and technology' and 'free entry and exit of firms' are regarded as being particularly conducive to the spread of knowledge and technical change.

Comparing East Asia with other regions shows that, unadjusted for quality, its rate of growth of labour input has not been greater than that elsewhere. It has however had a much faster growth of capital input. The latter is reflected in the comparative savings-investment records of a group of nine Asian and nine Latin American countries given in Tables 3.3 and 3.4. The comparison with Latin America is particularly interesting because in the 1950s and 1960s, it was the Latin American countries which saved more than the Asian countries. However, in the 1990s, the median Asian economy saved and invested nearly 30 per cent of GDP compared with a figure of about 20 per cent for the Latin American countries. It is notable that between 1955 and 1965, the average domestic savings in South Korea were only 3.3 per cent of GDP; this compares with a figure of over 35 per cent for the 1990s. The data show that of the six East Asian economies listed in Tables 3.3 and 3.4, five of them (the Philippines being an exception) have been able to attain exceptionally high savings and investment rates over the last fifteen years, and some (for example, South Korea) over a longer period.

Table 3.3 *Domestic savings in Asian and Latin American countries 1955–94 (gross national savings as a percentage of GDP)*

	1955–65	*1965–73*	*1973–80*	*1980–89*	*1990–94*
Asia					
China	–	28.7[1]	–	35.0[2]	39.3
India	–	17.9	22.3	21.5	20.8
Indonesia	–	13.7	24.6	27.6	31.2
South Korea	3.3	21.5	26.4	32.8	35.1
Malaysia	23.3	21.6	29.4	29.3	29.5
Pakistan	11.8	–	10.9	14.8	17.6
Philippines	10.9	20.6	24.3	17.6	18.1
Sri Lanka	13.5	14.6	13.5	15.6	12.7
Thailand	16.7	22.6	21.5	22.6	34.1
Median	12.7	20.6	23.3	22.6	29.5
Latin America					
Argentina	18.9	19.7	21.2	11.2	17.1
Bolivia	8.1	29.2	18.2	2.0	6.3
Brazil	16.0	24.3	21.7	19.7	20.4
Chile	10.8	12.9	12.2	9.7	24.4
Colombia	18.8	17.2	19.2	17.4	21.3
Ecuador	15.4	16.3	21.2	16.6	19.4
Mexico	14.6	19.9	21.3	21.3	17.2
Peru	20.9	27.2	24.9	22.0	18.9
Venezuela	32.0	30.0	34.5	23.6	19.8
Median	16.0	19.9	21.3	17.4	19.8

Notes: [1] Figure refers only to 1970
[2] Figure refers only to 1980

Sources: World Bank (1991); United Nations (1966); Asian Development Bank (1995); ECLA (1995).

Parenthetically, some readers may be puzzled by the fact that there is a discrepancy between saving and investment figures in Tables 3.3 and 3.4. Why, for example, was the South Korean domestic savings rate between 1955–65 only 3.3 per cent of GDP (Table 3.3), while the corresponding investment rate was 14.3 per cent (Table 3.4). How does one explain the difference since *ex-post* savings should be equal to investment by the national income accounting identity? Strictly speaking, such an identity holds only for a closed economy. In an open economy the accounting identity takes the following form:

$$Y = C + I + (X - M) \qquad (8)$$

where Y is national income
C is consumption expenditure
I is investment expenditure
X and M are expenditures on exports and imports respectively.

Readjusting equation (8) gives:

$$Y - C = I + (X - M) \qquad (9)$$

Given that Y – C = savings (S), substituting in equation (9) gives:

$$S = I + (X - M) \qquad (10)$$

Therefore:

$$I - S = M - X \qquad (11)$$

From equation (11), if investment is greater than savings ($I>S$), this implies that the country is running a current account deficit on its trade account ($M>X$), which is being financed by net capital inflows on the

Table 3.4 *Investment performance of Asian and Latin American economies between 1955 and 1994 (gross domestic investment as percentage of GDP)*

	1955–65	1965–73	1973–80	1980–89	1990–94
Asia					
China	–	28.5[1]	–	35.0[2]	36.8
India	–	18.4	22.6	23.9	23.9
Indonesia	–	15.8	24.5	30.4	30.2
South Korea	14.3	25.1	31.8	31.2	36.7
Malaysia	14.2	22.3	28.7	32.2	34.6
Pakistan	–	16.0	16.5	18.8	19.7
Philippines	11.4	20.6	29.1	21.7	23.1
Sri Lanka	14.0	15.8	20.6	25.8	23.0
Thailand	17.6	23.8	26.6	26.7	40.7
Median	14.2	19.5	25.5	26.7	29.0
Latin America					
Argentina	19.7	19.8	21.8	15.5	16.7
Bolivia	16.7	25.4	24.9	12.2	15.4
Brazil	16.4	26.1	26.2	21.5	20.5
Chile	11.3	14.4	17.4	18.1	25.3
Colombia	18.9	18.9	18.8	20.4	18.3
Ecuador	14.8	19.0	26.7	23.2	20.6
Mexico	15.1	21.4	25.2	23.1	22.4
Peru	22.4	27.7	28.9	26.2	21.5
Venezuela	22.0	29.3	32.6	22.0	16.3
Median	16.7	21.4	25.2	21.5	20.5

Notes: [1] Figure refers only to 1970
[2] Figure refers only to 1980

Source: World Bank (1996)

capital account through, for example, foreign aid, private investment or other capital inflows.

The answer to the South Korean puzzle above is therefore straightforward: during the earlier period 1955–65 South Korean domestic savings were being supplemented by a large injection of foreign capital inflows to bridge the current account deficit implied by the excess of investment over savings in that period. These inflows came mainly from the USA in the form of economic and military aid. As the South Korean economy became more developed and richer, more and more of the country's total investment was financed by domestic savings. Indeed, by the 1980s South Korean investment as a proportion of GDP was smaller than domestic savings (see the South Korean investment and savings figures in Tables 3.3 and 3.4). What this suggests is that in the period 1980–89, South Korea was running a current account surplus and was therefore most likely a net investor abroad.

The empirical analysis reported by the World Bank economists in *The East Asian Miracle* shows that the high rates of investment in East Asian countries have made an important contribution to their overall fast economic growth. However, this analysis also suggests that investments in these countries were more efficiently utilized, and hence were more productive than elsewhere. The study's estimates of the TFP growth rates indicate that these were considerably higher in the 'Miracle' countries than in other developing economies.

Market-friendly strategy of development and economic openness

As pointed out earlier, the next step in the World Bank economists' analysis is to suggest that these comparatively high growth rates of TFP of East Asian countries were largely due to superior economic policies which have been followed in these countries. Specifically, the economists call attention to two related aspects of economic policy. First, they argue that these countries implemented a so-called 'market-friendly' strategy of development. 'Market-friendly' is a vague term which can mean all things to all people and can also be a mere tautology. However, to their credit, the bank's economists defined the concept fairly precisely in *The Challenge of Development* (see Box 3.1). Government interventions are regarded as being market-friendly if they meet the following criteria:

1   *Intervene reluctantly.* Let markets work unless it is demonstrably better to step in ... [It] is usually a mistake for the state to carry out physical production, or to protect the domestic production of a good that can be imported more cheaply and whose local production offers few spillover benefits. (Spillover benefits are indirect benefits to the economy as a whole which arise from the local production of the goods whose imports are being restricted. Such benefit may include the stimulation of production of related goods, training of work force, etc.)

2 *Apply checks and balances.* Put interventions continually to the discipline of international and domestic markets.

3 *Intervene openly.* Make interventions simple, transparent and subject to rules rather than official discretion.

Overall, the state's role in economic development in this 'market–friendly' strategy is regarded as being at best limited to providing the social, legal and economic infrastructure, and to creating a suitable climate for private enterprise to flourish. In other words, the role of a 'market–friendly' government in this conception is essentially that of 'a night watchman' (i.e. a government which only provides the broad framework for the private sector to operate in, but does not actually interfere directly in its activities).

The second related set of policies to which the World Bank economists ascribe the superiority of the TFP growth of the East Asian economies is their greater openness and close integration with the world economy. Together with vigorous competition in the domestic markets, it is suggested that openness to international competition and foreign direct investment have forced East Asian corporations to be efficient; it has also enabled them to reap the full benefits of foreign technology.

3.4   The TFP approach: alternative estimates and interpretations.

The foregoing analysis of the World Bank's economists has been subject to serious criticisms both empirically and theoretically. A number of academic economists have produced empirical estimates of TFP growth in East Asia which contradict the World Bank's findings. In an important contribution, the US economist Alwyn Young (1994) has presented extremely interesting international evidence on TFP growth for a sample of over one hundred countries. Young's study shows that over the period 1960–85 the four leading East Asian NIEs (Taiwan, Hong-Kong, Singapore and South Korea) were among the top five in the world league in terms of growth of output per capita. However, as Table 3.5 indicates, in terms of TFP growth, which Young calculated for the same group of over 100 countries but over a somewhat shorter time period 1970–85, the NIEs performance was no longer so spectacular. (Table 3.5, for reasons of space, presents data only for the top 66 countries rather than the full sample of 118.) The table indicates that in the TFP league, Hong Kong ranked sixth, Taiwan twenty-first, South Korea twenty-fourth and Singapore sixty-third. The table shows that Bangladesh, a poor developing country with a large population and low growth prospects, ranked higher than either Taiwan or South Korea in terms of TFP growth. Bangladesh was ninety-fifth on Young's list of 118 countries in relation to per capita growth of GDP.

Other studies suggest that, for somewhat different periods than above, South Korea and Taiwan had almost zero TFP growth. In other words, in terms of the TFP methodology, most, if not all, of the extraordinarily high

Table 3.5 *Annual growth of 'total factor productivity' (1970–85)*

1	Egypt	0.035	23	Guinea	0.014	45	Turkey	0.008
2	Pakistan	0.030	**24**	**South Korea**	**0.014**	46	Netherlands	0.008
3	Botswana	0.029	25	Iran	0.014	47	Ethiopia	0.007
4	Congo	0.028	**26**	**Burma**	**0.014**	48	Austria	0.007
5	Malta	0.026	27	Mauritius	0.013	**49**	**Australia**	**0.007**
6	**Hong Kong**	**0.025**	**28**	**China**	**0.013**	50	Spain	0.006
7	Syria	0.025	29	Denmark	0.013	51	Kenya	0.006
8	Zimbabwe	0.024	30	Israel	0.012	52	France	0.005
9	Gabon	0.024	31	Greece	0.012	53	Liberia	0.004
10	Tunisia	0.024	**32**	**Japan**	**0.012**	54	Paraguay	0.004
11	Cameroon	0.024	33	Luxembourg	0.012	**55**	**Honduras**	**0.004**
12	Lesotho	0.022	34	Yugoslavia	0.011	56	Portugal	0.004
13	Uganda	0.021	35	Tanzania	0.011	**57**	**USA**	**0.004**
14	Cyprus	0.021	**36**	**Colombia**	**0.011**	58	Belgium	0.004
15	**Thailand**	**0.019**	37	Sweden	0.010	**59**	**Canada**	**0.003**
16	Bangladesh	0.019	**38**	**Malaysia**	**0.010**	60	Algeria	0.003
17	Iceland	0.018	39	Malawi	0.010	61	Cent. Af. Rep.	0.002
18	Italy	0.018	40	Brazil	0.010	62	India	0.001
19	Norway	0.017	**41**	**Panama**	**0.009**	**63**	**Singapore**	**0.001**
20	Finland	0.015	42	UK	0.009	64	Sri Lanka	0.001
21	**Taiwan**	**0.015**	43	W.Germany	0.009	**65**	**Fiji**	**0.001**
22	**Ecuador**	**0.014**	44	Mali	0.008	66	Switzerland	0.000

Note: Asia-Pacific countries are printed in bold type

Source: Young (1994, p 970)

economic growth of many East Asian countries can simply be explained by the fast expansion of factor inputs, including *inter alia* capital inputs arising from very high rates of capital accumulation (Rodrik, 1995). In that sense, it is suggested that there is no miracle about East Asia – it is basically a question of high rates of investment.

However, an interesting interpretation of these new empirical findings on TFP growth in East Asia is provided by another US economist Paul Krugman (1994). He argues, on the basis of these results, that the high growth rates of the 'East Asian Miracle' economies are not sustainable. This, in his view, is for the following reasons. It is unrealistic to expect that countries which are already investing 35–40 per cent of their GDP will be able to raise their rate of investment much higher still. Krugman goes on to point out that these countries similarly already have highly educated and high quality labour forces, which limits the scope for further improvement in these spheres as well. In these circumstances, without technical progress, eventual decreasing returns to investment will set in and limit the growth potential of these economies.

Krugman's interpretation can however be challenged on a number of grounds. First, it has been pointed out that even within the confines of the growth accounting framework (employed by Krugman himself), there is considerable scope for improving the quality of labour input in East

Asia. Educational levels in many East Asian countries are still considerably lower than those in advanced countries. Therefore, it will be a long time before decreasing returns of the kind Krugman is referring to set in.

Second, however, a more powerful critique of the Krugman interpretation is provided by those economists who do not accept the growth accounting framework and instead put forward an alternative non-neo-classical approach to economic growth. These economists suggest that the effects of technical progress cannot be separated from those of the expansion of capital input. This is because it is argued that technical progress can only take place through the introduction of new machines, i.e. through an increase in capital inputs. Even replacement investment is associated, in this view, with technical progress, because when an old machine is replaced by a new one the latter is likely to be technologically more advanced and not simply a new copy of the old one. Therefore, in this analysis, there is no reason for decreasing returns to occur since the higher the rate of investment, the greater would be the turnover of machines and the greater would be the technical progress. This in turn would also lead to greater learning by doing and, through a process of cumulative causation, should result in a virtuous circle of greater competitiveness and faster economic growth. According to non-neo-classical analysis, therefore, the high growth rates of the exemplar East Asian countries were mostly, if not entirely, due to their very high rates of capital accumulation, which embodied technological progress.

In conclusion, returning to the TFP analysis, it is important to observe that even if the measured TFP for a country like South Korea is zero, it certainly does not mean that the country has literally made no 'technical progress' in the common usage of the term. This would clearly be an absurd conclusion for a country which has, within a short period of 30 years, progressed from largely exporting agricultural and textiles products to exporting motor cars and advanced computer chips. All that the zero TFP result tells us is that the country's economic growth is entirely due to the increased use of inputs, rather than due to a greater efficiency in their use of inputs. Equating greater efficiency in this sense with 'technical progress' is significant and meaningful only within the framework of the TFP model. To re-iterate, one could argue that the TFP approach does not properly measure the contribution of technology to economic growth since much technology is embodied in capital goods, and this fact is not reflected in the simple model given in equation 5 in Box 3.2. Moreover, as noted in Box 3.2 on TFP earlier, critics are also right to suggest that the TFP approach overstates the contribution of labour relative to capital by ignoring the fact that an increased supply of labour by itself does not lead to more growth of output, unless there was also growth of capital stock. As the economist Joan Robinson pointed out earlier this century, capital is not malleable in the real world and therefore a given amount of capital cannot be stretched to provide productive employment to every size of the labour force.

3.5   Did East Asian NIEs follow a 'market-friendly' strategy?

Apart from the TFP analysis, other aspects of the World Bank's theses concerning East Asian development have also been subject to stringent criticism. The bank's economists' claim, that East Asian countries (including Japan during 1950 to 1973, when it was more like a developing country but also enjoyed rapid growth) followed a market-friendly strategy, has met widespread scepticism. The World Bank's critics have raised a number of questions: Did these countries follow the Bank's 'market-friendly' prescriptions in the precise sense outlined earlier? Did their governments intervene in the markets 'reluctantly'? Did they, for example, leave the prices and production priorities to be determined by the market forces and simply provide the necessary infrastructure for private enterprise to flourish? How 'transparent' was the government intervention in industry? To achieve their colossal economic success, how closely did these countries integrate with the world economy?

Unless otherwise specified, the following discussion, for reasons of space, is confined to the two leading East Asian 'tiger' economies of South Korea and Taiwan, as well as Japan during the period 1950 to 1973. There is overwhelming evidence to show that their governments did not intervene either (a) reluctantly or (b) transparently in any of these economies (see Chapters 4 and 6). Specifically, during their periods of fast economic growth, the governments in all three reference countries used a wide array of interventionist instruments including many of the following:

- import controls;
- control over foreign exchange allocations;
- provision of subsidized credit, often at negative real interest rates, to favoured firms and industries;
- control over multinational investment and foreign equity ownership;
- heavy subsidization and 'coercion' of exports, particularly in South Korea;
- a highly active state technology policy;
- restrictions on domestic competition and government encouragement of a variety of cartel arrangements in the product markets;
- promotion of conglomerate enterprises through mergers and other government measures (again particularly in South Korea);
- wide use of 'administrative guidance', indicating non-transparency of government interventions (see, for example, Amsden, 1989 and Wade, 1990).

In other words, the governments in Japan, South Korea and Taiwan did all the things which the 'market-friendly' strategy for development is not supposed to do. Above all, all three countries followed an 'industrial strategy' – a set of policies to deliberately change the market prices and production priorities – which is explicitly ruled out by this approach. The

World Bank economists acknowledge that there was significant state intervention in each of these countries, but argue that 'these economies refute the case for thorough-going *dirigisme* (state intervention in the economy) as convincingly as they refute the case for *laissez-faire*'. Critical economists agree that the experience of these countries is certainly an argument against *laissez-faire*; nor does it provide any support for 'command' planning of production of the Soviet-type, which in effect supplants the market altogether. However, for mixed economy developing countries with effective governments, these economists suggest that the post-war East Asian economic history is unequivocally an argument for adopting an industrial strategy, for guiding the market, and not following the hands-off 'market-friendly' approach recommended by the World Bank.

3.6 'Openness' and East Asian economic development

There is a great deal of evidence which also does not support the World Bank claim that these exemplar East Asian countries either sought or implemented a close integration with the world economy. Consider the following:

- As a result of its explosive economic growth at a rate of nearly 10 per cent per annum during the 1950s and 60s, by the end of that period Japan had graduated to the status of an OECD country, i.e. it had become a member of the developed country club. Unlike developing countries which under GATT were able to provide infant industry protection, OECD member countries were obliged to abolish such restrictions against freer trade. (Infant industry protection refers to restrictions on imports of products which a developing country has just begun to produce domestically. Since, compared with the older and larger competing firms from abroad, the domestic industry is likely to be at a lower or an 'infant' level of development, it will be at a competitive disadvantage in relation to those foreign firms. In these circumstances orthodox theory acknowledges the case for protection for a relatively limited period of time. This is to permit the infant industry to 'grow up' so as to be able to compete on more equal terms with foreign rivals.) Nevertheless, as late as 1979, manufactured imports amounted to only 2.4 per cent of the Japanese GDP; the corresponding percentages in the UK and other countries of the EEC was five to six times larger. Even in the USA, which traditionally because of its continental size has a relatively closed economy, the volume of imported manufactured goods in the late 1970s was proportionally almost twice as large as in Japan. Clearly, during the 1960s and 1970s (and even more so in the 1950s) the Japanese economy operated under a regime of draconian import controls, whether practised formally or informally.

- South Korea, during the last decade, has become a major producer and exporter of cars. It is expected to become the fourth largest car producer in the world by the year 2000. Even now, it has sizeable exports to the USA and Western Europe. And yet, in 1995, South Korea still imported only 4,000 cars from abroad. Essentially, the South Korean government has heavily protected its car industry for the last 30 years.

- Instead of welcoming foreign direct investment, the fact is that both Japan and South Korea (but not Taiwan) discouraged it, particularly during their respective periods of fast industrialization. It is not that the Japanese and South Korean governments were averse to obtaining technology from abroad, quite the contrary. Rather, these governments evidently took the view that it was cheaper and more conducive for national development to 'import' foreign technology through means other than FDI, e.g. licensing (Chapter 10).

- A useful measure of 'price distortion' for an economy is the extent to which its relative domestic prices differ from the international relative prices for the same products (see Chapter 2). On this measure, the estimates of which are presented by the World Bank economists in *The East Asian Miracle* itself, it turns out that Japan, South Korea and Taiwan were among the most distorted economies. Relative domestic prices conformed less to international relative prices in these countries than in Brazil, India, Mexico, and Venezuela. Most of the last mentioned countries are often held up by the Bretton Woods institutions as prime examples of countries which do not 'get the prices right'.

3.7   East Asian experience: alternative perspectives

The analysis of Sections 3.4 to 3.6 has indicated that the various World Bank theses on fast economic growth in East Asia can be argued to be deeply flawed, both empirically, as well as analytically. How can this phenomenon then be explained?

Government–business interactions, the financial system and successful co-ordination

There is a fair degree of agreement that the key to fast economic growth in East Asia lies in the very high rates of savings and investments attained by these economies. Savings and investments are the subjects of a separate chapter in this book (Chapter 4), where these issues will be discussed in detail. However, for the sake of completeness of the argument, it is necessary here to note that:

1   these high savings and investments were carried out largely by the private sector, particularly in Japan and South Korea;

2   they were not a spontaneous outcome of the working of the free market, but were policy induced.

Research shows that the close relationship between the government and business and their interactions, together with the 'long-termist' qualities of the financial system existing in these countries, played a key role in this process (see Chapter 4). For example, in Japan the government not only provided fiscal incentives to the corporate sector, but also implemented protection, had lax enforcement of anti-trust laws (designed to prevent excessive concentration of industry by a small number of firms) as well as practised financial repression (interest rates kept deliberately low, particularly for firms and industries favoured by government industrial policy). All this led to greater rents and profits for the private corporate sector than would otherwise have been the case. However, the government also ensured through other policies that these greater corporate profits were not simply to be consumed or paid as dividends to shareholders, but were in fact reinvested. The government's role was also crucial in raising and maintaining at a high level the corporate propensity to invest, primarily by addressing the problem of co-ordination failures which are ubiquitous in the real world of incomplete and imperfect markets. The US economist, Dani Rodrick (1994), particularly emphasizes the role of the government in this sphere in ensuring high rates of investment in the East Asian economies. The co-ordination problem was extremely important during Japan's high growth phase, as what in effect the Ministry of International Trade and Industry (MITI) did in that period was to orchestrate investment and technological races among oligopolistic firms in favoured industries. Such races were carefully controlled as, otherwise, excess capacity might have been created which would have adversely affected the future corporate inducement to invest.

In South Korea, the role of the government was even more pronounced in all these spheres. Here the government was not just a co-ordinator of investment decisions, but in fact a co-partner with the private sector. Research shows how government policies and government business interactions resulted in extraordinarily fast upgrading of the industrial structure of that country. The government's complete control over the financial system for much of this period was pivotal in this process.

The optimal degree of openness

Turning to the question of openness, the Indian economist, the late Professor Chakravarty, and the present author have suggested in Chakravarty and Singh (1988) that the fast growing East Asian countries did not seek close integration with the world economy (as the World Bank economists would have us believe) but implemented, rather, what may be called 'strategic integration'. In other words, Japan, South Korea and Taiwan were open to the international economy only up to the point that it was in their interest to be so in order to maximize national economic growth.

Chakravarty and Singh (1988) argue that 'openness' is a multi-dimensional concept: apart from trade, a country can be 'open' or not so open with respect to financial and capital markets, in relation to technology, science, culture, education, and inward and outward migration. Moreover, a country can choose to be open in some directions (say trade) but not so open in others (such as foreign direct investment or financial markets). Their analysis suggests that there is no unique optimum form or degree of openness which holds true for all countries at all times.

Indeed, as orthodox economic analysis now recognizes, in the real world of economies of scale, learning by doing and imperfect competition, even free trade is not necessarily optimal for a country. In the Chakravarty and Singh analysis, a number of factors affect the desirable degree and nature of openness: the world economic configuration, the past history of the economy, its state of development, among others. The timing and sequence of opening are also critical. They point out that there may be serious irreversible losses if the wrong kind of openness is attempted or the timing and sequence are incorrect.

The East Asian experience of 'strategic' rather than 'close' integration with the world economy is only comprehensible within this kind of theoretical framework. Thus, in terms of these concepts, countries like Japan and South Korea chose to be open with respect to exports and closed in relation to imports. Similarly, they were open with respect to the interchange of scientific and technical knowledge, but not so open with respect to foreign direct investment. They were also, for much of their fast growth periods, not open to free international capital flows.

It is also useful to consider the experience of the second-tier NIEs – Indonesia, Malaysia, Thailand – within the Chakravarty and Singh framework. As noted earlier, in these South-East Asian economies, foreign direct investment has played a far more important role than it did in Japan or South Korea. One interpretation of this phenomenon is that as a consequence of the fast development of the East Asian countries, the second-tier NIEs are faced with a different historical situation, which makes the optimal degree of openness different for these countries. In this new situation, it is advantageous for the South-East Asian NIEs to attract industries which are no longer economic in the first-tier countries because of the growth of their real wages – as suggested by the so-called 'flying geese' model of Asian economic development (see Chapters 2 and 10).

3.8 China: the plan and the market and fast economic growth

As indicated earlier, the extraordinary economic growth achieved by China during the last fifteen years is an epoch-making event. How has such fast growth come about? (The following section is based on Singh, 1996b.)

It is tempting to say, and is often asserted by orthodox economists, that the Chinese experience shows the virtues of the free market in unleashing entrepreneurship and rapid wealth creation. Such a story may meet the ideological predilections of the orthodox economists, as well as the international financial institutions, but is unfortunately greatly at variance with the facts. Although the Chinese Communist Party over the last two decades has progressively introduced markets and allowed a modest degree of private enterprise, China is very far from being a free market economy:

1   China does not have nationally integrated product markets compared, for example, with a country like India. Apart from the relatively poorer transport structure, Chinese provinces and municipal authorities are prone to impose restrictions on free movement of goods to protect local industry. This leads to imperfections and to the fragmentation of product markets.

2   Although China is attempting to establish capital markets, at the present stage of development these can only be described as embryonic. Investment allocation is essentially done by government controlled banks and the planning authorities, rather than by the free market.

3   China does not yet have free or competitive labour markets. People are still, by and large, allocated to jobs by government departments rather than by the market.

4   Although since 1978 China has been following a so-called 'open door' policy in its economic dealings with the rest of the world, and has benefited enormously from this, its economy is very far from being closely integrated with the world economy. The country maintains a whole plethora of restrictions on imports and on the free movements of capital. China in recent years has been a major recipient of foreign direct investment, but such investment is nevertheless subject to government controls and restrictions at the national, the provincial, and the local levels.

All this raises the question that if competitive markets are crucial to economic growth, as the Bretton Woods' institutions continually assert (IMF and World Bank), then how come the Chinese economy has had this extraordinary economic growth for a long sustained period with markets which are highly imperfect, segmented, or do not exist at all? Equally anomalously for conventional economics, a clear definition of property rights and private ownership of productive assets is thought to be critical for economic efficiency, for technical progress and for wealth creation. Yet in China 90 per cent of industrial capital is in state hands, and most land is still collectively owned. As *The Economist* (28 November, 1992, p.16) ruefully remarked, the story would be much simpler to tell if only the highly successful Chinese small scale enterprises – the so-called TVEs (township and village enterprises) – were privately owned. However, by and large, they are not; their assets being owned by the towns and the villages.

It could of course always be argued that the Chinese growth rate would have been even faster had they had free and competitive markets and private ownership of the means of production. This is, however, highly unlikely in view of the fact that for a large country the Chinese economy has recorded historically unprecedented growth rates in the reference period. What the Chinese story tells us so far is that a country can perfectly well grow extremely fast without having free and competitive markets and private ownership of productive assets.

Decentralization has breathed new life into country districts of China. Here new buildings rise in Kunming city centre in Yunnan Province

What then accounts for China's extraordinary economic performance during the last fifteen years? Research suggests that an important factor has been the very high degree of decentralization which the Chinese have carried out as a part of the economic reform programme. This has transferred most production decisions from the central ministries in Beijing to the provincial and local levels. Such decentralization may have some unfavourable side-effects, such as market fragmentation, mentioned earlier, but on the whole it has been a powerful force in promoting economic efficiency, in motivating people and releasing their creative energies.

Moreover, it must be emphasized that although the Chinese economic performance is anomalous from the perspective of the World Bank's competitive markets paradigm, it accords very well with the actual experience of the other East Asian countries as outlined in the previous sections. Starting from an extreme position where the 'plan' totally dominated the market, the Chinese are attempting to achieve, like the other highly successful East Asian NIEs, that desirable combination of the 'plan' and the market which is most conducive to rapid industrialization. Similarly, like these other economies, the Chinese are seeking strategic, rather than close, integration with the world economy.

3.9 The US economy: achieving full employment with rising real wages

As noted in Section 3.1, the USA, the world's most advanced economy, has performed very well in important dimensions during the last ten years. The rate of unemployment is low, as is inflation, and the economy is expanding at a trend rate of growth of 3 per cent per annum. This may appear small beer as compared with the contemporary East Asian rates of economic growth, but this pace is nevertheless faster than that of either Western Europe or Japan. A priori, economic growth in the world's most advanced economy may be expected to be slower than in others, mainly because it is at the technological frontier. Therefore, unlike the less advanced countries which can copy the leader's technology, the leading country is obliged to carry out the more difficult task of further technological development by itself. In that sense, the slower growth in the USA compared to China or South Korea does not necessarily reflect any economic inefficiency. By the same token, the faster US growth, compared to that of Western Europe or Japan during the last decade, is highly creditable. (See Singh 1995b, 1997a and 1997c for a fuller analysis.)

Nevertheless, there are chinks in the US armour. First, although the rate of unemployment is low, there is still considerable involuntary unemployment. As the US economist, Lester Thurow, notes:

> There are 8.1 million American workers in temporary jobs, 2 million who work 'on call' and 8.3 million self-employed 'independent contractors' (many of whom are down-sized professionals who have very few clients but call themselves self-employed consultants because they are too proud to admit that they are unemployed). Most of these more than 18 million people are looking for more work and better jobs. Together these contingent workers account for 14 per cent of the workforce.
>
> (Thurow, 1992)

Second, and more importantly, the US economy has not been delivering the increases in real wages (money wages adjusted for inflation), which American workers have traditionally come to expect. Until recently real wages of each generation of American workers have historically been twice as high as those of the previous generation. This process seems to have stopped in 1973, since when real wages, particularly of manual workers, have fallen rather than increased. The average real wage for non-supervisory workers in the USA declined at a rate of 0.3% per annum in the 1970s, 1.0 per cent per annum in the 1980s and 0.3 per cent per annum between 1990 and 1994. In the 1960s, in contrast, the corresponding average real wage rose at a rate of 1.4 per cent per annum.

Third, in addition to the huge under-employment and stationary or declining real wages, another unfavourable aspect of the labour market experience in the USA in the recent period has been the growing inequality of wages. Wage dispersion had decreased in the USA during the 1950s and 1960s, but wages have become much more unequal during the last two decades.

It is customary to suggest that the superior US performance, in terms of employment, is due to the greater wage price flexibility of the US economy, compared to European economies. However, the story must surely be more complicated than that in view of the fact that the US labour market is not only more flexible now in relation to the European economies, but it was also more flexible in the 1950s and 1960s. Yet Europe had more or less full employment in the earlier period, and that record was far superior to that of the USA. The essential point here is that Europe outperformed the USA at the time because the European economies were growing at twice their current rate, and at nearly one and a half times the then US rate. That enabled these economies not only to have fast employment growth, but also rising real wages.

Although the US growth rate in the 1950s and 1960s was slower than that of Western Europe, it was faster than its current rate. The higher growth rate of the earlier period enabled the country to have not only as good as, if not a better, employment record than it does today, but more significantly it also enabled real wages to rise appreciably in that period (as was noted earlier).

Clearly, to meet the historic aspirations of the American people, it is not enough to have high overall employment, but it is also essential to have growing real wages. This would require a trend increase in the rate of growth of the US economy to levels such as those attained in the 50s and 60s, when, as seen above, the economy was able to deliver on both these dimensions.

An important question which arises from the above analysis is whether the market forces left to themselves will be able to generate the required increase in the trend rate of economic growth. Since such fast growth has not materialized in the last two decades, the answer to this question may be presumed to be no. That then raises the issue of what kind of public interventions will help to achieve the desired objective, and whether or not such interventions would be acceptable in the USA's political culture.

3.10   Conclusion

This chapter has examined economic growth in East Asia, which has emerged as by far the most dynamic region of the world economy. Over the last four decades several East Asian countries have expanded for sustained periods at rates which are historically unprecedented. Alternative theories have been reviewed concerning the long-term growth processes in these countries, including China and Japan. The last part of the chapter has commented briefly on employment, real wages and economic growth in the world's most advanced industrial country on the other side of the Pacific – the USA.

What lessons can be drawn from the analysis of sources of economic growth in the capitalist East Asian NIEs, as well as China and the USA? The first point which emerges is that the East Asian countries have achieved extraordinarily high rates of overall growth, despite their comparatively poor performance in terms of growth of total factor productivity. Second, regarding proximate causes, we have seen that these high growth rates can be explained in terms of high rates of savings, investment and human capital formation. In that sense, it is right to suggest that the East Asian economic development is not a miracle – it is compatible with standard economic theory. Third, however, the previous analysis indicated that although these high savings and investment rates were by and large implemented by the private sector in most East Asian countries (other than China, see below), nonetheless government played a critical role. The government did not simply follow a hands off, market friendly approach in the World Bank sense, but rather played a crucial co-ordinating, as well as stimulating, role in this process. Further, contrary to the World Bank report, the integration of the East Asian countries with the world economy has been strategic, rather than close.

With respect to these proximate sources of economic growth, the Chinese story is similar, despite its not being a free enterprise economy. Most Chinese land and industrial capital is not privately owned but is under collective ownership. China has introduced markets in the last twenty years, but most product, capital and labour markets are highly imperfect, segmented and incomplete. Moreover, notwithstanding the 'open door' policy launched in 1978, the Chinese have also implemented a strategic rather than a close integration with the world economy. Thus in all these respects, the Chinese experience is not compatible with the World Bank paradigm of competitive markets being a necessary condition for fast economic growth.

The Chinese experience is also similar to that of other East Asian NIEs in another sense. In China also, the growth of factor inputs (specifically, high rates of human and physical capital formation) have been much more important than the growth of total factor productivity in accounting for its overall economic growth. Before Chairman Deng's reforms in 1978, China had a Stalinist command economy with a high degree of centralization of economic decision making. Under Deng's reform, the Chinese introduced markets and decentralization, but they are attempting to find an optimal combination of the plan and the market which will best promote the country's economic growth.

There are two further conclusions which emerge from the analysis of TFP growth in the East Asian NIEs which deserve to be highlighted. First, low TFP growth does not imply that a country has had no or slow technical progress in the ordinary meaning of these terms. That would be a silly conclusion for a country like South Korea in the light of its extraordinary success in continually upgrading its export structure. Thirty years ago it was exporting mainly textiles. Today much the larger part of its exports come from cars, computer chips and other technologically advanced products. The second and related conclusion is that Krugman's inference that these countries will not be able to sustain these high growth rates is only valid within his own neo-classical theoretical framework. In a non-neo-classical analysis where technical progress is embodied in new capital goods as well as replacement capital, there is no reason to expect that high rates of investment will necessarily lead to decreasing returns.

Before we conclude the discussion of East Asia and China, it is necessary to address the following puzzle which may have troubled many readers. The puzzle is why did the state succeed so spectacularly in East Asia when it failed elsewhere, for example in Latin America and Africa? This is a large question, but very briefly, the answer is that apart from the close relationship between the government and business in these countries, and the particular characteristics of their financial systems, there were two other factors which were extremely important. First, unlike many countries in Latin America and South Asia, although the East Asian countries implemented import controls, they also had export orientation. Indeed, export promotion and import controls in East Asia were organically linked. Import controls provided the Japanese and the South Korean corporations, for instance, with high profits which enabled them to raise their rates of investment and to increase their share in the world markets. The corporations in these countries were obliged to promote exports by government policies which made it clear to any corporation that to get ahead, to get help from the state or to be able to get a licence to import foreign technology, it had to export. The second factor which was extremely important is implicit in the above discussion. Unlike developing countries elsewhere which also provided subsidies or imposed restrictions on imports, the East Asian governments imposed strict performance standards on the recipients of the government largesse. These standards often took the form of specific targets for exports or for technological upgrading.

Finally, we turn to the case of the USA which differs from that of East Asia in two important dimensions which have been the focus of this chapter. First, unlike in East Asia, total factor productivity, in terms of conventional growth accounting, has been an important determinant of US economic growth. Second, the role of the state has been different, rather than being necessarily less extensive. The US government intervenes in the country's industrial development in a wide range of ways, for example, health and safety standards, antitrust laws, environmental control measures, government procurement, especially of military goods. Nevertheless, there is a qualitative difference between US interventions and, say, Japanese government interventions in relation to their respective economies. The latter are co-ordinated, primarily by MITI (see Chapter 6), and constitute an overall industrial policy, whereas in the USA there is no such strategic co-ordination. During Japan's high growth phase, MITI could use its arsenal of coercive laws, including, specifically, control over the allocation of foreign exchange to bring about the desired co-ordination of industrial investments. However, since Japan's graduation to membership of the OECD (the rich country's club) around 1970, MITI has to rely much more on its persuasive powers, but nevertheless it continues to carry out its tasks of strategic co-ordination of

Japanese industrial development in the light of evolving international competition.

This chapter has argued that although the US economy has performed well along some dimensions in the last decade compared with western Europe and Japan, it has been unable to meet the historic aspirations of its people. In order to provide both full employment and rising real wages to satisfy these aspirations, it is necessary to have a trend increase in the rate of growth of the US economy. The chapter suggests that market forces left to themselves are unlikely to generate the required rates of growth.

References

Amsden, A. (1989) *Asia's Next Giant*, New York, Oxford University Press.

Asian Development Bank (1995) *Asian Outlook*, Manila, ADB.

Chakravarty, S. and Singh, A. (1988) *The Desirable forms of Economic Openness in the South*, mimeo, Helsinki, WIDER.

ECLA (1995) *Statistical Yearbook for Latin America and the Caribbean*, Santiago, ECLAC.

IMF (1996) *World Economic Outlook*, Washington DC, International Monetary Fund.

Krugman, P. (1994) 'The myth of Asia's miracle', *Foreign Affairs*, vol.73, no.6, pp.63–75.

Nelson, R.R. (1981) 'Research on productivity growth and productivity differences: dead ends and new departures', *Journal of Economic Literature*, vol.XIX, pp.1029–64, September.

Rodrik, D. (1995) 'Getting intervention right: how South Korea and Taiwan grew rich', *Economic Policy*, no.20, April; pp.55–97.

Singh, A. (1994) 'Openness and the market friendly approach to development: learning the right lessons from development experience', *World Development*, vol.22, no.12, pp.1811–24.

Singh, A. (1995a) 'Institutional requirements for full employment in advanced economies', *International Labour Review*, vol.134, no.4–5.

Singh, A. (1995b) 'The causes of fast economic growth in East Asia', *UNCTAD Review*, Geneva, UNCTAD.

Singh, A. (1996a) 'Profits, savings, investment and fast economic growth: a perspective on Asian catch up and implications for Latin America', *Department of Applied Economics Discussion Papers in Accounting and Finance, no.AF33*, Cambridge, University of Cambridge.

Singh, A. (1996b) 'The plan the market and evolutionary economic reform in China' in Abdullah, A. and Khan, A.R. (eds) *State, Market and Development: Essays in Honour of Rehman Sobhan*, Dhaka, The University Press Limited.

Singh, A. (1997a) 'Liberalisation and globalisation: an unhealthy euphoria' in Michie, J. and Grieve Smith, J. (eds) *Employment and Economic Performance*, Oxford, Oxford University Press.

Singh, A. (1997b) 'Catching up with the West: a perspective on Asian economic development and lessons for Latin America' in Emmerij, L. (ed.) *Economic and Social Development into the XXIst century*, Washington DC, Johns Hopkins Press for the Inter-American Development Bank.

Singh, A. (1997c) 'Expanding employment in the global economy: the high road or the low road?' in Arestis, P., Palma, G. and Sawyer, M. (eds) *Markets, Unemployment and Economic Policy, Essays in Honour of Geoff. Harcourt, vol.2*, London, Routledge.

Thurow, L. (1992) *Head to Head: The Coming Economic Battle Among Japan, Europe and America's Business*, New York, Morrow.

UNCTAD (1996) *Trade and Development Review*, Geneva, UNCTAD.

Wade, R. (1990) *Governing the Market*, Princeton, Princeton University Press.

World Bank (1991) *The Challenge of Development, The World Development Report*, Washington DC, The World Bank.

World Bank (1992) *World Development Report*, Washington DC, The World Bank.

World Bank (1993) *The East Asian Miracle*, Oxford, Oxford University Press.

World Bank (1996) *Data Disk*, Washington DC, The World Bank.

Young, A. (1994) 'Lessons from the East Asian NICs: a contrarian view', *European Economic Review*, vol.38, no.3/4.

CHAPTER 4

Financial systems and monetary integration

Grahame Thompson

4.1 Introduction

A key element in the overall explanation of the growth record for the Asia-Pacific is the role played by the financial systems in the countries of the region. Financial systems serve to organize the flows of financial resources that are so important for investment and for the general operation of an economy. A modern economy is typified by the degree and sophistication of its financial system: how effectively it facilitates the exchange of goods and services by providing a measure of prices and means of payment function, and how it helps in the organization and allocation of economic resources so as to maximize investment and national income growth.

The way the financial system assists in these processes is often discussed under the heading of 'financial development'. 'By the process of financial development is meant the gradual evolution, in the course of economic development, of financial institutions – money, banks and other financial intermediaries, and organized securities markets' (Arndt, 1983, p.86). Financial development places command over the disposal of real resources in the hands of those agents that control flows of money, financial institutions and financial markets. Thus the holding of financial resources is in many ways just as important to the overall development process as is the control over land resources, or physical infrastructures such as transport, power and water resources, or the development of human capital and an educated workforce.

The idea of financial development allows an important distinction to be drawn between, on the one hand, *physical*, or 'real', resources and capital, and, on the other, *financial*, or 'money' resources and capital. Financial capital and real capital, whilst different and possibly subject to different processes of development and with different consequences for economic growth, may also be viewed as complementary to one another. The precise relationship between these two is the subject of a great deal of economic debate and is not settled. Some argue that 'real capital' is the key, and greater attention should be paid to developments in the real economy (the formation of physical capital, education and employment levels, the volume and composition of real output, etc.), while others argue that just as important as these are 'monetary capital' and the development of monetary variables and aggregates (interest rates, money supply, financial flows, and the asset and liability structures of various agents). What is happening to the financial dynamic of an economy is just as important as its real dynamic, if not more so, argue the latter group, because financial incentives are the key to the mobilization of these other real resources anyway. It was in the context of reviewing the development process in many of the East Asian economies in the 1960s and 1970s – particularly Taiwan and Korea – that the importance attributed to the purely financial side of the economy for development was stressed (McKinnon, 1973; Shaw, 1973). As we shall see, the debate originated by these analyses in the 1970s continues today.

For the most part this chapter concentrates upon financial developments and financial flows. This process is typified by the increased *monetarization* of the region's economies. But there is still a significant proportion of *subsistence* economic activity in many of the countries of the region, and barter remains an important means of exchange (see Chapter 12). This does not pass through a market exchange so is not registered in a financial form. However, for the most part, the monetarized sector has expanded in the regional economies to such an extent that concentrating upon this will not distort the analysis – though the extent of the non-monetarized sector was still perhaps surprisingly large even in the 1980s (Arndt, 1983, Table 2, p.92; Cole, 1988, p.28). The non-monetarized sector tends to be the greatest in those economies designated by Gangopadhy (Chapter 2) as the 'traditional developing nations' and 'almost-NIE' types, such as Indonesia, the Philippines, Burma and Laos.

The process of financial development has also involved the *deepening* of financial relationships in these economies. The development of the financial system leads not only to an extension of monetary relations – so that more and more economic activity is drawn in under the monetary net – but to an enrichment in levels of financial intermediation as well. Retail commercial banks are an obvious first institutional level in a monetarized economy. But they are then supplemented by the development of a set of secondary financial institutions such as specialist savings banks, mortgage lenders, merchant banks, insurance companies, discount houses, etc., and then further by the emergence of various types of security markets. These latter deal with the issue of commercial company shares and bonds and the secondary trading of these, and with the government bond market as the role of government expenditure expands. In addition, as the economy internationalizes another level can be added, which deals with all the international financial transactions that typify a sophisticated and increasingly open economy.

The central role of the financial system is to undertake the task of *financial intermediation*. Financial intermediation refers to the process of gathering financial surpluses from a large number of small savers, aggregating these, and then lending them on to borrowers who wish to use the surpluses for financial or real investment. The financial institutions and markets thus act as intermediaries between lenders and borrowers. They thereby help constitute aggregate savings and investments in an economy (see Chapter 3). But financial institutions and markets are not simply passive conduits for this process. They always establish terms and conditions by which they will borrow and lend. So a key element in the allocation of financial resources in any economy is the organizational structure of its financial system, and the terms and conditions under which its financial institutions and markets operate. There is a diversity in these as between the regional economies and they produce different outcomes as a result. Part of the debate is over how efficient these different systems are in terms of the growth performances they have contributed towards.

An additional complication here is that the process of financial development also implicates what has come to be known as *financial repression*. In some ways this is seen as the opposite of financial development. It refers to various controls put on the operation of the financial system, usually in the form of government action. Thus, various types of liquidity controls and capital adequacy constraints are placed upon banks, and legal ceilings on interest rates and credit access conditions have been implemented by governments. Governments have also subsidized credit, or physically directed credit and investment funds to favour different industrial sectors or product lines in the economy. They have used taxation to stimulate or repress certain activities and markets. Regulations on who can and who cannot operate in various parts of the financial system and markets have been operative. Foreign capital and exchange controls have been prevalent at times. All these go towards establishing restrictions and direct and indirect controls over the free operation of the financial system. Those advocating a 'market friendly' approach towards economic policy (such as McKinnon and Shaw mentioned above) have designated these as 'impediments' to the efficient operation of the financial system, with a concomitant loss of performative outcomes. On the other hand, those less wedded to the market-friendly approach have designated these practices as precisely the ones that have helped the regional economies to achieve their spectacular successes. There are some advantages in the 'rigidities' that these practices have installed in the economies, and these have positively worked to enhance economic outcomes (Wade, 1985; Harris, 1988).

A final introductory point is that this chapter concentrates on the financial systems in what might be termed the mainstream market economies of the region. There are two exceptions to these which are not discussed at any great length here.

The first is the remaining communist states. Here the state directly allocates credit through its control of the financial system and banking organizations. It is the state banking system that gathers surpluses from its productive organizations and citizens, and then passes these on to those organizations responsible for investment as and where the plan targets dictate. In fact, there are always informal lines of credit operating in even the most closely controlled and state directed economies of this kind. For instance, productive organizations can extend trade credit between themselves within the various chains of raw materials, component and goods supply. Also, although in theory the state should exercise central control over the money supply in these countries, in fact, this is often not the practice and rampant inflation can result from lax controls. In addition, the state banking system is often over-burdened with 'non-performing assets' which are debts that state enterprises will never be able to repay.

The second exception to the main thrust of this chapter involves Islamic banking. This is important in Malaysia and to a lesser extent in Indonesia, the main Islamic countries of the Asia-Pacific region. Islamic banking forbids the operation of interest payments. As a result, the Islamic banking sector of these economies places the emphasis on the participation of lenders in the normal profits that emerge from enterprise. Fixed interest rate returns are replaced by variable returns dependent upon profitable successes (or losses) of the borrowing enterprise.

The plan of the rest of the chapter is as follows. The next section looks at the general trends in financial development in the regional economies, concentrating upon the East Asian nations. Then the chapter reviews issues associated with financial liberalization. This is followed by an analysis of international financial developments. The chapter then moves on to look at the role of the financial system in various macroeconomic management issues. The final main part of the chapter raises issues of financial integration across the Pacific Rim and beyond. This is followed by a short concluding section.

4.2   Financial development in the Asia-Pacific

The economies of East Asia have had a long history of financial development, the origins of which lay in the historic importance of rice and other grain production to their economies. Combined with a monsoonal climate that sharply delineated the growing season from the dormant one, and which often resulted in crop failure, this led East Asian societies to develop a sophisticated grain surplus and reserve system. The legitimacy and survival of early political formations in these countries were highly dependent upon how well they administered and protected their grain reserve and redistribution systems. This resulted in an early and easy move from a grain based credit system to first a metallic coinage based financial one, and then into a fiat or paper system (see, for instance, the case of China discussed in Yang, 1952).

In addition, this early encounter between proto-state political formations and the protection of the credit systems – which eventually evolved into genuinely financial systems – led to the strong predisposition in these countries towards modern governments' involvement in the raising and allocation of financial resources. This is something deeply embedded in these societies, a legacy of a particular historical trajectory, and one which marks them off from the more privately commercial evolution of Anglo-American type financial systems. The role of government has always been ambiguously placed *vis-à-vis* the development of the financial system in the Anglo-American historical experience. The consequences of these different historical experiences linger even today.

Herein, in part at least, lies the origin of one of the enduring points of debate about the form and organization of the financial system in the economies of East Asia and those of the Anglo-American type; the proper role and consequences of governmental regulation or guidance of the financial system – what in modern parlance is argued to lead to 'financial repression' as mentioned above. We return to this issue in a moment.

Explaining high levels of savings and investment

One of the most significant features of the growth experience of the East Asian nations is the high levels of investment in their economies. This is argued to be a key element in their economic success (Chapter 2). Supporting these levels of investment has been the phenomenal growth in domestic savings, particularly household savings. Aggregate Taiwanese savings, for instance, increased from about 5 per cent of GDP in 1950 to over 30 per cent in the late 1970s (Wade, 1985, p. 107); Korean savings increased from 3 per cent in the 1950s to 35 per cent in the early 1990s (Chapter 3, Table 3.3). Why have these countries been able to save so much?

To begin with, the underdeveloped nature of the state sector and government expenditure may have had something to do with it. A low ratio of government expenditure to GDP means that even if the government sector displays net dissavings, that is, if government expenditure is higher than government revenues (which was often the case in the 1950s and early 1960s in the NIEs and almost-NIEs), then its impact on the economy's savings rate overall is still small. In fact, particularly since the mid 1960s, the government sector had mainly been in surplus in these countries, as Table 4.1 indicates, which added to the positive savings rate. Government savings represent the vigorous use of fiscal policy to mobilize surpluses, via means of taxation, and any surpluses generated by publicly owned enterprises. But the main bulk of the savings is undertaken by households (and to a lesser extent by firms – the other contributor to private savings as shown in Table 4.1). Here a number of considerations enter the picture.

One element involves another aspect of a relatively low state involvement in the economy. The absence of a developed welfare and social security system means that households have had to save to provide for this themselves. Similarly, with the absence of a large public housing stock the pressure to save for private housing is greater. And with the

Table 4.1 *Public and private savings in a selection of Asia-Pacific developing economies*

Economy/year	Public savings	Private savings
East Asia		
Indonesia 1981–88	7.7	14.0
Japan		
1945–54	5.3	12.0
1955–70	6.2	17.2
1971–80	4.6	20.1
1981–88	5.1	15.8
Malaysia		
1961–80	3.2	18.7
1981–90	10.3	19.1
Philippines		
1980–83	10.4	11.5
1984–87	1.4	14.1
Singapore		
1974–80	5.5	22.6
1981–90	18.5	24.0
Thailand		
1980–85	14.3	4.7
1986–87	8.6	14.6
Latin America		
Chile		
1980–84	3.9	2.3
1985–87	7.9	0.6
Mexico 1980–87	4.3	17.5

Source: adapted from World Bank (1993, Table 5.6, p.210)

underdeveloped nature of the financial system the ability to raise finance for house purchase – and additionally, consumer durable purchase – is restricted. Combined with the practices of demanding very large down payments for housing and consumer credit, all these have contributed to a high savings propensity.

In addition, the actual form of the financial system can make a significant impact. The East Asian economies established means of mobilizing small savings through postal savings institutions very early in their development processes. These proved to be a low cost and secure means of raising the savings ratio (World Bank, 1993, pp.218–20). In Japan, Post Office savings accounts paid no tax on interest earned, and they received favourable rates compared to commercial banks.

Another feature concerns the access to finance by small and medium sized businesses. By and large, the banking sectors in the East Asian economies have either been government owned or highly concentrated in private hands (cartelized and obligopolistic). As discussed further in a moment, governments have used their powers here to direct credit in various ways, and this has traditionally favoured their own publicly owned enterprises or large private companies (for example, the *chaebol* in Korea), or those companies attached to the large manufacturing and trading groups (for example, the Japanese *keiretsu*, which each include a bank as a central part of their conglomerate structure). Small independent companies have been disadvantaged as a result, and they had to resort to their own savings to invest. Given the importance of the 'family firm' in these countries, this often takes the form of personal and household savings. (For a full explanation of these different business arrangements amongst the East Asian countries see Chapters 6 and 9.)

A further aspect of the way the financial systems have operated relates to their regulation and control. Governments have been loath to see any part of their financial system collapse. They have supervised them closely in terms of their solvency, risk profiles and capital adequacy ratios, regulating spreads and non-performing assets. They have exercised tight controls over licensing arrangements and ownership structures. Prudential regulation has been the order of the day. In addition, during periods of financial distress – when an actual crisis strikes – governments have quickly come to the rescue to bail out the banks in difficulty, or to press other stronger financial institutions to lend their support or take them over. This has produced a general climate of confidence and security for depositors. Coupled with a commitment to a stable macroeconomic environment and low levels of inflation, lenders have been well served by their governments, with positive long-term results in terms of their attitudes towards savings. This is not to say that there have been no financial crises or bouts of inflation – there have been many serious incidents of these – but it is to say that they have occurred less often, and been generally better controlled events, than in other comparable countries.

A final issue in terms of the characteristics of the financial system is the question of 'forced' savings. Some East Asian governments (for example, in Japan, Malaysia and Singapore) have in effect made saving mandatory, in terms of pension plans, welfare provision, and for the purchase of consumption goods. The most spectacular example of this is Singapore's Central Provident Fund (CPF), into which citizens are forced to invest their savings for all manner of welfare benefits (see **White, 1998**). (The CPF, which is an off-balance sheet item in the government accounts and thus not part of government revenues or expenditures, has become an attractive model for many in Europe and North America who are seeking to 'reform' their own welfare systems.) It is argue that the CPF boosted savings in Singapore by four per cent of GDP per year during the 1970s and 1980s (World Bank, 1993, p.219).

What role for interest rates?

One of the most controversial aspects of East Asian financial development in the post-Second World War period concerns the impact of the regulated, guided and directly controlled financial systems found there. A key element in this form of government intervention has been control of the interest rate and, in particular, the artificial repression of the rate to below what might have been its market rate. The imposition of such 'interest rate ceilings', often implemented along with the deliberate direction of credit into certain favoured areas of the economy, is generally recognized to have been prevalent in most of the economies at least at some time in the post-war period. This experience is contrasted to the much more 'open' and market friendly nature of US interest rate determination, but also of the other Anglo-American economies in the region (along with Hong Kong, which took a more *laissez faire* attitude towards the development of its financial system under UK guidance). In a moment we come to the whole debate about the liberalization and deregulation of these economies, but it is generally recognized that such controls have existed (and continue to exist in many cases).

To put this into a slightly more formal framework, consider Figure 4.1 which sketches the relationship between real deposit interest rates and real growth rates ('real' rates are money rates adjusted for inflation).

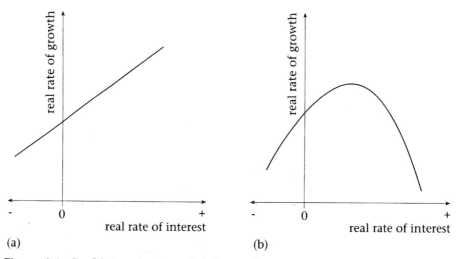

Figure 4.1 *Real interest rate and real growth rate*

A simple traditional view is illustrated by Figure 4.1(a), where there is a linear relationship between the interest rate and growth rate. As the real deposit interest rate increases we might expect the real growth rate to increase since there is an incentive for both savers to save and borrowers to borrow, resulting in investment and growth. Both savers and borrowers receive real returns to their activity as the economy moves into the positive real-valued right hand quadrant of the diagram. Even with negative real interest rates, however (though positive money rates), some real growth is likely since 'money illusion' is a commonly observed phenomenon (savers and investors do not totally discount for inflationary conditions).

But probably a more adequate picture is illustrated in Figure 1.4(b). Here the effect of real interest rates on growth is a quadratic one. First the real growth rate increases as the real interest rates increase. But then it peaks and falls away as the real interest rates expand further. At low real interest rates, the growth rate is low because of the lack of incentives to invest. This incentive expands as the interest rates increase, but after a while the growth rate increase falls away as fewer and fewer attractive investment opportunities present themselves. Eventually the schedule turns down and the growth rate declines. Why might this be the case? At very high real interest rate levels too many risky and adventurous investments are undertaken, which, as they prove unsuccessful, produce lower growth rates. It could even be the case that the schedule moves into a negative real growth rate phase if the interest rate were so high as to lead to purely speculative activity and investment in very risky ventures.

In both cases (a) and (b) discussed above the suppression of interest rates (or higher inflation) will lead to lower growth rates than would otherwise have been the case. In fact, attempts to test a model such as that shown in Figure 4.1(b) on the empirical conditions found in the Asia-Pacific economies have not proved very successful, mainly because the real deposit rates of interest have not varied over a wide enough range to register sufficient observations on the horizontal axis (Fry, 1995, p.43). But the figure still provides us with a convenient framework for discussing further the possible impacts of the interest rate on savings and investments.

Looking towards investment

Other things remaining equal, lower interest rates would normally lead us to expect lower savings and lower investment in an economy. But despite the restrictions on interest rates and credit mentioned above, the East Asian economies have displayed very high comparative savings and investment ratios, and historically spectacular GNP growth rates. This is the apparent paradox that lies behind the big debate about the actual effects of government interventions in the financial system of the economies in question. Might these interventions be the actual stimulus for that growth rather than a constraint upon it?

Before we pursue this directly, it is important to recognize another endemic feature of these economies' financial systems. This involves an 'unorganized' part of that system, what is termed the 'curb market'. Most of the economies have experienced a two-tier financial system: an organized and formal part and an unorganized and informal part. Many of the restrictions put on the formal market may have led to the stimulation of the informal, 'curb-side' part. Alternatively they may have operated as complementary to each other. Curb-markets are usually viewed as inefficient, since they may have to cater for only those borrowers rejected by the formal sector, who are thereby thought to be more risky to lend to, and curb market interest rates are therefore much higher than they need be. The overall result is a less than optimal outcome for everyone.

However, curb markets seem to have played an important part in the financing of the small and medium sized family business enterprises disadvantaged by the 'big firm' bias of the formal financial sector, in providing consumer credit, and in the crucial area of export finance (particularly before the governments took this up with a vengeance as they turned to an export orientated growth strategy in the late 1960s and 1970s – see Chapter 2). As financial development proceeded, the curb market seems to have become gradually absorbed into the formal sector, though it remains important in some of the almost-NIEs and traditional developing countries of the region. Export credit became a key provision of the formal systems, along with priority finance for the small and medium sized businesses. Both of these were once again guided and organized by the governments themselves, however. So we have yet other instances of governments intervening strongly to promote their particular policy goals as their economic priorities changed.

The traditional way that finance is thought to be raised for investment in the Anglo-American systems is via the stock market. Companies can float their shares on the market and use the proceeds to expand their business. In fact this is of less importance than is often recognized, even in the Anglo-American systems, since it is internal savings that contribute the greatest proportion of resources for company investment, via depreciation allowances and retained earnings. Only a minor proportion is generated from external sources such as the stock market or as loans from banks.

As Figure 4.2 demonstrates, the stock markets in the Asia-Pacific region vary considerably in size. Of the East Asian economies, only Japan had a sizeable stock market in terms of capitalization (the worth of the shares traded) in the mid 1990s. In addition, the number of companies traded on the East Asian markets (and in Australia) remained modest, as shown in Figure 4.3. Hong Kong, the largest of the region's emerging markets, is only about 5 per cent of New York's and 9 per cent of Tokyo's.

Thus the role of the equity market in these economies remained small, at least until the mid 1990s. Their main activity had been in the secondary market of buying and selling already listed shares. To some extent this is the result of government restrictions put upon the operation of stock markets in the countries, which have not favoured their development. Similarly with the corporate bond market. But more recently these markets have expanded, particularly in Korea, Taiwan and China, and with further liberalization their role in mobilizing financial capital might be expected to expand.

All the East Asian developing countries have established specialist financial institutions explicitly designed to provide long-term development finance at favourable rates. These development banks have been a central part of the governments' overall attempts to mobilize domestic savings for investment, and to attract foreign capital. They have been substantial long-term lenders in Indonesia, Japan, Korea, Taiwan and China in particular. There remains a debate about the effectiveness of these institutions, however. Some have argued that they have made a significant contribution to rapid industrialization (World Bank, 1993, pp.226–8), while others have

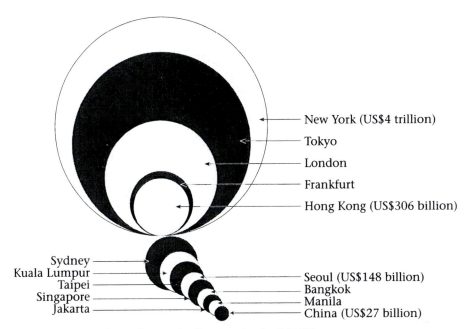

Figure 4.2 *Stock market capitalization (end of 1993)*

Source: Pacific Economic Cooperation Council (1994, Figure 19.5, p.117)

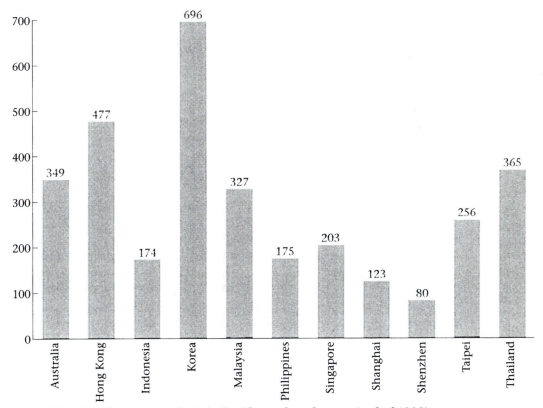

Figure 4.3 *Listed companies in Asia-Pacific stock exchanges (end of 1993)*

Source: Pacific Economic Cooperation Council (1994, Figure 19.5, p.116)

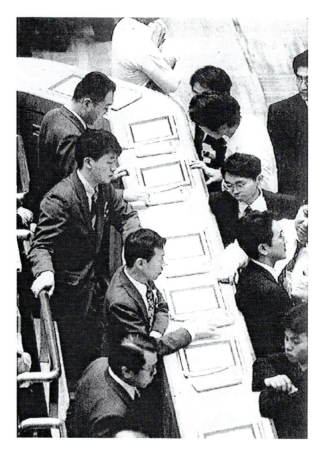

Tokyo stock exchange

suggested that their record is a poor one, that they have not become self-supporting, autonomous institutions capable of mobilizing resources on entirely commercial terms (Fry, 1995, pp.50–1).

An additional reason for the high levels of domestic investment, and one of the most controversial, is controls on capital outflows. Japan, Korea, Taiwan, China, Indonesia, Thailand and Malaysia have all employed these kinds of restrictions in the formative period of their economic take-offs. Put alongside the repression of interest rates discussed above (which encourages investment), and the important role of direct government investment in infrastructure and in the enterprises owned by the public sector in various countries, the basic explanation for investment becomes clearer. What is impressive about these countries is the wide range of institutions and policies all designed to meet the single target of increasing investment, and the determination of the authorities to activate these at any time. Thus, in many ways, the direct and indirect involvement of the government in these economies would seem to have stimulated the high levels and rates of investment, rather than to have restricted them.

4.3 Pressures for liberalization and deregulation

As mentioned above, the trajectory of financial development is towards a wider and wider embrace of the financial system, and for its deepening in terms of levels and markets. This is not a smooth evolutionary process, however, nor may it quite capture the full complexities of the historical experience of all the countries of East Asia. An added element involves the relationship between government controls and financial liberalization.

A simple evolutionary approach might suggest that at first the systems were characterized by heavy government involvement, which was then followed by successive rounds of decontrol and liberalization. In fact the relationship between control and decontrol has also been complex and non-linear. There have been rounds of liberalization in parts of the economies' financial systems throughout their development processes, with often quite rapid and radical changes in policy direction. Nor have these changes been all in the single direction of a more market-friendly approach. They have oscillated between more liberalization and less. The 1960s saw some early liberalization in Korea and Taiwan in particular, which stimulated the work of Shaw and McKinnon referred to in Section 4.1. This was followed by the almost reinvention of regulation in the late 1960s and into the 1970s. Then there was another round of deregulation in the very late 1970s and into the 1980s as the economies reacted to the adjustments pressed upon them by the turbulence in the international financial system. Once again, however, the effects of deregulation seem to have melted away as the recovery took place in the 1990s.

Thus perhaps the best way of viewing the question of regulation and deregulation is not along a single dimension but as involving multidimensional adjustments and manoeuvrings, in which the governments have been most concerned to maintain their capacities to 'supervise' their financial systems in the interest of their own domestic economic development. Often this has frustrated those pressing for greater overt 'disengagement' from intervention, but the records seem to show that this has not too adversely affected their growth rates, at least during the period of the main growth and maturity of their economies. Thus the governments have shown a very pragmatic attitude towards liberalization, bending to pressures and circumstances when that has seemed necessary, and then regaining the initiative as the pressures subsided.

However, a number of more recent developments may be conspiring to alter quite radically the possibilities of this pragmatic and careful approach. There has been a much more sustained change in the sentiment of economic policy making in the world at large, which is deeply affecting the economies of East Asia, just as it affected the Anglo-American ones beforehand. The momentum of a neo-liberal, *laissez faire* deregulatory programme, which is much more sustained and thoroughgoing than any before, is having a major impact on the economies generally, not just in respect to their financial systems. Pressures to sell off public assets and to denationalize the banking systems, to remove any remaining government restrictions on the operations of financial markets, to use competition policy to push private markets to reduce cartels and widen ownership, and generally to withdraw from all but the most minimal of intervention, are more intense than ever before.

This programme is aided by two further developments: the slowdown in the growth of many of the economies (Chapter 1 and Figure 4.7 below), which was led by the Japanese economy in the early 1990s, and the increasing internationalization of the financial markets throughout the region. Both of these have added to the calls, from domestic as well as from international sources, for the further opening up of the economies to the freer operation of market forces. And these calls will be increasingly difficult to resist, so that a radical change in approach may be under way. These calls are particularly intense in the case of Japan, whose financial system is generally agreed not to have developed sufficient flexibility as its economy has matured into an advanced-country status.

Whether these liberalization moves will be for the good of all the economies in the region is another matter. For those wedded to the market-friendly approach it goes without saying that it will be. They have led the calls for this kind of deeper deregulatory programme ever since the 1960s. But, as we have seen, this may not have been in the best interests of the economies concerned. It will affect the almost-NIEs and traditional development economies of the region in particular, since they will not be able to develop behind the protective barriers that were operative for Japan and the first tier of NIEs in the 1960s and 1970s.

What this brief analysis of the pressures for further and rapid deregulation reveals is the need for further analysis of where these economies stand in an international context. Up until now we have been dealing with what is an essentially closed economy model. It is time to reconsider this, now set within the terms of the international economy.

4.4   The internationalization of the financial systems

There are three main initial aspects to discuss, which serve to introduce the international relationships in which the economies are located. As indicated in both Chapters 2 and 3, savings and investment need not be confined to the domestic economy if there is some international transmission mechanism that redistributes financial resources from one country to another. Here we refer to official and unofficial development assistance, to FDI flows and to portfolio investment as separate mechanisms for the international flows of capital into and out of a country. These make it possible for domestic investment not to be matched by domestic savings.

Forms of international financial investment

Because of the strategic importance of the Asia-Pacific region, particularly its East Asian part, financial assistance from the USA was an important early source of capital for development. Post-war reconstruction in Japan became a US priority. In addition, strategic considerations led to a good deal of military aid to Japan, Korea and Taiwan in particular. This aid was important in launching these economies onto a growth trajectory, but the direct significance of non-military aid soon fell away as their internal growth dynamic began to emerge in the 1960s (for example, as their internal savings rates escalated – see Section 4.2). However, military aid has remained indirectly important in that it has released these countries from some of the expenditure involved in providing for their own defence. The USA carried much of the burden from its own expenditures. Other official development assistance has been in decline in the region, though that originating from Japan remains an important source, particularly for the almost-NIEs and traditional developing countries. Indonesia remains the most important recipient of official financial assistance in the region.

Probably of much greater long-term significance are FDI flows, which add directly to the potential real productive investment in an economy. The trajectory of these flows was extensively discussed in Chapter 2. Inflows played only a very small part in the Japanese economy, and they were similarly low in the early years of Korea's take-off. Only after 1965 did FDI flows into Korea begin to expand. Taiwan followed soon after. Singapore has been the country most dependent upon FDI flows for its investment (responsible for 37 per cent of capital formation between 1991 and 1993), followed by Malaysia (25 per cent over the same period). In 1970 FDI inflows within East Asia and the Western Pacific were US$270 million. By 1994 these had expanded to US$42.7 billion. As pointed out in Chapter 2, the striking feature of the region's FDI flows is the growing intra-regional nature of the investments involved. In the mid 1990s the five main capital exporting countries were Japan, Taiwan, Korea, Singapore and Thailand. Japan is by far the largest intra-regional investor, followed by Korea and Taiwan, and more recently by Singapore and Thailand. The major recipients were Thailand, Malaysia, Indonesia and China. China became the single largest developing economy recipient of FDI in the world in the mid 1990s. While it remains the most alluring prospect to international investors, overheating of its economy and infrastructural problems could make China increasingly less attractive. Vietnam (along with India) looks to be the next hottest target for international investors.

In recent years the East Asian countries have also attracted substantial volumes of portfolio capital. Unlike FDI, portfolio investment represents the purchase of stocks and bonds. It is financial investment as opposed to the real investment associated with FDI. A number of developments have aided the trend towards portfolio investment. As the economies have matured, their stock markets and bond markets have grown, though as pointed out above their stock markets in particular remain thin in terms of the number of participants and operators and the size of investments. But the rate of growth of these markets in the 1990s has been particularly sharp, especially those involving the participation of foreign investors. Foreign portfolio investment in East Asia and the Western Pacific rose from

US$2.3 billion in 1990 to over US$18 billion in 1995. However, there remain some restrictions on the short-term inflow of capital in many of the countries and also, perhaps more importantly, on the outflow of capital. But, in general terms, it is the marked liberalization of the economies in the region since the early 1980s that has opened them up to portfolio and other financial investments. It is Hong Kong and Singapore that carved themselves out a strong regional position as financial centres, largely because of their perceived stability and open nature, depth of participation, and low risks.

Another development that has made the East Asian economies attractive for portfolio investment is the growth of the bond issue made by governments. Governments have found this a convenient method of raising finance, and the growth in the credibility of governments in the region has added to their ability to attract foreign funds. The general macroeconomic stability in the region has also enhanced this kind of finance, since investors can be more certain of their returns, particularly as the exchange rates were stabilized. Following from this has been a growth in derivatives trading, particularly in Japan and Singapore. Derivatives are pure monetary instruments – options taken on the movement in prices of the underlying financial assets or commodities.

But portfolio capital is very volatile capital. It can represent 'hot money', that moves in an out of an economy quickly according to only slight changes in market sentiment. Thus the rise in importance of this kind of investment can increase the instability in an economy. Given the rapidity of its build up, the potential for instability is magnified as it increases very quickly relative to GDP growth. When the size of foreign inflows is large relative to the size of market capitalization, the potential for uncontrollable financial bubbles increases with higher foreign participation.

Some macroeconomic considerations

Hot money of this kind not only flows into countries because of the underlying attractiveness of the conditions there, but also because of changes in the condition in the traditional alternative sites of investment, notably the older advanced industrial economies. Thus the recession and slow down in growth in the USA and Europe may have stimulated the move into the East Asian market. As real interest rates increase in the traditional countries, and as they come out of recession, that money can quickly flow out of the East Asian economies if it is allowed to. In relation to this, however, studies have shown that securitized capital flows to the East Asian economies are much less sensitive to changes in US interest rates and economic conditions than are comparable flows into Latin American countries (Das, 1996, pp.329–30). So hot money has been more stable in East Asia than it has been in Latin America.

Large capital inflows into the South-East Asian economies indicate to a deterioration of their current accounts. Given that the balance of payments overall has to balance, an increase in one part implies a decrease in another; as current flows decrease, capital flows increase. This means that the trading account has moved into deficit, which is exactly what tended to happen as these countries built up large deficits with Japan in particular. They had been importing capital equipment from Japan to feed their development processes. Additionally, capital inflows mean interest payment outflows on the current account, which can also lead to a further deterioration in the current account.

Another consequence is that capital inflows will put pressures for an appreciation of the exchange rates of the countries in receipt of them. The need for capital inflows can also affect domestic interest rates and the money supply, which means that macroeconomic conditions change. The reaction of the monetary authorities to financial inflows is important for the overall consequences and impact on the domestic economy. In particular, the domestic authorities can try to 'sterilize' the inflows in various ways, so as to minimize their impact on the domestic economy (Dean, 1996).

For instance, as money moves in, one reaction would be to try to 'mop it up' by buying up the foreign currency and storing it as reserves. This kind of 'open market' sterilization is the traditional one used by the East Asian economies, but it was in decline in the mid 1990s because it was costly for governments and proved not to be too effective. Instead they were moving towards sterilization by requiring commercial banks to hold much higher reserves, in effect by putting added restrictions on the ability of those banks to create their own liquidity and hence the domestic money supply. Finally, several of the Asia-Pacific countries, such as Indonesia, Malaysia, Singapore, Taiwan and Thailand, have moved pension fund money from commercial banks into the central bank, again to try to restrict the growth in the domestic money supply. These measures are just another manifestation of the guided and controlled nature of the financial systems in these countries. Of course they have also resorted to fiscal policy to try to mop up the added liquidity that capital flows induce.

All these responses point to the difficulty of conducting an independent macroeconomic policy in an increasingly interdependent and integrated international economy. This is the issue taken up more explicitly in the next two sections.

4.5   Exchange rate regimes

An important aspect of exchange rate stability is the relationship of the domestic currency to the main currencies used in international trade and finance. All international trade is invoiced in a particular currency, and investments are denominated in the main currencies as well. Thus what is happening to the values of these main currencies relative to one another, and to the currency of the domestic economy, can have a considerable impact on economic performance. It affects the competitiveness of economies, the returns they gain from trade and the worth of their underlying assets.

Table 4.2 puts this into perspective for a number of different indicators of international trading and financial activities. The US dollar remains the dominant currency used in international trade (b). This is also true of official currency holdings (a), and in terms of transactions on the foreign exchange markets (c), and finally in terms of the currency in which assets and liabilities are denominated (d). Thus the US dollar continues as the *lingua franca* of the international economic system (Frankel, 1995). But, as the table indicates, the dollar has lost ground, particularly to the German mark (DM) and the Japanese yen. This is significantly so in the case of the currency of denomination of financial assets and liabilities (d). Here it was the ASEAN economies and China that had been most rapidly diversifying their official reserves by reducing their commitments to the dollar and increasing those of the yen and the DM. However, overall, it is important to note the continued commitment to the US dollar by the East Asian countries, particularly the ASEAN members. There is as yet no strong indication, for instance, that the yen is poised to replace the dollar as the currency of choice for these transactions. More on this in a moment.

Table 4.2 *The international role of the main currencies*

(a) Official role

	Share of total official currency holdings (per cent)		
	end 1973	end 1983	end 1995
US dollar	76.1	71.1	61.5
European currencies[1]	14.3	15.8	20.1
of which: German mark	7.1	11.7	14.2
Yen	0.1	4.9	7.4

[1] Pound sterling, German mark, French franc, Dutch guilder.

Number of currencies linked to:	1983	1994	1994 (percentage of world GNP)
the dollar	34	25	1.53
European currencies (including the ecu)	18	19	0.25

(b) Currency use in international trade

	Share of the main currencies as regards use in international trade			
	1980		1992	
	Percentage of world exports	Internationali-zation ratio[1]	Percentage of world exports	Internationali-zation ratio[1]
US dollar	56.4	4.5	47.6	3.6
German mark	13.6	1.4	15.5	1.4
Yen	2.1	0.3	4.8	0.6

[1] Ratio of world exports denominated in currency relative to that country's exports.

(c) Transactions on foreign exchange markets

	Breakdown of transactions by currency[1]		
	April 1989	*April 1992*	*April 1995*
US dollar	90	82	83
German mark	27	40	37
Yen	27	23	24
Other	56	55	56
Total as %[2]	200	200	200

[1] Gross turnover. Daily averages.

[2] Since any transaction on the foreign exchange market involves two currencies, the total of the proportions of transactions involving a given currency is 200 per cent.

(d) Currency in which financial assets and liabilities are denominated

	Share of outstanding international bonds		
	end 1981	*end 1992*	*end 1995*
Dollar	52.6	40.3	34.2
European currencies	20.2	33.0	37.1
of which: German mark	NA	10.0	12.3
Yen	6.9	12.4	15.7

NA = not available

	Share of world private portfolio		
	end 1981	*end 1992*	*end 1995*
Dollar	67.3	46.0	39.8
European currencies	13.2	35.2	36.9
of which: German mark	NA	14.7	15.6
Yen	2.2	6.9	11.5

NA = not available

Source: European Commission (1997, Annex 2, p.18)

This continued commitment to the US dollar is confirmed if we look at the actual way these economies conduct their exchange rate operations. Table 4.3 specifies the official exchange rate regimes of a selection of East Asian economies as notified to the IMF. But this in fact disguises how they actually conduct their exchange rate operations, since most of the managed/free floats actually involve surrogate alignments to the US dollar (this is measured by calculating the degree of variation of domestic exchange rates to the US dollar and to other currencies; the lower the degree of variation, the closer the effective alignment – see Bénassy-Quéré, 1996, pp.19–38). Most of the East Asian economies thus anchor their currencies to the dollar and not to the yen. The questions are, why is this the case and what might its consequences be?

To begin with, let us look at the broad pattern of intra-Asia-Pacific trade, as indicated by the data plotted in Figure 4.4. This shows the aggregated direction of intra-Pacific exports: East Asia ⇒ East Asia compared with East Asia ⇒ USA. On the basis of this comparison there looks to be a clear move towards the development of an East Asian trading

Table 4.3 *Official exchange rate regimes (end of 1994)*

Hong Kong	Pegged to the US$
Korea	Managed float[1]
Singapore	Managed float
Taiwan	Not IMF member
Indonesia	Managed float with US$ reference
Malaysia	Managed float
Philippines	Free float
Thailand	Pegged to a basket[2]
China	Managed float
Myanmar	Pegged to the SDR[3]

[1] Managed float = currency allowed to float, but managed by the authorities to smooth out fluctuations in value.

[2] Basket = group of currencies weighted by their importance in country's trade.

[3] Special drawing rights (SDR) = an international money equivalent managed by the IMF.

Source: adapted from Bénassy-Quéré (1996, Table 2.2, p.18)

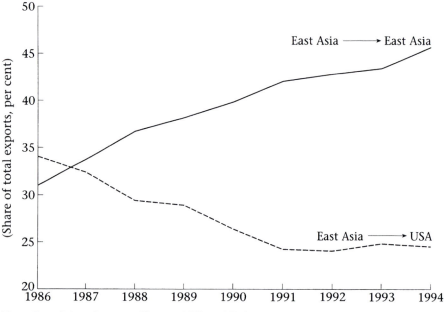

Note: East Asia = Japan + China + NIEs + ASEAN

Figure 4.4 *Intra-East Asian trade compared to East Asia–US trade*

bloc, at the expense of East Asia–USA trading relationships. It looks, therefore, as though there might be an incentive for the East Asian countries to form a single currency bloc as well, perhaps organized around the yen (Kwan, 1996). However, this is misleading if one does not look more closely at the *disaggregated* trading relationships between the country groups involved, and at their trading relationships beyond the purely Asia-Pacific arena.

Such a richer pattern is demonstrated by the data included in Table 4.4. Here we see the trade relationships between the NIEs, the ASEAN countries, Japan, the USA, Europe and elsewhere for a selection of the East Asian countries separately, 1973 compared to 1993. Within just the intra-Asia-Pacific trade some important trends and changes can be identified:

1   intra-NIEs trade is developing at the expense of exports to the US and Japan;

2   the NIEs have also become major suppliers for ASEAN countries, at the expense of Japan;

3   Japan's trade intensity with East Asia declined, while it increased a little with the USA (see also Chapter 1, Table 1.1).

In addition, the NIEs and ASEAN countries continue to build very important trade relationships with Europe and elsewhere. Thus, broadly speaking, the data in Table 4.4 indicate to the continued *diversity* of the trading relationships of the main East Asian countries, and particularly no

Table 4.4   *Overall patterns of East Asian external trade, 1973 and 1993*

Orientation of exports by selected East Asian countries (% of total exports of each country)

Exporting country	To the USA		To Japan		To NIEs		To ASEAN		To the EU15		Elsewhere	
	1973	1993	1973	1993	1973	1993	1973	1993	1973	1993	1973	1993
Japan	27.7	29.4	–	–	13.5	19.1	7.4	9.2	14.3	16.2	37.1	26.1
Hong Kong	35.3	22.5	5.7	4.0	5.0	8.9	2.7	3.7	32.6	21.6	18.7	39.3
Korea	33.6	21.3	37.8	14.3	5.7	11.1	2.0	7.7	10.7	12.1	10.2	33.5
Singapore	16.6	21.9	10.3	7.0	9.2	15.6	22.4	23.4	16.2	14.5	25.3	17.6
Taiwan	42.1	28.3	14.8	11.2	9.4	9.9	4.1	7.1	13.0	15.3	16.6	28.2
Indonesia	12.1	13.0	56.3	31.7	14.9	21.1	1.1	3.9	11.5	14.8	4.1	15.5
Malaysia	13.3	21.0	29.7	15.5	16.1	29.4	1.4	5.5	23.0	14.9	16.5	13.7
Philippines	35.2	38.2	40.4	18.9	4.7	12.2	1.2	3.5	13.0	16.4	5.5	10.8
Thailand	10.7	22.2	28.3	17.9	14.8	15.5	12.1	4.3	19.4	18.9	14.7	21.2
China	1.4	29.0	20.1	19.8	19.3	9.0	1.1	3.2	13.8	20.5	44.3	18.5

Origin of imports of selected East Asian countries (% of total imports of each country)

Importing country	From the USA		From Japan		From NIEs		From ASEAN		From the EU15		Elsewhere	
	1973	1993	1973	1993	1973	1993	1973	1993	1973	1993	1973	1993
Japan	24.6	22.1	–	–	6.5	11.8	12.1	12.3	9.2	13.8	47.6	40.0
Hong Kong	13.4	9.1	21.1	18.7	10.3	23.3	3.3	6.0	18.7	22.0	33.2	20.9
Korea	27.2	19.3	13.0	26.0	1.8	4.4	8.1	6.6	7.2	13.7	42.7	30.0
Singapore	15.5	14.3	20.6	22.6	5.9	9.6	17.1	21.5	15.9	13.1	25.0	18.9
Taiwan	22.4	20.5	38.8	32.8	4.4	7.3	4.5	6.3	13.9	14.5	16.0	18.6
Indonesia	17.4	10.8	36.5	23.6	9.4	20.5	2.6	3.0	20.5	21.6	13.6	20.5
Malaysia	8.2	16.0	22.1	26.7	13.9	26.1	7.7	5.3	22.0	14.1	26.1	11.8
Philippines	26.9	19.3	33.7	27.2	4.2	17.3	1.5	5.0	13.3	12.6	21.5	18.6
Thailand	13.1	9.1	38.3	31.2	8.1	17.2	1.3	5.7	20.4	16.6	18.8	20.2
China	13.8	11.6	20.3	26.7	3.7	27.7	1.7	3.1	16.3	14.5	44.2	16.4

Source: adapted from Bénassy-Quéré (1996, Box 3.2, p.39)

clear trend towards a greater reliance on trade just with Japan (indeed, to some extent the opposite). So there was no obvious incentive for these countries to change the currency in which they had traditionally invoiced their trade, and hence to which they anchored their domestic currencies.

What is more, this incentive not to change was all the greater given what had been happening to the relative exchange rates of the three largest international currencies discussed in relationship to Table 4.3 above, at least up until the mid 1990s. As Figure 4.5 shows, the Japanese yen was appreciating against the German mark and particularly against the US dollar after 1975, and most rapidly since the Plaza Accord of 1985 (see Chapter 2). Given that the East Asian currencies were mainly linked to the US dollar, which was depreciating in value, this meant that their currencies had been depreciating as well, compared to the DM and the yen. A depreciating currency makes an economy's exports more attractive and imports into it less so. Thus, in part, one of the reasons for a better than otherwise competitiveness of the East Asian economies has been this downwards pressure on their currency values produced by their anchor to the US dollar. This has made them more competitive in relationship to Japan, and partly explains the changing pattern of their trade relationships referred to in connection to the discussion of the data in Table 4.4. There has clearly been no incentive to switch to a yen anchor whilst that currency had been appreciating in value. From the point of view of the ASEAN countries in particular, macroeconomic stability is more likely to have emerged from a continuation of the existing policy. There was no obvious

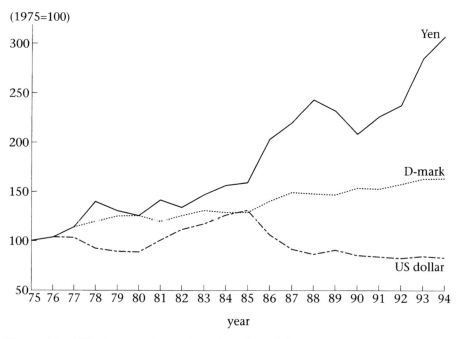

Figure 4.5 *Effective yen, Deutschmark and US dollar exchange rates (1975–94)*
Source: Kwan (1996, Figure 1, p.4)

yen bloc forming in East Asia. However, things did begin to change in the mid 1990s. The dollar began to *appreciate* against the yen after 1995, so the yen began to *depreciate* in value relatively. This could have longer-term consequences in changing the patterns so far described if the depreciation of the yen continues.

Of course, these potential favourable exchange rate movements are not the only determinant of the underlying competitiveness of an economy or its overall balance of payments position. They only represent pressures and tendencies, which can be overwhelmed by other trends and underlying structural features. As mentioned above, capital flows as well as trade flows determine the overall balance of payments, and a number of the ASEAN economies experienced growing trade deficits as they stocked up with capital goods, despite the favourable pressures on their exchange rates (see Table 4.5 in Section 4.6). In an increasingly open and internationalized economy, competitiveness also attracts capital inflows, which puts upward pressures on a currency. In terms of assets, holding these denominated in a currency that is appreciating in value will mean they are worth more in terms of the home currency, which could account for the move by the East Asian countries away from dollar denominated assets and into those denominated in yen, as mentioned above. So there are always trade-offs, conflicting pressures and counter-dilemmas involved with international financial activity. The next section focuses upon the issue of the possible growing financial interdependence and integration of the Asia-Pacific economies.

4.6 An Asia-Pacific financial integration?

The economies of the Asia-Pacific region are increasingly becoming interlinked as trade and financial activity expands across national borders. This interlinking is enhanced by the growth of the real integration of the economies as production networks stretch out across the Pacific Ocean (see Chapters 2, 8, 10 and 14), but this section concentrates upon the growth of purely financial integration. In part this is a truly global phenomenon as the financial markets of the international economy expand their range and integration. Thus in some ways it is difficult to discuss the nature of just trans-Asia-Pacific financial integration, since this is itself set within the growth of what is for many a global phenomenon. There are as many links between the Asia-Pacific economies and those financial markets that lie *beyond* the region as there are between the markets of those economies *within* the region. Thus, in part, the discussion must be conducted at two levels: the first in respect to the international economy in general and the second in respect to just the Asia-Pacific region.

As already indicated in this chapter there are plenty of examples of financial interlinkages between the economies of the region. But *financial interlinkages* are not quite the same as *financial integration*. The first has been a feature of economies ever since national borders were established. International financial interlinkages express the way two or more economies are linked as a financial transaction takes place between them. It is a fairly simple economic relationship: a discrete one-off exchange, and one that does not necessarily imply a change in the nature of the agents or economies involved with that transaction. However, financial integration implies the establishment of a much deeper and more continuous relationship that somehow binds the agents or economies together and changes the way they operate. It would establish a newly integrated entity, the parts of which operate in conjunction with one another. The question is, then, how to measure whether this process of integration has actually happened in the international financial system.

Traditionally there are a number of ways this is done or approached. The first is to look at the relationship between aggregate national savings and domestic investments in an economy, to see how closely they are correlated. If they are closely correlated (as one changes so does the other), then the argument is that the international financial system is *not* that integrated. Financial integration allows for flows between countries, so that domestic savings and investments can diverge. A close correlation implies that the domestic economies remain relatively closed to these cross border flows. The same applies with another measure, consumption patterns between countries. These are the flip-side of savings and investment. A high degree of financial integration would imply that consumers have access to finance on the international markets and can thus vary their consumption patterns accordingly so as to match lifetime earnings with lifetime consumption demands. This would imply the emergence of similar patterns of lifetime consumption for different countries. The continued differences in lifetime consumption patterns would indicate to a continued non-integration of the financial systems.

In fact, attempts to establish whether these measures operate for the APEC countries have been largely unsuccessful (Kearney, 1996, p.352). In part this is because the testing techniques are not robust enough to sort out the issue properly, but at another level it indicates to the continued non-integrations of the economies in question. Indeed, this result is one confirmed at the global level by looking at a wider set of OECD countries (Thompson, 1997, Table 2, p.164).

Other measures can also be used to test the integration hypothesis. One is to investigate the degree of real interest rate convergence between economies. If the financial systems were closely integrated, then real interest rates would also be at a similar level. This implies that the return on assets will be converging amongst the economies, as capital moves freely between them. Another related measure would be the way stock market prices move in similar directions in the different markets, or the way adjustments in the exchange rates take place so as to equalize the real convergence between different countries.

In fact, all of these measures are extremely difficult to properly operationalize because of a number of technical difficulties in making

(a) The stock markets take fright ...

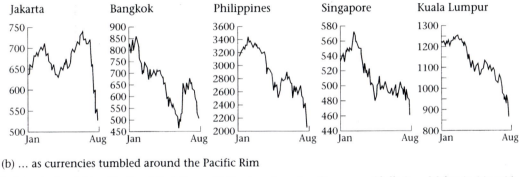

(b) ... as currencies tumbled around the Pacific Rim

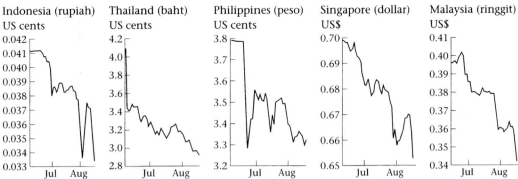

Figure 4.6 *East Asian stock prices and currency falls in 1997*

Source: *The Observer*, 31 August 1997

valid comparisons between different countries' systems (Kearney, 1996). This is nowhere more so than as between the Asia-Pacific countries as a whole, or even between a subset of the East Asian/ASEAN ones. All the diverse mechanisms of 'financial repression' discussed above serve to undermine a legitimate comparison.

Although not as rigorous, there is, however, some other rather more superficial evidence that integration is happening between the East Asian financial systems. In July and August 1997, for instance, a serious financial crisis seemed to hit a set of the ASEAN economies more or less simultaneously, and overflowed into Singapore and Korea as well. In technical parlance, their markets suffered from 'contagion' (as from a contagious disease), where the crisis in one market quickly spreads to others. The way this affected the markets is shown in Figure 4.6. Stock market prices and currency values fell as capital tried to move out of the economies simultaneously. They seemed to suffer a genuine co-ordinated attack from disillusioned foreign investors.

But what were the reasons for this attack? An answer to this could tell us something more general about the state of these economies in the late 1990s. The authorities in some countries tried to blame it on 'foreign speculators', but the real sources of the crisis lay elsewhere, and mainly on the domestic front. Financial panics of this kind happen quickly and dramatically after pressure has built up over a longer period of time. The first point to recall is that the countries in question experienced an unexpected downturn in their growth rates in 1995–96 (with the exception of the Philippines), and an added sudden fall in their export growth rates (Chapter 1). Figure 4.7 reminds us of the trajectory of growth rates over the 1990s, clearly indicating to the fall in 1996. Second, as mentioned above, most of the countries in question were running a current account deficit, indicating to their underlying 'uncompetitiveness'. This is shown in Table 4.5. What is more, countries such as Malaysia and Thailand were suffering from a considerable over-heating of their economies, given the large inflows of portfolio capital and FDI investment, much of which had found its way into construction and real estate developments and not into directly productive activity. Finally, the consequences of the dollar appreciation after 1995 were also important, since these economies had attached their currencies to a now increasingly *uncompetitive* currency. Thus all the ingredients were present for a crisis of this kind to emerge, most of which were home-grown and to do with the state of the real economies.

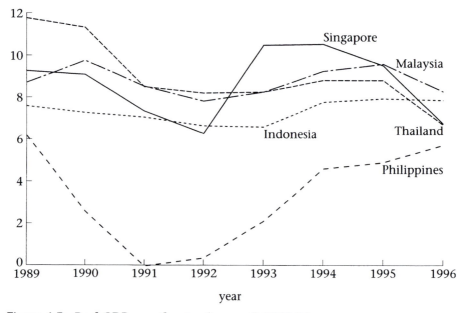

Figure 4.7 *Real GDP growth rates (per cent) 1989–96*
Source: *The Observer*, 31 August 1997

But what does this say about financial integration? First, the coincidental downturn in these financial systems need not *necessarily* indicate to a high degree of such integration *amongst themselves* since the immediate stimulus for it came from a common 'outside', amongst an amorphous mass of foreign investors. Second, although Indonesia, Thailand, the Philippines and Malaysia did demonstrate a large current account deficit, Korea (not shown in these figures, but which also suffered some contagion) did not, and Singapore shows a massive current account surplus. (Note also

Table 4.5 *Selected Asia-Pacific countries' current accounts 1993–96 (% of GDP)*

	1993	1994	1995	1996 (estimate)
USA	-1.5	-2.2	-2.1	-2.0
Japan	+3.1	+2.8	+2.2	+1.9
Australia	-3.7	-4.8	-5.3	-4.6
Indonesia	-1.6	-1.7	-3.7	-4.1
Korea	+0.1	-1.2	-2.0	-1.5
Malaysia	-4.6	-5.9	-8.5	-7.9
Mexico	-6.4	-7.7	-0.1	-0.9
Philippines	-5.5	-4.4	-3.3	-2.7
Singapore	+9.1	+17.3	+18.3	+14.7
Taiwan	+3.0	+2.6	+1.6	+1.8
Thailand	-5.4	-5.7	-7.1	-7.0

Note: - in deficit; + in surplus

Source: derived from International Monetary Fund (1996, Table 7, p.37)

that Taiwan had such a surplus and was not so affected by contagion.) What is more, much larger current account deficits were demonstrated by Australia, but it was not involved. Thus if there were any genuine integration, it probably involved only a few countries in the East Asian region, was not strongly embedded, and certainly did not involve the entire Asia-Pacific economy.

Finally, what might have been the consequences of these events in the summer of 1997? In part a response to this depends upon an issue raised at the beginning of this chapter.

Those who look upon the financial aspects of an economy as being the most important would view these events as very significant in their own terms. They demonstrated a lack of confidence by the international financial community in the future of these economies. They were also used to press for further deregulation on those economies, particularly in respect to the freedom of capital movement *out* of the countries concerned. One of the reasons advanced for the growing lack of confidence of international investors was that financial capital could not be easily enough withdrawn for the ASEAN economies, although it was always welcomed as an inward investment.

On the other hand, those who remain wedded to the real side of an economy as providing the key indicators of success would probably remain a little more ambiguous in their judgements. The causes of the financial crisis looked to be real ones, associated with a downturn in real growth rates (see Figure 4.7). That was bad news. But growth rates were still running at around 6 per cent, an exceptionally buoyant position compared to the growth rates being experienced in the advanced economies of North America and Western Europe. The question was whether the financial crisis would further exacerbate the real downturn, or whether a rapid recovery was possible as the effects of the financial downturn were quickly reversed (see also Chapter 3).

4.7 Conclusion

This chapter has reviewed the role of the financial systems in the economies of the Asia-Pacific region, concentrating upon the high performing economies of East Asia. The initial problem set for the chapter was to explain the very high investment rates found in these economies, and to assess their possible contribution to overall economic performance. In particular, here was a debate about the relative merits of a 'market-friendly' as opposed to a 'government-friendly' approach to economic policy making. The conclusion was that systematic government involvement in the financial systems did not seem to have hindered these economies in their development processes as much as the market-friendly theorists might have expected.

However, times are changing. The possibility of the governments maintaining a tight control over their financial systems in the traditional way looks unlikely as the world's economies internationalize further and the tide of neo-liberal policy advice and pressures for deregulation continue to gather force. The economies of Asia-Pacific are probably in a unique period of transformation in this respect.

But we should not expect radical structural change quickly or precipitously. The economies and their financial systems are tied into a complex set of domestic and international economic relationships, not all of which are driving towards disruption of the existing patterns of financial organization. There remains plenty of scope for a consolidation around existing patterns and practices. In addition, the extent of genuine financial integration (as opposed to financial interlinkaging) still looks to be marginal, again leaving opportunities for the re-establishment of effective national responses to the changing international environment.

References

Arndt, H.W. (1983) 'Financial development in Asia', *Asian Development Review,* vol.1, no.1, pp.86–100.

Bénassy-Quéré, A. (1996) 'Potentialities and opportunities of the Euro as an international currency', *Economic Papers No.115*, Brussels, European Commission.

Cole, D.C. (1988) 'Financial development in Asia', *Asian-Pacific Economic Literature,* vol.2, no.2, pp.26–47.

Das, D.K. (1996) 'Emerging markets and macroeconomic stabilization: with special reference to Asia-Pacific economies', *Journal of the Asia-Pacific Economy,* vol.1, no.3, pp.319–46.

Dean, J.W. (1996) 'Recent capital flows to Asia-Pacific countries: trade offs and dilemmas', *Journal of the Asia-Pacific Economy,* vol.1, no.3, pp.287–317.

European Commission (1997) 'External aspects of economic and monetary union', *Euro-Paper No 1*, July, Brussels, European Commission.

Frankel, J.A. (1995) 'Still the lingua franca: the exaggerated death of the dollar', *Foreign Affairs,* vol.74, no.4, pp.9–16.

Fry, M.J. (1995) 'Financial development in Asia: some analytical issues', *Asian-Pacific Economic Literature*, vol.9, no.1, pp.40–57.

Harris, L. (1988) 'Financial reform and economic growth: a new interpretation of South Korea's experience' in Harris, L., Coakley, J., Croasdale, M. and Evans, T. (eds) *New Perspectives on the Financial System*, London, Croom Helm.

International Monetary Fund (IMF) (1996) *World Economic Outlook*, May, Washington, DC, IMF.

Kearney, C. (1996) 'International financial integration: measures and policy implications', *Journal of the Asia-Pacific Economy*, vol.1, no.3, pp.347–64.

Kwan, C.H. (1996) 'A yen bloc in Asia: an integrative approach', *Journal of the Asia-Pacific Economy'*, vol.1, no.1, pp.1–21.

McKinnon, R.I. (1973) *Money and Capital in Economic Development*, Washington, DC, The Brookings Institution.

Pacific Economic Cooperation Council (1994) *Pacific Economic Development Report 1995: Advancing Regional Integration*, Pacific Economic Cooperation Council, Singapore.

Shaw, E.S. (1973) *Financial Deepening in Economic Development*, Oxford, Oxford University Press.

Thompson, G.F. (1997) 'Globalization and the possibilities for domestic economic policy', *Internationale Politik und Gesellschaft*, no.2, pp.161–71.

Wade, R. (1985) 'East Asian financial systems as a challenge to economics: lessons from Taiwan', *California Management Review*, vol.XXVII, no.4, pp.106–27.

White, G. (1998) 'Politics of welfare' in Maidment, R., Goldblatt, D. and Mitchell, J. (eds) *Governance in the Pacific*, London, Routledge in association with The Open University.

World Bank (1993) *The Asian Miracle*, Oxford, Oxford University Press.

Yang, L.S. (1952) *Money and Credit in China: A Short History*, Cambridge, Mass, Harvard University Press.

CHAPTER 5

Engendering the 'economic miracle': the labour market in the Asia-Pacific

Lucie Cheng and Ping-chun Hsiung

5.1 Introduction

Since the late 1960s, following the phenomenal recovery of the Japanese economy after the Second World War, a number of East-Asian countries have seen unprecedented economic growth. The great diversity in area and population size, culture, social organization and historical legacy among these countries continues to frustrate scholars who struggle to find 'grand theories' or linear explanations for these 'economic miracles'. The rise of Asia-Pacific and the corresponding decline of the hegemonic 'West' provide a fertile ground for competing theories of capitalist economic development that generally focus on one or more of the following: cultural values, social institutions, a strong state, geopolitical factors and the world economic system. While the role of labour figures prominently in these theories, it is generally more taken for granted than given serious analysis. When it is examined, labour is either genderless or male. It is not until very recently, with the increasing awareness of the gendered nature of relationships between economic policy and labour use and the penetration of feminist thought into Asia-Pacific studies, that we began to see discussions of the different roles of male and female labour in the East-Asian 'economic miracle' and of how this 'miracle' has impacted on male and female labour differently.

This chapter will summarize these discussions, focusing especially on women's labour and the strategies pursued by selected Asia-Pacific nations and the consequences of those strategies for gender equality in terms of women's access to jobs, entrepreneurship, mobility and security. We will show that while women are absorbed by global capitalism into the labour force, their reproductive roles have not diminished. Women are also resisting global capitalism in a variety of forms. We argue that only by 'engendering' the 'economic miracle' can we reach an adequate understanding of the rise of the Asia-Pacific.

Workers in a surgical glove factory, Penang, Malaysia

5.2 Economic development and gender equality

Discussions of the relationship between economic development and gender equality the world over have been controversial. In general they revolve around two opposing arguments. One side contends that notwithstanding the fact that there is still some way to go, economic development has created jobs for women which have led to independent incomes and self-confidence. The integration of women into the labour force has been advantageous in achieving equality with men (Jaquette, 1982). The general growth of the economy has 'trickled down' more or less automatically, so that those previously disadvantaged have also received some reward.

The opposing view sees economic development as somewhat detrimental to gender equality because it either marginalizes women, pushing them into secondary, peripheral or informal jobs that earn a fraction of men's wages (Boserup, 1970), or leads to a double burden on women by proletarianizing their productive roles while insisting on the maintenance of their conventional reproductive functions (Mies, 1986). Thus there is no automatic advantage accruing to women in particular, but simply a continuation, or even a deterioration, of their relatively disadvantaged status.

This chapter evaluates these three positions *vis-à-vis* women's labour in selected countries of the Asia-Pacific. Since other chapters discuss women's subsistence and reproductive work, the focus here is on a gender analysis of women's income-generating activities in both traditional and non-traditional economic sectors (see also Chapters 11 and 12). Through a systematic examination of available statistics, the chapter discusses whether or not women have achieved, or are closer to achieving, parity in the labour market in terms of gender division of paid work, comparable worth and access to promotion and mobility. It also considers intra- and inter-country differences and the Asia-Pacific as a region in comparison with the rest of the world.

Women and men in paid work: a narrowing divide?

Over the last three and a half decades, as the economy of the Asia-Pacific region has grown, an increasing number of women have been drawn into the labour force. This pattern of increase is similar to the history of the industrialized countries in the West. Worldwide, more than 40 per cent of women over fifteen years of age are now in the labour force, the percentage having grown almost twice as fast as that of the male labour force. Of the ten Asia-Pacific countries examined, only two, the Philippines and Indonesia, show a lower female labour force participation rate than the worldwide average.

Despite the overall increase in women's labour force participation, Figure 5.1 shows that the percentage of women in the labour force consistently lags far behind that of men. Except for Thailand and the People's Republic of China (PRC), where differences between the two rates are less than 20 percentage points, men's labour force participation rates exceed women's by a large margin. In Singapore, for example, men's rate was higher than women's by 52 percentage points in 1970, and even in 1995 the difference was still more than 30 points.

Figure 5.1 also indicates that while the overall rates for men and women have generally increased, the patterns are by no means uniform. For the more industrially advanced countries such as Japan, Singapore and Hong Kong, men's rates show a downward trend until 1995, while women's rates increased continuously during the same period. Taiwan and Korea show some slight variations, where women's rates first increased from 1970 to 1990 and then declined in 1995. For most late-comer countries, such as the Philippines and Indonesia, men's rates increased continuously throughout the period whereas women's rates show a marked decline from 1990 to 1995. For Malaysia both men and women's labour force participation increased sharply, while for Thailand both declined during the last five-year period. The PRC has the highest labour force participation rate for women (80 per cent) and men (96 per cent), partly due to a difference in its measurement system. Unlike other countries in the region that report labour force participation rates based on the population of 15 years and older, the PRC uses 16 to 59 years old for males and 16 to 54 for females as bases for their calculation.

Additional statistical data also reveal a persistent gender division of labour by industry and inequalities in terms of occupational distribution and remuneration. As Table 5.1 indicates, for all countries, women are concentrated in manufacturing and trade and service industries, but are almost absent from the construction, mining and utilities industries.

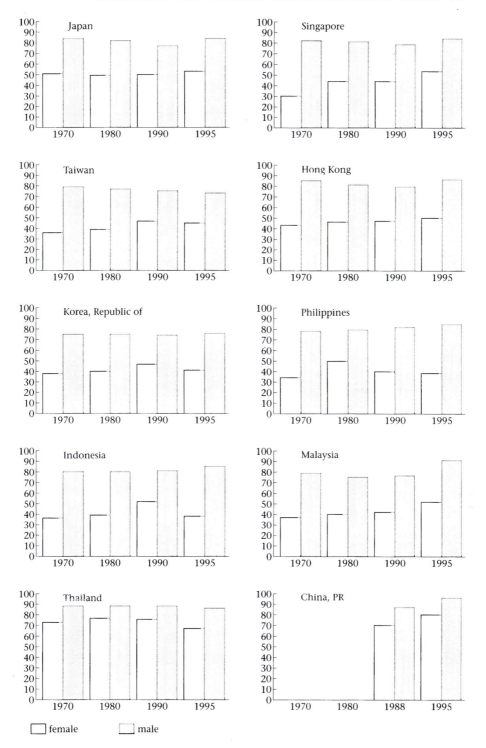

Figure 5.1 *Labour force participation rates for those fifteen years and older by gender (per cent)*

Sources: International Labour Organization (various years); 1995 data from The World Bank (1996, p.3); Taiwan data from Republic of China (various years; 1993a)

Table 5.1 Distribution of women's employment by industry (women as a percentage of total employment in that sector)

Country	Year	Economic sector									
		A	B	C	D	E	F	G	H	I	J
Japan	1970	50.85	15.00	37.62	10.71	13.45	45.95	12.96	46.21	44.30	28.57
	1980	49.05	9.09	38.55	13.33	14.03	46.15	11.71	42.45	45.95	30.77
	1990	47.78	16.67	39.53	13.33	16.33	48.69	14.63	44.96	47.93	36.67
Singapore	1970	21.36	9.46	33.63	7.00	6.53	18.96	4.99	33.24	16.54	44.65
	1980	25.17	18.75	46.10	11.34	9.09	35.23	16.98	46.96	33.96	5.26
	1990	15.38	12.50	46.78	14.93	6.88	39.59	21.43	48.06	51.15	0.00
Taiwan	1970	32.31	11.55	29.37	9.43	3.27	20.78	10.57	NA	15.84	18.62
	1979	36.35	14.54	44.21	9.55	9.00	14.22	13.81	40.97	25.28	17.39
	1986	NA	15.51	49.58	12.12	11.69	46.06	17.48	40.71	55.03	NA
Hong Kong	1970	23.18	11.65	12.70	6.41	2.93	21.96	8.22	NA	12.55	28.22
	1980	25.09	NA	50.21	8.60	4.31	30.37	20.83	38.70	44.82	23.79
	1990	29.96	0.00	41.87	8.99	4.42	39.39	14.71	42.77	48.47	0.00
Republic of Korea	1971	12.57	3.04	23.55	0.85	0.94	27.42	1.93	NA	24.40	46.67
	1980	43.77	8.87	39.28	11.63	8.56	48.61	9.05	31.02	34.49	0.00
	1990	46.18	10.13	42.44	12.86	10.10	52.96	8.67	37.84	43.01	0.00
Philippines	1970	19.18	5.77	54.14	3.03	0.68	54.71	2.21	NA	55.78	25.68
	1977	18.57	5.56	43.88	16.70	1.83	61.56	4.89	NA	50.04	24.80
	1990	25.18	9.02	45.75	17.58	1.85	63.69	3.96	39.41	55.59	26.67
Indonesia	1971	18.06	4.77	56.48	14.08	0.79	43.45	1.51	17.67	23.92	NA
	1980	31.28	17.74	42.40	12.45	3.15	47.52	1.68	15.46	31.77	43.31
	1990	30.06	16.22	45.28	8.09	2.88	52.20	2.30	26.07	35.36	55.00
Malaysia	1970	38.00	12.60	28.13	5.35	6.78	18.23	4.36	NA	28.90	47.83
	1980	38.96	10.36	40.07	6.98	7.12	29.27	6.26	29.54	29.42	32.83
	1990	34.52	11.38	47.68	9.45	4.65	37.50	11.46	36.60	39.49	0.00
Thailand	1970	14.50	NA	42.06	NA	10.00	51.70	1.28	NA	44.92	23.53
	1980	50.44	30.47	46.61	14.90	18.54	58.71	7.84	35.32	41.25	41.58
	1990	47.38	14.84	49.92	20.26	16.64	53.77	10.62	NA	51.87	40.93
China	1980	36.17	22.69	42.21	41.53	24.79	40.03	21.43	20.63	54.13	30.26
	1990	37.44	25.28	44.34	35.94	13.28	47.06	21.45	35.15	34.73	32.39

Note: A = agriculture, forestry and fishing; B = mining and quarrying; C = manufacturing; D = electricity, gas and water; E = construction; F = trade and commerce; G = transport, storage and communication; H = financing, insurance, real estate and business services; I = community, social and personal services; J = non-classified activities. NA = not available.

Sources: International Labour Office (various years); Taiwan data from Republic of China (various years; 1993a); China data from People's Republic of China (various years)

In 1990, for example, women comprised more than 40 per cent of all manufacturing workers in all countries except Japan (column C); and less than 20 per cent in mining except China (column B). When Asia-Pacific countries are compared with each other, we find that as the economy of the country shifts away from labour-intensive manufacturing women's pattern of employment also changes. Their concentration in manufacturing decreases while that in trade and services increases. This is clear with Japan and the four 'little dragons': Singapore, Hong Kong, Taiwan and South Korea.

Economic development has not yet brought gender equality in paid work. Similar to the worldwide position, women in the Asia-Pacific continue to be under-represented in the more prestigious and well-paid occupations and over-represented in the lower status and less well-paid ones. The extent of inequality varies across countries in the region. Take managers, for example. The most blatant case is represented by South Korea, where women made up only 4.2 per cent of all managers in 1993. Even in the best case, Singapore, male outnumber female managers by almost three to one. A similar discrepancy between men and women in the managerial category is observed in 1990 for all countries (Figure 5.2). In contrast, proportionately more women than men are found among clerical and service workers in most of the countries.

The professional category indicates an interesting though somewhat misleading situation. As Figure 5.2 shows, for almost all countries proportionately more women than men are employed in this category. This is especially glaring for the Philippines and Malaysia. There are two reasons for this: the rising levels of education for women in all Asia-Pacific countries and the increasing demand for educated women to fill occupations that are extensions of traditional female roles, such as nursing and elementary and kindergarten teaching. These occupations are included in the professional category shown in Figure 5.2, and they are at the lowest rung of the professional ladder. Both the similarities and diversities in gender distribution of occupations are clearly demonstrated by the varying heights of the bars.

As in Western industrialized countries, women's wages in Asia-Pacific are only a fraction of those of their male counterparts. Generally speaking though, women's access to jobs in the modern sectors tends to narrow the gender gap in earnings. This is indicated by data in Table 5.2. In the USA, while women's wages were only 64 per cent of their male counterparts in 1980, by 1990 they rose to 70 per cent. In the Asia-Pacific the most dramatic case of wage gap reduction is found in Malaysia, where the female/male wage ratio was reduced by 12 percentage points in ten years. In some countries, and for some industries, the gap between male and female earnings has not only persisted but has widened over the past two decades. An example is provided by Taiwan. In five out of nine industries – agriculture, mining, manufacturing, construction and commerce – the gains in wage equality observed in the 1970s had been largely eroded by the 1980s.

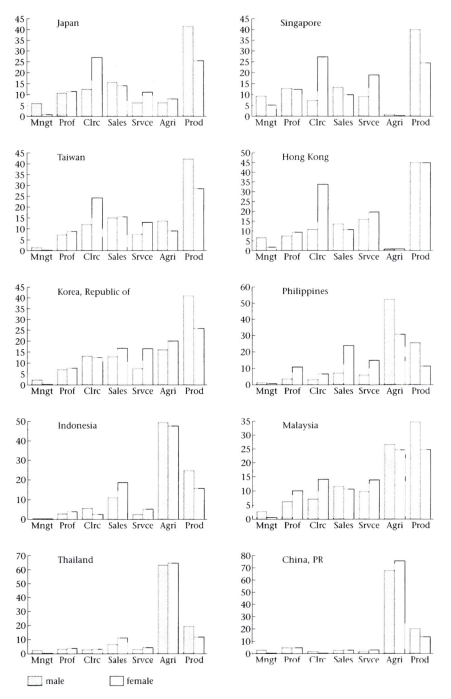

Figure 5.2 *Gender distribution of employment by occupation, 1990 (shown as a percentage of either total male or female employment)*

Sources: International Labour Organization (1992); Taiwan data from Republic of China (1993a); China data from All China Women Federation and Shaanxi Provincial Women Federation (1991); Hong Kong data from Hong Kong Census and Statistics Department (1991)

Table 5.2 *Ratio of female to male earnings in selected Asia-Pacific countries, various years (per cent)*

Country	Year	Female/male wage	Year	Female/male wage
Japan	1982	43.1	1991	42.9
Taiwan	1988	64.5	1992	67.1
Hong Kong	1987	74.0	1996	80.0
Republic of Korea	1984	41.9	1988	51.0
Philippines	1978	70.9	1988	80.0
Indonesia	1986	55.6	1992	60.0
Malaysia	1973	56.8	1984	69.3
Thailand	1980	73.5	1990	79.8
China	1978	82.3	1988	85.6
USA	1980	64.0	1990	70.0
Australia			1987	87.0

Sources: China data from All China Women Federation and Shaanxi Provincial Women Federation (1991, pp.318–19); Hong Kong data (excluding unpaid family workers) from Hong Kong Census and Statistics Department (1997, p.95); Taiwan data from Republic of China (1993a, p.32); others from The World Bank (1996, p. 21)

While part of the wage gap can be explained by differences in educational attainment and work experience between men and women, studies failed to account for this persistent wage inequality by human capital factors alone. The overall gender gap in wages has been attributed to differential access to education and jobs, interruptions in women's employment due to child rearing and other family responsiblities, and to the seniority system in industries. Korean women are paid less than men with the same education and in the same industry. Moreover, the differential increases rather than declines as women gain more education. Scholars maintain that this phenomenon is largely a function of the under-employment of women caused by pervasive discrimination.

The overall diversity in labour force participation among countries in the Asia-Pacific is clearly reflected in the hierarchical nature of the wage structure. Figure 5.3 shows the huge difference in earnings between an engineer in Hong Kong and Tokyo on the one hand, and one in Manila and Jakarta on the other. The most dramatic is the wage differential between a female unskilled industrial worker in Jakarta and an engineer in Hong Kong. The latter's earnings are more than 30 times the former. The huge variance in earnings is a major driving force towards international labour migration in the region (see Chapter 2).

In summary, despite the increasing participation of women in the labour force, gender division of labour has persisted and women are still concentrated in less prestigious, less responsible and less well-paid jobs. When women and men both work full time in the same industry, women still receive lower wages than men. Beyond these similarities among countries, there are significant variations. No single theory can explain the complexities. Commonly accepted explanations include the different timing and trajectory of economic growth in different countries, different

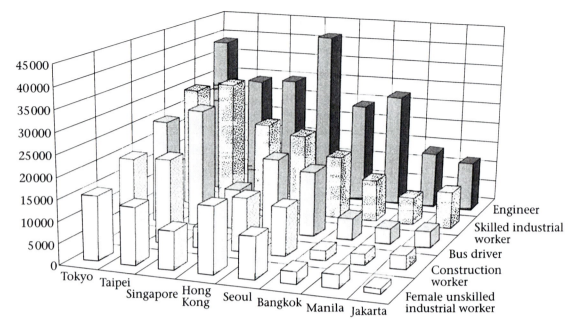

Figure 5.3 *Wage hierarchy in the Asia-Pacific, 1994 (US dollars per year)*
Source: The World Bank (1996, p.4)

institutional arrangements and different cultural and ideological systems. Our data do not reflect women's work in general, since they seriously undercount those in the non-traditional sectors or in the informal economy and disregard completely those engaged in unpaid work, the two categories where women are over-represented. In terms of gender differences in paid work, the general pattern observed for this region indicates a persistent but narrowing, rather than widening, divide.

Education: women's capital resources or entrapment?

Scholars and other observers have attributed the 'economic miracle' of Japan and the newly industrialized countries in the Asia-Pacific to a well-educated, hard-working and disciplined labour force. While women's educational attainment has improved during the last three decades, for all countries, as Table 5.3 shows, women still lag behind men in terms of access to college education. However, again, there are important differences among the countries. For comparable years, Korea has the best educated labour force regardless of gender, while the People's Republic of China has the least. In terms of gender, the largest difference in educational attainment between men and women is observed in Indonesia. Similar to what has been reported in the West, gender continues to be a significant variable in tracking students into specific subjects and fields of study. While male students are counselled towards careers in science and engineering, women students are channelled towards the humanities.

Table 5.3 *Percentage distribution of educational level by gender*

Country	Year	Women			Men		
		1st level	*2nd level*	*3rd level*	*1st level*	*2nd level*	*3rd level*
Japan	1980	51.40	41.54	7.06	48.17	38.92	12.91
Singapore	1980	58.46	37.75	3.79	59.18	35.28	5.54
Taiwan	1992	40.64	49.32	10.04	33.60	51.59	14.81
Hong Kong	1996	26.20	58.36	15.44	23.91	57.99	18.10
Republic of Korea	1990	46.63	42.78	10.58	41.35	39.49	19.16
Indonesia	1992	73.34	25.23	1.43	66.73	25.91	7.36
Malaysia	1990	61.14	36.08	2.78	61.72	34.99	3.29
China	1992	70.69	28.38	0.92	66.87	31.56	1.57

Note: 1st level = completion of compulsory education, 6 to 9 years of schooling; 2nd level = completion of middle school or vocational school, 12–14 years; 3rd level = 15 years and above

Sources: Taiwan data from Republic of China (1993b, pp.90–5); Hong Kong data from Hong Kong Census and Statistics Department (1997, p.67); other data from The World Bank (1995)

As more and more women become college educated, they often face serious barriers in comparable employment and advancement. Newspapers report that many bright young women in East Asia, notably in Japan, are trying to escape corporate sexism and bleak job prospects by finding work overseas. At the same time, an increasing number of East-Asian women have successfully broken into the corporate and political worlds. The implication of education for gender equality in employment and promotion remains controversial.

Two important aspects of the relationship between gender, education and economic development in the Asia-Pacific experience bear specific scrutiny. On the one hand, gender inequality is perpetuated in the process and content of schooling. At the same time, however, the educational system has been transformed to facilitate a capitalist production that relies heavily on female labour. Let us examine these two aspects one by one.

Similar to the West, schooling in the newly industrialized economies (NIEs) is an engendered socialization process where male and female students are taught to develop gender-proper roles, behaviours and career aspirations. Textbooks at all levels continue to portray stereotypical images of women as being caring and loving and men as strong and independent. Nurses, mothers and school teachers are represented by female figures while men are the doctors, soldiers, pilots and engineers. We therefore caution against an overly optimistic interpretation of numerical increases in women's educational access, since access alone does not automatically or necessarily bring about a more gender equal society, unless the process and content of schooling are altered.

An even more pertinent aspect of education in relation to the region's economic growth is the emergence of a partnership between school and factory systems that tends to entrap students, especially rural females, into early labour force participation. This plays out in two distinctive ways. First, the school is converted from an educational institution into a brokerage agent which prepares its students for the employment demands of the newly flourishing manufacturing sector. In April or May each year, factories send representatives out to junior middle schools in rural areas to recruit potential workers, usually 15 or 16 year olds.

Small industry car-seat cover manufacturing in Yen Bai, North Vietnam

The representatives, armed with official endorsements from school principals, placement counsellors and teachers, meet with the local elites. As a result of such networking, parents of school graduates who give consent to have their children work in the factory often believe they are doing something in accordance with the wishes of the schools and the local authorities. Sometimes, the new factory pays a placement counsellor from the school to accompany the new recruits on their first trip from home to work. At other times, the principal or a teacher is brought in to visit and comfort the youngsters after they have worked in the factory for a month or so. The visit often coincides with the period when many of the young workers are most inclined to quit, either because of homesickness or the hardship of factory work.

The transformation of the school into a recruiting agency for the factory suggests that capitalist production has tapped into the pre-existing hierarchical structure of the school system to meet its need for a stable supply of malleable labour. In other words, the school system has been integrated into the NIEs developmental process not only on the basis of its formal, educational function, but also as an institution that is capable of extending its influence and control over its students even after their graduation.

Furthermore, since the mid 1960s, under state support, co-operative programmes have been widely set up at the junior and senior middle school levels through which students engage in full-time factory work during the day and take part-time courses for educational credits at night. Under these programmes, factory employers pay part of the tuition fees for their student workers. In exchange, a portion of the student workers' monthly pay is kept by the employer. The student worker can retrieve the money only upon completion of his/her three-year tenure at the factory. That is, a student worker automatically loses part of his/her wages for changing jobs within a three-year period.

These co-operative programmes serve multiple functions. First, the prospect of earning a high school diploma while working in the factory is enormously appealing to student workers, especially female junior middle school graduates in rural areas whose parents were mostly unwilling to support them for further schooling. Second, the programme helps to stabilize and sometimes discipline a capitalist labour force through various mechanisms. In particular, the three-year contractual arrangement with an automatic wage forfeiture proviso ties the worker to the employer. This is especially favourable to the factory employer, since student workers are quickly worn out by the repetitive and monotonous routine and without the proviso may decide to leave the factory. Many female student workers cite the aspiration of getting a high school diploma as their main reason for enduring the type of factory employment which otherwise would be unbearable. The co-operative programme is advantageous to the employer in yet another way. Whenever conflict arises on the shop floor, the school authority is called upon to resolve it. This ranges from negotiating wages and work schedules to settling in-fights among student workers. It is not uncommon for teachers to side with the employer, rather than the student workers, when it comes to capitalist discipline. The co-operative programme has been widely adopted by private vocational schools in the region which otherwise would have difficulty in retaining high levels of student enrolment.

The above discussion suggests that capitalist development in the East-Asian NIEs has been nourished by cultural norms that value education. Such symbiotic relationships are embedded in the way that educational and manufacturing systems sustain each other.

The role of the state: perpetuating the double burden?

In studies of the origins of the economic development of the NIEs, the state is often recognized for its strong, active involvement in financial policies, market management and labour regulation. A less articulated area has been the implication of various regulations and policies on gender equality. Here we focus our discussion on the gender implications of the export-oriented growth strategy of development pursued by Japan and the NIEs.

In the 1960s, all the first-tier NIEs shifted from import substitution to export-led industrialization (see Chapter 2). The main objectives were to draw their under-employed and unemployed population into the export sectors, while at the same time overcoming limitations that had prevented them from further pursuing an import substitution strategy. Policy makers at the time engaged heavily in debates about the merits of such policy shifts, because a labour-intensive, export-led industrialization entails suppressing labour's wages for the enrichment of foreign investors and subjecting workers in the Export Processing Zones (EPZs) to abuses and exploitation. (EPZs are special areas giving tax and other advantage to companies operating there.) Taiwan's experience provides an example.

The idea of EPZs emerged in Taiwan in 1956. It took ten years before a proposal was approved and the actual construction of the first EPZ began. Li, an economist heavily involved in Taiwan's economic policy formation process, recalls debates at the time. According to Li, supporters of the EPZ downplayed the prospect of foreign investors' exploitation by arguing that 'it was better to provide a job to someone who would otherwise be unemployed than to be concerned with the profits of the employer' (Li, 1985). In retrospect, Li states, 'it was largely an investor's market in the 1960s and 1970s, whether one likes the fact or not' (ibid.).

It is beyond the scope of this chapter to discuss whether or not a labour-intensive, export-oriented strategy was the government's best choice at the time. We do want to point out, however, that the consequences of such a choice have not been gender neutral. The manufacturing sector, which has been the motor of the NIEs export-led growth, has relied heavily on female labour force participation; women have been over-represented in the manufacturing sector (see Table 5.1). This has been the case for every listed country. For the four 'little dragons' – Singapore, Hong Kong, Tawain and South Korea – between one-fifth and two-thirds of the entire female labour force participated in manufacturing production in 1980.

Since the state's own political legitimacy is founded on continuing economic growth and social stability, it is not surprising to find that labour regulation and developmental programmes often have these twin goals in mind. Two programmes of the ruling Nationalist Party in Taiwan aimed at incorporating married women into its manufacturing production are illustrative.

In distinction to South Korea and Singapore, where large-scale factories employing mainly young single girls have dominated the manufacturing sectors, more than 85 per cent of factories in Taiwan's export sector have fewer than 30 workers, with married women as their main source of labour. The Living Rooms as Factories programme was part of the government's effort to target an under-utilized labour reserve – married women and their children – for informal homework or to turn their own living rooms into factory production sites. Its parallel programme, Mothers' Workshops, on the other hand, emphasized the importance of married women's traditional familial responsibilities as mothers, wives and daughters-in-law. Taken together, these two programmes constitute the state's intentional effort to facilitate Taiwan's export-led industrialization on the one hand, and to reconcile the potential conflict between female labour force participation and women's roles in the family on the other. Married women are incorporated into the labour force not as regular workers but as homeworkers, and the subsidiary and supplementary character of their employment reinforces their subordinate and dependent status at work and in the family.

5.3   Gender, entrepreneurship and the family firm

In Asia-Pacific, entrepreneurship, the key to capitalist development, is often linked to the family firm (see Chapter 9). Scholars have considered Asia-Pacific familism as both a detriment and as an advantage to economic development. Many have pointed out that Asia-Pacific businesses rely on kinship networks and familial ties for financial and labour needs (Redding, 1993). Commitment to the well-being and prosperity of the family is said to be the driving force behind numerous men and women whose extraordinary work behaviour is being held up as a model for the rest of the world. Although these scholars have captured the significance of familism in East-Asian societies, such an approach assumes that family members constitute a homogeneous group with identical interests and equal power in decision making. The approach fails to recognize individual member's positional relationship with each other and with the collective unit. Nor does it explore how the supposedly 'collective' interest is constructed. While Chapter 9 in this book discusses the role of 'the Chinese family firm', here we examine the dynamics within family enterprises characteristic of several Asia-Pacific countries. Specifically, we discuss women's role in household-based entrepreneurship and the impact of household-based entrepreneurship on gender relationships.

Women's roles in household-based entrepreneurship

Although East-Asian family businesses are typically owned by men, women play a very central role. The owner's wife is indispensable to the establishment and success of a small-scale family business: her dowry is pulled in as start-up capital; her women-centred social network is activated for labour recruitment; the technological know-how she acquired from working before marriage gives the family business a competitive edge; and her bookkeeping skills are employed to keep transaction records straight. For factories that provide room and board for out-of-town workers, the owner's wife becomes the natural and unpaid cook and housekeeper.

In addition, the labour of an owner's wife is indispensable because she can always be counted on for overtime work. She is also the most loyal, reliable supervisor that a factory owner can ever find. By providing close supervision on the shop floor, a wife serves to maximize productivity, minimize possible waste of materials and, consequently, increase business profitability. The following description of the work process in a Taiwanese wooden jewellery-box factory illustrates how the owner's wife acts as a supervisor and rate-of-work setter:

> Today I [Hsiung] was assigned to wrap every wooden jewellery box with a piece of paper. Show-Li [fellow worker] stood to my right putting each wrapped jewellery box into a coloured paper box. Ching-may, the owner's wife, performed the next steps in the process by putting four Styrofoam protectors on the bottom of each jewellery box, closing the bottom of the paper box and then passing it to the next person, Ya-ling. Ya-ling in turn had to right the paper box, put another four protectors on the top of the jewellery box and then close the cover of the paper box before passing it to the next person for final packing. Across the table, there were four workers doing the same job we were doing. I had to keep up the pace so that Show-Li and the rest of the workers on my side would not be standing there without anything to do. Ching-may kept yelling to the workers who did the final packing to speed up. 'Hey you, don't stand there. Hurry up!' she said. She yelled at San-mi, who stood across from me, 'You are too slow. Go and switch with Jin-pao.' San-mi went over to take Jin-pao's place to do the final packing. Jin-pao came and took over San-mi's job. Ching-may's yelling and giving orders were quite intimidating. While I was trying to push myself to go faster, I heard her say to Jin-pao, 'Smart guys should avoid standing next to me. They get exhausted easily.'
>
> (Hsiung, 1996, p.105)

Although the growth of small-scale, family-centred factories make experienced, hardworking female workers attractive marital partners for the male owners, their indispensable role and contribution have not allowed them to achieve equal partnership with their husbands. Besides, their contribution has been invisible and unrewarded in monetary terms. Women who marry factory owners are more likely to work as unwaged family workers than the workers' wives. Although the owners' wives as a group enjoy higher social status and more luxurious lifestyles than their female worker counterparts, they have not been able to surmount gender disparities in relation to their husbands. More importantly, household-based entrepreneurship has made it possible for many skilled male workers to experience upward mobility by setting up their own businesses, which in turn strengthens their status as head of the household. Unfortunately, such rewards and opportunities are not equally available to their wives, or to women in general.

In summary, the family firm, touted by scholars and writers as the engine of Asian economic success, is rooted in gender ideology and held together by the waged and unwaged labour of women. Gender and class intersect in the complex relations between owner and his wife and between owner's wife and female employees. The family firm works to facilitate upward mobility for some while keeping others down.

5.4   The feminization of intra-regional migrant labour

Until the 1980s, most research on international migration and work focused on men and the role of women was largely unrecognized. Women migrants' economic and social contributions were generally considered trivial or irrelevant, because when women migrated they were routinely viewed as 'tied-migrants', either dependants of male migrants or passive participants in migration. However, the migration of women has become an important issue due to the increase of independent women migrants. This is especially true for the Asia-Pacific (Chapters 2, 10 and 11).

During the last three decades the intra-regional flow of women in Asia has been higher than in any other region. In 1976 women constituted less than 15 per cent of the 146,400 Asians who left their countries to work overseas; by 1987 they comprised some 27 per cent of Asians who left that year to work temporarily abroad. In the early 1990s, approximately 1.5 million Asian women were legally and illegally working abroad, with an outflow of 800,000 a year from Asian countries of origin. Major sending countries have been the Philippines, Indonesia, Sri Lanka and Thailand; and those receiving have been the Middle East – particularly Saudi Arabia and Kuwait – Hong Kong, Japan, Taiwan, Singapore, Malaysia and Brunei.

There is a clear gender difference in the migration process, perhaps related to geographic proximity between countries of origin and desti-nation, specific labour needs in the receiving country, the employment situation in the sending country and cultural and social factors. For example, Filipino women emigrants outnumbered their male counterparts by twelve to one for Asian destinations, although they accounted for less than a third of Filipinos going on contract work to the Middle East. Indonesian female migrant workers outnumber their male counterparts by nearly three to one, the proportion having increased sharply during the last decade. Though total numbers are lower for other Asian countries, they nevertheless have high proportions of women overseas, working mainly as domestic workers.

We attribute the feminization of migrant labour to several factors. First is the generalization of gender stereotypes in the division of labour across national borders, which matches women with 'feminine jobs' overseas. Second, it is the outcome of mature labour markets, with their high rate of participation of women in the local labour force and the consequent demand for women in traditional reproductive jobs such as housekeeping and care-giving. Third, the development of tourism and new service industries has created certain employment opportunities for women overseas. Fourth, uneven economic development in the region has increased the gap between rich and poor countries, as well as polarized intra-country rural–urban and class differences, creating a pool of potential migrant workers, including women. Last, but not least, is the penetration of global capitalism into the region, incorporating all countries into a world market of commodities and services which makes it mandatory for these countries to obtain as much foreign exchange as possible to help balance international trade. Labour supply and demand, facilitated by global capitalism, result in a transnational network of organizations that profit from human trafficking.

Concern for national image, reports of physical abuse, and pressure from humanitarian groups and women's organizations have led several countries to establish specific policies regarding female labour flows. Indonesian women must be at least 22 years old to be employed overseas. In addition, when women are recruited through authorized agents there are various restrictions regarding place of employment for household workers and the male/female ratio, although these restrictions may be lifted under certain conditions. In Thailand there is a ban on the recruitment of women for overseas work in general except in the case of selected countries of employment. The Thai government, under domestic and international pressure to curb its notorious image as a haven to the sex trade, now requires entertainers to hold a diploma from a school of arts and a license, and forbids them to perform in night clubs abroad.

An extreme contrast in government policies on women emigrant workers is provided by Malaysia and the Philippines. While the former does not seem to have any restrictions, the latter has developed a set of explicit and detailed rules according to the type of work and country of destination. Filipino women domestic workers must be at least 25 years old and they are banned from employment in certain countries where serious abuses have been reported. The government requires a minimum age of 23 for women entertainers and has a similar ban on selected countries. Women entertainers must also pass the required academic and skills tests, possess an Artist Record Book and undergo a pre-departure showcase preview. Nurses employed abroad must be at least 23 years old, possess a Bachelor of Science degree in nursing and have one year's work experience in the Philippines.

Perhaps as might be expected, women migrant workers in the receiving countries do not seem to comply with these elaborate regulations. Female migration for overseas employment shows an almost exclusive concentration in the services sector, namely domestic workers and entertainers, or sex service providers. A significant number of women working overseas are nurses, although their destinations are not concentrated in other Asian countries as they are with the other two occupations. The social construction of gender and racial stereotypes within the labour recruitment process help to channel women migrants into these jobs.

Domestic workers

The increasing flow of female domestic workers is evidence of a new transnational division of labour between middle class women in the receiving countries and working class women in the sending countries. The use of domestic workers enables middle class women to join the labour force, leaving childcare and other household chores to the migrant women workers. This is certainly true in major East-Asian cities such as Singapore, Hong Kong and Taiwan. These three cities have emerged as the main destinations of employment for women migrating for domestic services in the Asia-Pacific since the mid 1980s. By the end of 1995, there were 152,000 migrant domestic workers in Hong Kong, more than 80,000 in Singapore and approximately 10,000 in Taiwan. In Hong Kong, migrant women come mainly from the Philippines and Indonesia. In Taiwan, women from the Philippines make up more than 90 per cent of the domestic workers on the island. In recent years, women domestic workers from mainland China are increasingly found in Chinese-speaking Taiwan and Hong Kong.

The Philippines is by far the most important source of Asian domestic workers, and their major destinations are the Middle East, Singapore and Hong Kong. In 1992, Hong Kong reported 66,000 Filipino domestic workers, Singapore 50,000 (1993) and Malaysia 10,000. The number of Filipino domestic workers in Hong Kong had almost doubled to 125,000. Women migrating from the Philippines are mostly from 20 to 34 years old, although there are 5.5 per cent between the ages of 15 and 19. These domestic workers are well-educated women, between 30 to 43 per cent having completed college.

In response to reports of serious abuse, the Philippines imposed a ban on the exit of domestic workers to Singapore in 1987, but this did not mean a drop in the flow as work permits approval would be issued in Singapore to those arriving with tourist visas. In fact, these attitudes in the two countries led to the growth of private, often disguised recruitment agents and the informalization of migrant domestic work.

The execution of a Filipino domestic worker convicted of the murder of her employer by the Singaporean government, in spite of diplomatic and social protests in the Philippines, brought another ban on the deployment of domestic workers to Singapore in 1995. However, it only affected the medium-sized agencies, leaving the large and small agencies untouched. The latter still offer domestic workers to interested employers in Singapore. This ban was further circumvented by the re-routing of Filipinos via Kuala Lumpur, Brunei and Hong Kong. Any reduction in the number of Filipino workers is now made up by increases in Sri Lankan (from 12,000 to 16,000) and Indonesian (from 11,000 to 23,000) domestic workers.

Migrant domestic workers are usually paid substandard wages which are sometimes delayed or withheld. Days off are not observed, food is inadequate, accommodation is poor and unsafe, medical benefits are nil and mobility is limited. Furthermore, they are subject to maltreatment, sexual harassment and other abuses such as excessive workloads and working for additional households. Workers unwilling to endure these abusive conditions often seek refuge in their embassies. Some run away from their employers and may become super-exploited illegal workers, liable to be arrested by the police and deported or returned to their employers.

Workers of different nationality and ethnicity are subject to different discriminatory treatment. For example, Filipinos earn 50 per cent more than women from Indonesia and Sri Lanka because of their command of the English language. Domestic workers are not considered as 'labour' in many receiving countries, which helps to explain their abusive treatment by employers. In Japan, migrant women domestic workers are seen as housewives' and mothers' helpers, filling voids created by the occupational advancement of Japanese women.

In comparison with other Asia-Pacific countries, Hong Kong seems to have the most progressive legal system for the protection of domestic service workers. Both foreign and local domestic workers are protected by the labour law with a minimum wage system. This is probably the consequence of the strong presence of non-government organizations (NGOs) in the territory. Migrant women domestic workers are more vulnerable both in Taiwan and Singapore due to the lack of legal protection, the denial of access to the redress system, the inadequacy of the legal infrastructure, the transfer of responsibility from the state to individual providers, intrusive immigration regulations and the limited function of the NGO community. They are excluded from the protection of labour laws.

Employers have the power to terminate the contracts of migrant workers without due notice, cancel their work permits and repatriate the workers as long as no legal action has been initiated. In both Singapore and Taiwan, migrant women domestic workers even have to go through pregnancy tests every six months, and if the result is positive they are subject to immediate deportation. Singapore has the additional requirement of a security bond of US$5,000 for each migrant domestic worker from her employer, higher than any other category of foreign workers. The bond is forfeited if the maid becomes pregnant.

Entertainers and sex service providers

As is the case with domestic workers, the outflow of entertainers is dominated by the Philippines, although Thailand and mainland China are now playing an increasingly important part. The main destinations for entertainers are Japan, Hong Kong and Taiwan, through both legal and illegal channels. Although some women are indeed professional entertainers or artists, the name is also a euphemism for sex service providers. We discuss the sex industry in Section 5.5; here we focus on the situation of foreign migrant sex service providers.

The export of entertainers to Japan represents a reverse of 'sex tourism' which has escalated in Asia-Pacific since the 'economic miracle' first appeared in Japan in the 1960s. Organized by tour operators and tacitly, sometimes even blatantly, promoted by governments eager to gain foreign exchange, 'sex tourism' has brought millions of men, mostly Japanese, to other Asia-Pacific countries. As 'sex tourism' became less overt and blatant following strong protests from origin and destination countries, there was a corresponding rise in the intra-regional movement of female tourists who often ended up working illegally as 'entertainers'.

Murata Noriko estimates that there are more than 100,000 foreign women working in the sex industry in Japan, a lucrative business which brings in trillions of yen a year (AMPO, 1996, p.115). Filipinos were the first large group to come in the early 1980s, followed by Thai women. Entertainers from the Philippines could earn US$1,500 per month but, due to exorbitant brokerage fees and transportation debts, they would usually receive only about one-third of this amount.

Compared with Filipinos, Thai women are easily victimized since they tend to come from rural communities and cannot speak Japanese or English.

> Many find it impossible to escape from forced prostitution at small bars (called snacks) or regular bars in city red light districts or at local hot spring resorts. An especially large number of Thai women are tricked into coming to Japan by agents working for local and international human smuggling gangs. They are lured by promises of jobs in factories and told that they will be able to pay their debts off in a very short time, send considerable amounts of money home to their families and make their parents happy.
>
> (AMPO, 1996, p.116)

Just like the Filipino domestic workers in Singapore who rebelled against oppressive conditions of employment and were deported, imprisoned or even executed, Thai migrant women workers trying to escape from sex slavery by killing their owners or managers were prosecuted for their 'heinous' crime. Murata quotes a letter written by one of the accused to the Thai embassy in Tokyo:

> There are no factories where we can work, there are only bars and pubs and men who only think about drinking and having sex. I really suffered a lot. We had to go to bed with dirty men and strangers. If you don't do whatever you are told to do, you are beaten by the boss or the proprietress (mama-san).
>
> For them we Thai women are mere animals. They have the power of life and death over us. Japan is not heaven but hell for us Thai women. It's a barefaced lie that the cherry blossoms are waiting for you. What is waiting for you are men whose only concern is having sex.
>
> No matter how hard you work, putting your life on the line, there are no rewards, not even a single baht (Thai denomination of money). If you don't obey them, they'll hit you, beat you and do whatever they want. To them, we have no value other than that of a tool they use to make money by entertaining drunks and providing sex.
>
> Japan is not a place for Thai women who are eager to work. Please stay in Thailand. In our country people still have sympathy. No matter how much you have to suffer, no matter how hard you have to work, it's far better than being trapped in hell like me.
>
> (AMPO, 1996, p.118)

5.5 The sex industry and child prostitution

The exploitation of sex, and especially child prostitution, is linked to the globalization of the sex industry, tourism and the uneven economic development in the region. In the last section we focused on the situation

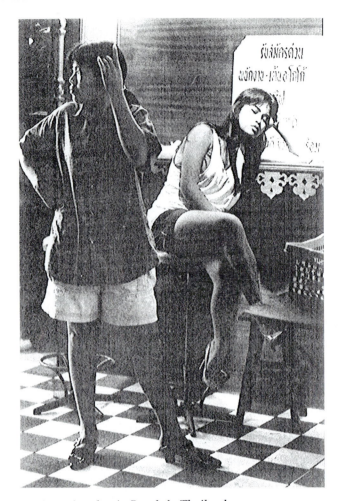

Prostitutes in a bar in Bangkok, Thailand

of foreign sex workers; here we discuss the sex industry and efforts to curb child prostitution.

Japan's phenomenal economic growth was quickly followed by a tremendous change in the lifestyles of the Japanese. Instead of preaching frugality and the delay of gratification, the Japanese government, together with the media, promoted mass consumption, even calling it a virtue in 1961. Japanese scholars and writers have attributed the commodification of sex, the rise of pornographic culture, the development of sex tourism and child prostitution to the sudden prosperity of Japan *vis-à-vis* its neighbours. What Japanese men could not easily obtain at home, they sought elsewhere in the Asia-Pacific. Taiwan and South Korea, both once colonized by Japan, were the favourite destinations in the 1960s. But as these two countries achieved newly industralized economy (NIE) status, concerns of international image and the growth of a protest movement tipped the cost-benefit calculus of sex tourism. The *nouveaux riches* Taiwanese and Korean men joined their Japanese brothers in seeking sexual gratification in their less fortunate neighbouring countries.

Airline magazines, tourist guide books and even the government tourist bureau publications promoted the 'buying of spring'. Travel agencies organized package tours on the principle of 'sightseeing by day and devouring women at night'. As recently as September 1994, four Japanese writers calling themselves the Asian Sexual Customs Study Group published a book entitled *The Thailand Prostitution Guide*, which became a best seller.

Thailand and Taiwan are notorious for the availability of child prostitution even though both countries have laws against it. Girls as young as eleven are found as prostitutes. The traditional ideology of self-sacrifice and submissiveness plays an important role in child prostitution, as girls, mostly from rural areas, 'volunteer' or are forced by their real or adoptive parents to trade sexual services for family betterment or for the education of their male siblings. Wiping out child prostitution has been a very prominent goal of women's movements in the Asia-Pacific. Activities include pressuring the government to pass and enforce laws against human trafficking and the buying and selling of children's sexual services, building networks of rescue, providing health care and shelter and establishing rehabilitation centres to help former child prostitutes to return to school and the community.

5.6 Women's resistance, agency and compliance

With the exception of South Korea and, to a lesser extent Taiwan, workers' struggle against capitalist exploitation in NIEs rarely takes the form of collective, organized and large-scale union movements. This has to do with the suppressive nature of state legislation on labour and the lack of formal, institutional protection for workers. However, this does not imply that Asia-Pacific workers are mindless victims. Recently, with capitalists relocating their factories and firms to countries with cheaper labour within and outside of the region, workers' class consciousness seems to be on the rise in Taiwan. In this section we focus on women workers' resistance to capitalist exploitation and their struggles for a better life.

The range of issues subjected to on-going negotiation and resistance is rather wide. It includes standard, contractual issues such as product quality, production quotas, overtime and overtime payment, as well as non-contractual issues such as eating and talking at work, dress codes, etc. This suggests that Asia-Pacific capitalists seek to extend their control beyond workers' physical labour to include also workers' attitudes and social behaviour, perceived as having an effect on production and the image of the firm. The employers' profit-driven and production-oriented managerial focus is in direct conflict with the multiple objectives that workers intend to accomplish through employment.

In addition to conventional means of resistance such as verbal negotiation and absenteeism, workers in the NIEs' manufacturing sector employ other ways of defining their own boundaries and guarding their integrity. For example, in order to avoid undue exploitation of their skills by the owners, male workers in Hong Kong's carpentry industry and in Taiwan's wooden jewellery box factories deliberately terminate regular daily exchange with others by displaying moodiness or 'bad temper' attitudes. In contrast, female workers in Taiwan and Singapore deliberately engage in wrangling and teasing with their supervisors and/or owners to skilfully set a boundary of acceptable labour extraction and a limit to the relationship.

The fact that negotiation and resistance have been carried out on an on-going basis suggests that managerial effort to control is constantly challenged. While none of the negotiation tactics and resistant strategies are aimed at challenging the production regime as a whole, or the workplace hierarchy in particular, women workers do pursue their daily struggle with concrete, subjective objectives. For example, despite legislative regulations concerning overtime and overtime payment in many of the NIEs, in practice frequent violations and inefficient law enforcement compel the workers to negotiate individual arrangements with their employers. This piecemeal method allows the workers to accomplish their individual, immediate goals without calling upon any abstract notion of justice or law enforcement. The relative absence of an organized union movement in the Asia-Pacific has fostered the development of a form of workers' resistance that is individualistic and clandestine. Our analysis leads us to an appreciation of the workers' own perception and definition of the situation, and their corresponding tactics and strategies of struggle.

Asia-Pacific NIEs are noted as having some of the most notorious and oppressive labour regimes, while their workers are portrayed as suppressed, mindless victims. This fails to include the workers' subjective understanding of their experiences. A comparison of the experiences of married female workers in Hong Kong with those of single female migrant workers in Canton, China, is instructive. According to our research, married women in Hong Kong are unwilling to endure on-the-job stress, or to invest a substantial amount of time and effort in acquiring additional skills or qualifications. They perceive factory work as a job, not a career, and therefore refuse to let it override their real priority, their familial responsibilities. They are confident of being capable of becoming the foreladies, technicians, or supervisors if they were willing to put aside their familial role. In this context, married women in Hong Kong easily accept their subordination to their male superiors. Nevertheless, such acceptance does not render them mere passive followers of ruthless capitalist disciplines. From time to time, married female workers in Hong Kong strategically call upon their familial responsibilities to put off unwarranted demands from their supervisors.

In contrast, employment opportunities in China's newly established coastal factories provide single, migrant female workers not only with precious cash earning opportunities and an escape from the agricultural backwater, but also the chance to meet potential marriage partners. For a supposedly promising future, these girls choose to leave family lives behind, take the risk of looking for jobs in strange cities and endure hardship in a factory job. Within this political, economic context, single, migrant female workers in Canton are more likely to comply, rather than challenge capitalist control. Again, to appreciate the engendered agency behind such compliance, one needs to go beyond the simple, rigid notion of passivity and self-victimization.

5.7   Summary: towards a feminist perspective on the 'economic miracle'

This chapter has sought to uncover the gendered nature of Asia-Pacific economic growth by examining the labour roles that women have played in the development process and the consequences this economic growth has had for them. We argue that, in many ways, women receive the short end of the stick. They have been incorporated into the labour force, but their significant contribution to the 'economic miracle' has not yet won them gender equality. Although more and more women are entering the labour market, they are still concentrated in just a few industries, unlike their male counterparts. Women workers are also concentrated in the lower end of the occupational structure and wage hierarchy. Even within the same occupation, women are paid less than men. These general patterns are similar to the experience of women worldwide. Our discussion does not include work in the reproductive area, where women are disproportionately concentrated. Suffice to point out that women everywhere have taken on waged work in addition to their unwaged family labour. While economic development has opened up many opportunities for waged work for both men and women, women have been incorporated into capitalist production in a quite different way. Global capitalism, intra-regional economic disparities and the social construction of gender roles operate together to track and sometimes trap women into conventional jobs, and to thwart their advancement in education, work and pay.

Our analysis points not only to the general pattern of women's experience in Asia-Pacific development, but also to experiences related to class and to particular countries. As more middle-class women enter the labour force in economically more developed countries such as Japan and the four 'little dragons', migrant women from poorer neighbouring countries fill their domestic labour needs. Increased labour force participation of women in one country has consequences for the socialization and commodification of housework as well as the engendering of intra-regional migration. The differences we have observed among the countries are a function of their position in the world economy, the development strategy of the state and their cultural and ideological systems.

Furthermore, we argue that the subjective meaning of work is not the same for women as it is for men, and that women in the Asia-Pacific have developed their own particular forms of resistance to gender discrimination and class exploitation. Any approach that seeks to understand women workers' compliance with, and resistance to, global capitalism must begin with an appreciation of their own definitions.

References

All China Women Federation and Shaanxi Provincial Women Federation (eds) (1991) *Statistics on Chinese Women (1949–1989)*, Beijing, China Statistical Publishing House.

AMPO-Japan Asia Quarterly Review (ed.) (1996) *Voices from the Japanese Women's Movement*, Armonk and London, M.E. Sharpe.

Boserup, A. (1970) *Women's Role in Economic Development*, London, Allen and Unwin.

Cheng, L. and Hsiung, P-C. (1992) 'Women, export-oriented growth, and the state: the case of Taiwan' in Appelbaum, R.P. and Henderson, J. (eds) *States and Development in the Asian Pacific Rim*, London and New Delhi, Sage Publications.

Gelb, J. and Palley, M.L. (eds) (1994) *Women of Japan and Korea: Continuity and Change*, Philadelphia, Temple University Press.

Hong Kong Census and Statistics Department (1991) *Population Census Main Report 1991*, Hong Kong.

Hong Kong Census and Statistics Department (1996) *Hong Kong Annual Digest of Statistics*, Hong Kong.

Hong Kong Census and Statistics Department (1997) *1996 Population By-Census Main Report*, Hong Kong.

Hsiung, P-C. (1996) *Living Rooms as Factories: Class, Gender, and the Satellite Factory System in Taiwan*, Philadelphia, Temple University Press.

International Labour Organization (ILO) (1992) *Yearbook of Labor Statistics*, ILO, Geneva.

International Labour Organization (ILO) (various years) *Yearbook of Labor Statistics*, ILO, Geneva.

Jaquette, J. (1982) 'Women and modernization theory: a decade of feminist criticism', *World Politics*, vol.34, no.2, pp.267–84.

Li, K.T. (1985) 'Contributions of women in the labor force to economic development in Taiwan, the Republic of China', *Industry of Free China*, vol.64, pp.1–8.

Mies, M. (1986) *Patriarchy and Accumulation on a World Scale*, London, Zed Press.

People's Republic of China (PRC) (various years) *Yearbook of Labour Statistics*, Beijing, PRC.

Redding, S.G. (1993) *The Spirit of Chinese Capitalism*, Berlin and New York, de Gruyter.

Republic of China (RC) (1993a) *Report on the Manpower Utilization Survey Taiwan Area, Republic of China, 1993*, Taipei, Directorate-General of Budget, Accounting and Statistics.

Republic of China (RC) (1993b) *Statistical Yearbook of Taiwan Province*, Taipei, RC.

Republic of China (RC) (various years) *Yearbook of Labour Statistics*, Taipei, RC.

The World Bank (1995) *Toward Gender Equality: The Role of Public Policy*, Washington, DC, The World Bank.

The World Bank (1996) *Involving Workers in East Asia's Growth*, Washington, DC, The World Bank.

CHAPTER 6

The role of the state in economic development

Stephen W. K. Chiu and Tai-lok Lui

6.1 Introduction

By now it is customary to attribute the economic success of East Asia to the special role played by the state in the development process. Here we follow Rueschemeyer and Evans' conception of the state as 'a set of organizations invested with the authority to make binding decisions for people and organizations juridically located in a particular territory and to implement these decisions using, if necessary, force' (1985, p.47). It is argued that in contrast to the Anglo-American model of regulatory states which play a refereeing role only in the economy, East Asian states are directly involved in the economy and have a significant influence on private decisions. Even the World Bank, long a bastion of free market philosophy, has recently admitted that the state could play a larger role than neo-classical economics would call for. Its 1993 report on the Asia-Pacific observes that: 'More selective interventions – forced savings, tax policies to promote (sometimes very specific) investments, sharing risks, restricting capital outflow, and repressing interest rates – also appear to have succeeded in some HPAEs (High Performing Asian Economies) especially Japan, Korea, Singapore, and Taiwan, China' (World Bank, 1993, p.242).

Yet this in fact represents a sea change in the assessment of the contribution made by the state in East Asian development. In the 1970s, when world-wide attention first focused on the economic success of the East Asian newly industrialized economies (NIEs), these states were hailed as models *par excellence* of a growth strategy based on an unfettered market mechanism. Against the contemporary Keynesian orthodoxy in development economics, some neo-classical economists argued that the East Asian NIEs' high speed growth came about only after the state dismantled restrictive, protective industries policies and set prices (interest rates, wages and exchange rates) correctly (see also Chapter 3). Into the 1980s, however, a new orthodoxy in development economics and a different interpretation of the East Asian experience emerged. Studies began emphasizing the idea of the 'developmental state' itself as responsible for East Asia's success.

Chalmers Johnson's (1982) study of Japan pushed this perspective to the forefront of academic discourse, while the *IDS Bulletin*'s special 1984 issue on the East Asian developmental states reflected the growing importance of this 'revisionist' perspective, as opposed to the neo-classical orthodoxy (Wade and White, 1984). Country studies of the East Asian NIEs, such as Amsden's on Korea (1989) and Wade's on Taiwan (1988), developed a state-centric account of development in the region. Comparative analyses, be they monographs (Haggard, 1990), or anthologies (Deyo, 1987; Appelbaum and Henderson, 1992), also began to anchor in the statist line in their interpretation of the East Asian experience. The concept of the developmental state also became increasingly current in East Asian studies (Castells, 1992). Both the neo-classical and statist approaches are often analytical and prescriptive in nature. They are based on a particular conception of the development process and its requirements and offer a specific description and empirical generalization of the role of the state. More importantly, these accounts also propose a prescription about the best mix of public policies to promote economic development. Focusing on the East Asian NIEs and Japan, this chapter will trace the changing perception of the role of the state in East Asian development, with an emphasis on the diversity of the relationship between public policy and the economy.

6.2   The market-led model

The magnitude of change in the mainstream view of the role of the state in development in general, or East Asian development in particular, can perhaps be gauged by the view of the World Bank itself. Wade (1996) provides a fascinating account of this change in the World Bank's view of the East Asian miracle. Until the 1980s the World Bank was the ultimate institutional anchor of a market-led model of development and East Asia was taken as the epitome of this development strategy. In the *World Development Report 1987*, it offers a direct statement consistent with the mainstream neo-classical view in economics (the stream of economics originating from Alfred Marshall which stresses the positive effect of an unrestricted market in the optimal allocation of resources) in support of the free trade and free market model of development. In its lending policy, the World Bank strives to coax developing states to adopt a more 'market-friendly' programme of development, as do other multilateral financial bodies such as the International Monetary Fund.

Accounts of East Asian development that emphasize the importance of market forces are best represented in the writings on the East Asian NIEs of economists associated with the World Bank in the 1970s and 1980s, such as Ian Little and Bela Balassa (Little, 1981; Balassa *et al.*, 1982; Balassa, 1988). In this model, the state's role is relatively limited to catalyst and corrector of market failures. Occupying the centre stage are private entrepreneurs who respond eagerly to market stimuli, capitalizing on cheap, plentiful supplies of labour. This interpretation starts with a free trade regime, whereby national policy allocates resources in accordance with the country's existing comparative advantage (see Chapter 2). Thus, Little (1981) stresses the positive effects of 'almost free trade conditions for exports' in East Asian NIEs' success. By 'getting the price right' through trade liberalization and exchange rate reform, East Asian NIE states provide the optimal environment for the growth of private enterprise.

During the East Asian NIEs' transition to industrial capitalism, the states in Korea and Taiwan removed fetters surrounding private industry, by abolishing restrictions on trade and devaluing currencies. In the case of Hong Kong, the maintenance of a free trade regime accounted for the city's successful industrialization. Freed from the fetters of government inter-vention, capitalizing on their comparative advantage, the East Asian NIEs therefore embarked on export-oriented, labour-intensive industrialization. Government stability is also important because it provides a stable, long-term horizon for private business calculations. A regulatory framework and infrastructural capacity is seen as beneficial, but any interference in private decision making is not. Hence, as Balassa remarks in his study of the 'lessons' of East Asian development:

> the principal contribution of government in the Far Eastern NIEs has been to create a modern infrastructure, to provide a stable incentive system, and to ensure that government bureaucracy will help rather than hinder exports ... More generally, less use has been made of government regulation and bureaucratic controls in East Asia than elsewhere in the developing world. Finally, there have been fewer policy-imposed distortions in labour and capital markets, and greater reliance has been placed on private enterprise.
>
> (Balassa, 1988, pp.286–8)

It is interesting to note, however, that in the same issue of the journal *Economic Development and Cultural Change* in which Balassa's article appeared, another eminent development economist, Paul W. Kuznets, also compares Japan, Taiwan and South Korea and concludes with a diametrically different view of the state from that of Balassa. As Kuznets states, in these three countries, '[g]overnment intervention, though restricted by the need to keep exports competitive, has been pervasive' (Kuznets, 1988, p.S36).

According to the mainstream World Bank view, however, the protagon-ists of the East Asian industrialization narrative are the private entrepreneurs, and the state's role is best conceived as catalytic rather than 'pervasive'.

Latin America vs. East Asia: the secret of export-led growth

Focusing on the East Asian NIEs, Balassa (1988) observes that these countries (apart from Hong Kong) have passed through the first stage of import-substituting industrialization (in which the local market is primary and imports of labour-intensive consumer products are 'substituted' by local production). However, instead of following the path of the Latin American NIEs in adopting the second stage of import-substituting industrialization (local production of capital-intensive producer goods substituting for imports), the East Asian NIEs shifted to a new developmental strategy called export-oriented industrialization, with export manufacturing as the engine of economic growth (see Chapters 2 and 3).

For Balassa it was the growth of exports in the East Asian NIEs that accounted for their GDP growth rates being the highest amongst developing countries. First, Balassa states that 'exports contribute to resource allocation according to comparative advantage. At the same time, these gains cumulate over time as the efficiency of new investment is enhanced through its orientation toward industries that correspond to the comparative advantage of the countries concerned' (Balassa, 1988, pp.280–1). Second, exports make it possible for the East Asian NIEs to overcome the limitations of their small domestic markets by ensuring full utilization of resources and reaping the advantages of large-scale production. Third, while import substitution often leads to protectionism and monopolies, export-oriented industrialization provides the 'carrot and the stick' of competition, inducing technological change in export industries that must keep up with modern technology in order to improve their position in the world market.

According to Balassa, the four determinants of the East Asian NIEs' favourable economic performance are: stability of the incentive system, limited government intervention, well-functioning labour and capital markets, and reliance on private capital (1988, pp.286–8).

First, the East Asian NIE states have a long tradition of encouraging exports by establishing incentives, eliminating administrative obstacles, and creating a favourable environment for exporters. In addition, the incentive system for exporters is relatively stable. For instance, the East Asian NIEs avoid the appreciation or fluctuation of the exchange rate, and exporters can usually expect that the incentives they receive will be maintained in the future. This is in contrast with the Latin American NIE states, which allow the export exchange rate to fluctuate and wages to rise, thereby greatly reducing the profitability of exporters.

Second, although the states in East Asia actively work to create a positive environment for economic growth, they rarely stray outside this limit and they do not interfere with the free workings of markets. As a result, the scope of administrative control is much more limited in East Asia than in Latin America. In the latter case, not only are there pervasive controls over investment, prices, and imports, but decisions are also generally made on a case-by-case basis, thereby creating uncertainty from a business perspective.

Third, states in the East Asian NIEs have instituted fewer policy-imposed distortions over labour and capital markets. While labour markets are generally free in the East Asian NIEs, they are highly regulated in the Latin American NIEs. Balassa complains that prohibitions on discharging labour and high severance payments in the Latin American NIEs have increased their cost of labour. Moreover, capital markets are also freer in the East Asian NIEs than in the Latin American NIEs. In the East Asian NIEs, interest rates are tied to market rates to provide incentives for domestic savings and to discourage the outflow of capital. In the Latin American

NIEs, by contrast, artificially low interest rates have reinforced the effects of overvalued currency rates in encouraging the outflow of capital.

Finally, greater reliance has been placed on the private sector in the East Asian NIEs than those in Latin America. In the East Asian NIEs, private enterprise takes the lead in making the necessary investments, and, through exposure to international competition, in becoming efficient and profitable. On the other hand, public enterprise tends to play a more important role in the Latin American NIEs than in the East Asian NIEs. In the early 1980s, the outlays of public enterprise accounted for 26 per cent of GDP in Mexico compared to only 4 per cent in South Korea. Balassa argues that economic growth is negatively correlated with the size of the public sector, the share of government expenditures in GDP, and the tax burden (see also Chapter 3).

Problems of the neo-classical imagery

As a set of empirical generalizations, neo-classical accounts of Asian industrialization have been under heavy fire lately, especially in terms of the applicability of the model to all of East Asia. Even if Hong Kong and Singapore were indeed perfect examples of the free market theory (we shall return to this question later), the same does not apply to Japan, Taiwan and Korea. In emphasizing the efficacy of the market, free marketeers are liable to overlook the fact that Japan, Korea and Taiwan's economic structures and policies are a far cry from the image of the unfettered market. Neo-classical theories argue that the establishment and maintenance of a free trade regime has been critical to the industrial take-off of East Asia. Hence they trace the explosive industrial growth of Taiwan and Korea in the 1960s to policy reforms in the late 1950s and early 1960s liberalizing international trade. Nonetheless, subsequent scholars such as Luedde-Neurath (1986) and Wade (1988; 1993) question the extent of such liberalizing measures.

First, they argue that studies conducted by neo-classical theorists such as Balassa are methodologically flawed, and that the picture of Taiwan and Korea as free trade regimes compared to other industrializing countries is highly misleading. These neo-classical theorists argue that Taiwan, Korea and Singapore have much lower levels of protection over manufacturing than such countries as Israel, Colombia and Argentina. Balassa's calculation of effective protection was based on a comparison of the prices of domestically produced commodities and foreign produced versions of the same item. Given the existence of tariff and trade restrictions, the domestic price is expected to be higher than the international free trade price. Balassa and his associates reject the use of legal tariffs and quantitative restrictions on imports for their analysis, relying instead on direct price comparisons. However, while direct price comparisons of domestic and international markets yield low rates of protection for the East Asian NIEs, we cannot ignore the fact that both Korean and Taiwanese legal tariff rates for imports averaged over 60 per cent in the 1960s. Furthermore, in Korea in 1968, some 294 (74 per cent) out of 396 commodities were subject to quantitative import controls (Wade, 1988). In a word, the trade regimes in Korea and Taiwan, with their full array of both quantitative and qualitative controls, cannot be characterized as *laissez-faire* (Wade, 1993).

Second, market-led approaches also assume a supply of production inputs free from administrative encumbrances, another pillar of the East Asian NIEs' market mechanism. One prominent fact disproving this account is that the East Asian financial system, a key source of funds, is never as free as the economists expect (see Chapter 4). Almost all the commercial banks in Taiwan and Korea were owned by the state until the late 1980s. Woo (1991), furthermore, contends that Korea's financial reforms of the early 1960s in fact strengthened, not loosened, state control over the financial system. Given these circumstances, it is difficult to sustain the view that fund allocation is unaffected by state actions. While Hong Kong and Singapore's financial systems are relatively 'undistorted' by government intervention (in the neo-classical sense), the Korean and Taiwanese states' allocation of funds is a critical component of their development strategies.

Third, few can deny that the Korean and Taiwanese states implemented an extensive industrial policy that shaped the course of development. In Korea, the state funnelled a large amount of capital into large-scale conglomerates (or *chaebol*), enabling them to invest in new ventures and expand their existing production lines. Again, this contradicts the theories of neo-classical economics and *laissez-faire*, which would emphasize the importance of small-scale competitive firms as the ideal 'market structure' for successful capitalist development. In Taiwan, as late as the 1970s, the public enterprises' share in production and investment was among the highest in the capitalist world. Taiwan possessed more the characteristics of a 'mixed economy' during its early stage of industrialization than that of a free market economy.

Chaebol

Chaebol are the Korean equivalent of the Japanese *keiretsu* (described in Section 6.4). They can be defined as business groups consisting of large companies in highly diversified business areas, owned and managed by family members or relatives (Steers *et al.*, 1989). It is a tricky business to count which ones are *chaebol* and which are not, but it is common for observers to include at least 30 such groups in the rank of the *chaebol* (Jones, 1994; *The Economist*, 1996). All of the *chaebol* are highly diversified. The largest of them, Samsung, has products ranging from aeroplanes and semiconductors to flour and printing paper. It also operates a wide range of service firms such as insurance, hotels and department stores.

The economic might of the *chaebol* is formidable, although estimations of their size vary. One estimate puts the combined sales of the four biggest *chaebol* – Hyundai, Samsung, LG and Daewoo – as equivalent to 80 per cent of GDP and 60 per cent of exports (*The Economist*, 1996, p.58). These four are also among the top Fortune 100 multinationals outside the USA. Their presence is no longer confined to South Korea, and a few of them have, since the 1980s, become household names in the USA and Europe (automobiles from Hyundai and Daewoo and electrical and electronic appliances from Samsung).

The rise of the *chaebol* to economic dominance has always been attributed to the heavy-handed intervention of the South Korean state in the economy. By allocating loans made by state-owned banks to the *chaebol* and guaranteeing their foreign borrowing, the state funnelled massive amounts of capital to these groups and helped their expansion and diversification. For example, during the 1980s the *chaebol* received a large amount of such 'policy loans' so that they could enter the high-tech electronics sector. With state assistance, Samsung Electronics has become a major player in the mass production of memory chips.

(See Chapter 9 for further elaboration of the nature and importance of the *chaebol*.)

The cases of Singapore and Hong Kong, as well as those of Taiwan and Korea, seem at odds with the neo-classical description. Singapore, for instance, fits the *laissez-faire* image poorly. The state distributes extensive incentives to foreign investors in strategic sectors, and also provides infrastructural assistance selectively to firms that the state considers beneficial to industrialization. The state also exercises heavy-handed control over the labour movement and the determination of wages. Even in Hong Kong, the state is intricately linked to economic development in various ways. For example, the state is heavily involved in the reproduction of labour power through provisions in public housing and education (see Castells, 1992; Chiu *et al.*, 1995).

6.3   The state-led models

Revisionist interpretations of the East Asian NIEs provide a diametrically different picture from the neo-classical perspective, epitomized by the concept of the developmental state (see Johnson, 1987; Castells, 1992). This intellectual paradigm draws historical sustenance from the argument that successful 'late development' takes a very different form from that of earlier industrializers (Gerschenkron, 1962); the former's developmental process becomes less 'spontaneous', with the state assuming the role of the major agent of social transformation. Partly in reaction to the neo-classical onslaught, two major studies on East Asian industrialization are devoted to this theme (Wade and White, 1984; Deyo, 1987). As Wade and White observe:

> If we turn to Japan, South Korea, and Taiwan, among the most dramatic and equitable cases in the history of capitalist development, industrialization has in each case been accompanied by aggressive government intervention. The authorities have acted to guide markets and moderate the competitive process in a way that neo-classical economics says public officials cannot get right.
>
> (Wade and White, 1984, p.1)

Deyo also concludes his volume on the 'new East Asian industrialism' by proposing a 'strategic capacity' model, emphasizing that:

> [the] state's commitment to economic expansion and, more important, its *capacity* to implement well-chosen development strategies differentiates these NIEs from other developing countries better endowed in natural resources, scale of domestic markets, and other economic assets.
>
> (Deyo, 1987, p.228: emphasis original)

The statist perspective emerged as a critique of the free market interpretation of developing countries. Instead of emphasizing free markets, trade liberalization, private enterprise, and the restricted role of the state, the statist perspective contends that states have a strategic role to play in taming domestic and international market forces and harnessing them to national ends. Instead of focusing on maximum profitability on the basis of current comparative advantage, the statist perspective focuses on the phenomenon of 'late industrialization'. In this respect, the statist perspective is still sharing the Gerschenkronian view of late development, arguing for the importance of a strong state to overcome market imperfections and the various bottlenecks of industrialization (Gerschenkron, 1962; Rueschemeyer and Evans, 1985).

According to the statist view, state intervention is necessary for successful late industrialization. Following Gerschenkron, Amsden (1989) contends that East Asian industrialization is characterized by its 'lateness' rather than by its 'newness' (as in 'newly' industrialized economies). As latecomers, East Asian firms must compete with established Western firms that can introduce new technologies quickly and thereby earn higher profits. This does, of course, allow the East Asian firms to acquire, 'learn,' or 'borrow,' the more codified elements of a given technology from the West without having to develop them for themselves. Nevertheless, there is generally a great gap between buying, borrowing, or stealing the codified elements on one hand and mastering the technology in production on the other. In other words, the magnitude of the problems facing latecomers called for the developmental states to offset the disadvantages faced by East Asian firms in international competition and to move the NIEs' industrial structure toward more technologically dynamic activities (Wade, 1992).

The capitalist developmental state

In the spirit of this line of argument, Johnson first popularized the idea of the capitalist developmental state. Contrasting it to the states in socialist and Western capitalist economies, he contends that the socialist state seeks to substitute administrative commands for private entrepreneurship and market mechanism, while in Western models the state is primarily regulatory and is expected to play the role of a neutral umpire in the marketplace. The capitalist developmental state does not attempt to replace the market mechanism and private decision making, but neither does it abdicate to private profit-seeking behaviours in the development process. It will strive to *influence* private business decisions by persuasion, coercion, and by manipulating the parameters of private decision making. In

Johnson's words, the 'logic of such a system derives from the *interaction* of two sub-systems, one public and geared to developmental goals and the other private and geared to profit maximization' (Johnson, 1987, pp.141–2, emphasis original).

The developmental state, according to Johnson's (1987) conception, possesses the following features:

1   As the name implies, economic development (in terms of growth, productivity, and competitiveness) is the foremost priority of state action. The state single-mindedly adheres to economic development even at the expense of other objectives, such as equality and social welfare. 'Developmental elites are generated and come to the fore because of the desire to break out of the stagnation of dependency and underdevelopment; the truly successful ones understand that they need the market to maintain efficiency, motivate the people over the long term, and serve as a check on institutionalized corruption while they are battling against underdevelopment' (Johnson, 1987, p.140).

2   Since the developmental state is not a socialist state, it has a firm commitment to private property and the market. The market, however, is closely governed by state managers who formulate strategic industrial policy to promote development. In other words, the developmental state elite actively intervene in the economy, but in a 'market-conforming' manner.

3   Within the state bureaucracy, a pilot agency (such as MITI in Japan) plays a key role in strategic policy formulation and implementation. This agency is given sufficient scope to take initiatives and operate effectively, and is staffed by the best managerial talent available to the state bureaucracy. Johnson suggests that the strictly meritocratic recruitment into the bureaucracy not only ensures a high degree of bureaucratic capability, but also generates a sense of unity and common identity on the part of the bureaucratic elite. Their long-term, often lifetime, service in the same bureaucratic agency also reinforces this *esprit de corps* among the bureaucrats and enables them to accumulate experience and expertise in economic matters.

MITI

The Japanese Ministry of International Trade and Industry (MITI) was established in 1949 and is generally recognized to have been a key institution in the emergence of Japan as a major economic power. MITI took responsibility for Japanese 'industrial policy' (*sangyo seisku* – a term reportedly invented by the Japanese) which, particularly in the 1960s and 1970s, guided both the private sector firms and the public sector in a direction of rapid economic growth. It represents a 'pilot agency' designed not so much to direct investment and trade into particular sectors or branches of industry, but to persuade, through consensus building measures, the big Japanese manufacturing and trading companies to enter new areas of economic activity and exporting. It has never espoused an ideology of public ownership. Rather, MITI is run by highly trained 'pragmatic bureaucrats', whose role has been to spot the new trends and product areas, to assess the strengths and weaknesses of Japanese producers in these fields, and to propose policies to strengthen the ability of the private sector to compete in these areas. On occasions this has meant that MITI has tried to organize and re-organize the domestic productive structure to meet its objectives: to encourage the merging of domestic production, to help establish new lines of production, to organize co-operative activity amongst firms, etc.

But MITI has not been without significant powerful policy instruments designed to push companies in particular directions. Technological transfers, joint venturing, patent rights, royalty conditions, licensing agreements: all were subject to its jurisdiction during the rapid phase of industrialization from the 1950s to the 1970s. In addition, MITI has had responsibility for everything from the setting of domestic electricity prices through to the regulation of bicycle racing. Through a series of high-powered advisory committees it has scrutinized all aspects of Japanese industrial performance and actively encouraged 'high speed growth'.

MITI was credited with being the main instrument of the 'developmental state' idea first popularized by Chalmers Johnson (1982). Ever since then, this thesis has itself been the subject of refinement and criticism. MITI is often credited with failing to spot developments in key areas such as information technology. Its success in encouraging private companies to act together has been questioned, for example, in the case of the development of the petro-chemical industry. Whether MITI was quite as central to the industrial development process of the 1950s to 1960s, compared to the importance of ordinary commercial decisions made by Japanese companies without its involvement, is the subject of fierce controversy. Also, MITI's role may have declined in importance as the Japanese economy matured and its companies transformed themselves into world class operations with outstanding international competitive success.

With respect to how the state promotes late industrialization, Amsden's (1989) study on South Korea emphasizes the dual policies of 'subsidies' and 'discipline'. If the first Industrial Revolution was built on *laissez-faire*, and the second on infant industry protection (see Chapter 2), then Amsden argues that South Korea's late industrialization was founded on subsidies. The allocation of subsidies has rendered the South Korean government not merely a banker but an entrepreneur, using subsidies to decide what, when, and how much to produce, and which strategic industries to favour. Subsidies are necessary because South Korean firms cannot initially compete against Japanese products, even in such highly labour-intensive industries as cotton spinning and weaving. Needless to say, the long gestation periods and relatively low profitability (through industries' adolescent period) make capital-intensive industries rather unattractive investments to South Korean firms. According to Amsden, South Korea's entry into heavy industries, and the emergence of cotton textiles as its leading export industry, provide graphic evidence of the need for state intervention under conditions of late industrialization.

Nevertheless, while the South Korean government subsidizes strategic industrial firms, it also imposes 'discipline' on them. For example, the government specifies stringent performance requirements (notably in the field of exports) in return for the subsidies it provides. Such discipline over private firms involves both rewarding good performers and penalizing poor ones. 'Carrots and sticks' take the form of granting or withholding industrial licensing, government bank loans, advanced technology acquired through the government's investment in foreign licensing and technical assistance, etc. Since the South Korean government deliberately refrains from bailing out firms which are badly managed in otherwise profitable industries, government subsidies do not lead to a waste of resources, as they do in the case of socialist countries and many developing countries in Latin America. Thus Amsden asserts that '[w]here Korea differs from most other late industrializing countries is in the discipline its state exercises over private firms' (1989, p.14). This interpretation of the development process is also argued to apply to Taiwan (Wade, 1992).

Finally, what is the relationship between the developmental state and other social institutions in the society? Onis (1991) points out that East Asian industrializing states are unusual because they experience both bureaucratic autonomy and public–private co-operation. On the one hand, there is a high degree of bureaucratic autonomy and capacity facilitated by meritocratic recruitment and a sense of unity and mission among state managers. This allows the state and bureaucratic elites to avoid being 'captured' by their private-sector clients and to develop national strategic developmental policies independent of the other powerful groups in society. Bureaucratic autonomy is also safeguarded by the depoliticization of major economic decisions, or what Johnson calls the separation between 'reigning' and 'ruling': 'the politicians set broad goals, protect the technocratic bureaucracy from political pressures, perform "safety valve" functions when the bureaucracy makes mistakes, and take the heat when corruption scandals are uncovered ... the official bureaucracy does the actual planning, intervening, and guiding of the economy' (Johnson, 1987, p.152).

On the other hand, there are close institutional links between the developmental state and private sector conglomerates, banks, and trading companies that dominate strategic sectors of the economy. The state attempts to implement its industrial policy through the various sector 'peak associations', that is, the largest business or industrial associations. In Johnson's (1987) words, 'administrative guidance' often works without the backing of legislative coercion because of the long-term informal relationship between bureaucrats and businessmen. Of course, the omnipresent threat of the withdrawal of state support and incentives is also an instrument to 'discipline' the private sector. As a result, the private sector is highly co-operative with the state policy of subsidies and discipline. Onis argues that this unusual mixture of bureaucratic autonomy and public–private sector co-operation brings about the emergence of a strong autonomous state which is not only capable of formulating strategic developmental goals, but is also able to translate these broad national goals into effective policy action to promote late industrialization in East Asia.

The limitations of the strong state model

In spite of the popularity of these stylized 'models' of East Asian development in academic and non-academic discourses, their limited validity and applicability are easily discernible. In invoking the 'East Asian model of development', we must consider Colin Bradford's early warning: 'The real story of what constitutes successful development [in the East Asian NIEs] is more subtle and indeed quite different from what the stereotypes [of development models] suggest' (Bradford, 1986, p.122). Subscribing uncritically to either of the two dominant interpretations of East Asian industrialization causes a real problem: a lack of depth in the comparisons. There are two symptoms of this problem. First, researchers are prone to generalize across East Asian NIE cases without systematically comparing relevant phenomena. Second, they sometimes overuse the single case that most proves their theoretical position at the expense of paying attention to others. By positing a 'unique' East Asian model of development generalizable to the whole region, discussions of the region's developmental experiences assume too much uniformity within the 'East Asian phenomenon'.

If not the free market, is a strong, developmentalist state the motor behind the 'East Asian miracle'? Here we argue that statist theorists' imagery is also overdrawn and cannot capture the nuances of Japan and the East Asian NIEs' actual developmental experiences. Once again, deeper comparative analysis reveals a more complex picture: only Japan and Korea among the East Asian economies seem to conform to the expectations of the developmental state model; the other three NIEs deviate from this norm to varying degrees and towards different directions.

The case most clearly deviating from the statist model is Hong Kong. While Hong Kong is hardly a neo-classical utopia, it is also a far cry from the developmental state. The public sector accounts for only a modest share of the economy and public ownership of productive enterprises is almost negligible. As much as possible, the state refrains from intervening in the allocation of resources as well as in their management. It performs no industrial targeting, and encourages labour and management to determine conditions of employment 'voluntarily' by negotiation. The state elite even actively espouses a *laissez-faire* philosophy to justify its non-intervention in the economy.

In Singapore, though the state appears omnipotent and omnipresent, its role in industrialization is rather complex. The state does take an active role in indicative planning and invests in productive enterprises. Nevertheless, foreign enterprises remain the most important agents in the industrialization process. The state's role is actually more indirect than in the other NIEs and not as great as the statist literature leads us to believe. We argue that the Singaporean state's interventions centre mainly on fiscal incentives, infrastructural provisions, and the labour market; the state is neither capable of, nor willing to, offer financial assistance to the manufacturing sector.

Taiwan also seems enigmatic judging from the statist point of view. The Taiwanese state was one of the heaviest investors in production among the capitalist economies, but most of its export industries were privately owned, and the state's relationship to these operations was at best arm's length. The multitude of small and medium-sized export enterprises basically thrive on their own, competing on managerial ability and cheap labour (Amsden, 1985; Ho, 1980). The linkages between the public enterprise sector and the private sector are also far from organic, as the state is more concerned with maintaining a monopoly of key sectors through state enterprises. Based on these observations, we agree with Evans' exhortation: 'it is more important to ask "what kind" of state involvement rather than "how much"' (Evans, 1995, p.11). To understand the role of the state in development, we need to depart from the dichotomous duplex of free markets and strong states and move towards a more nuanced analysis of the diverse roles assumed by the state in East Asia.

6.4   Towards state–business interdependence?

Statist theory emphasizes the state's autonomy in making decisions and its dominating capacity to bring about results in the marketplace. The state-led view of East Asian development, however, quickly gives rise to a theoretical reaction which emphasizes the interactions and institutional linkages between the state elite and societal actors. This new, broadened focus on state–society relations echoes Gilbert and Howe's call for the need to examine the convergence of state and class capacities in bringing about a particular outcome:

> We argue that state-centred theorists disregard the *interrelation* of state and society; in viewing the state as an independent entity, they fail to see how it is related to the wider society. Further, they oversimplify societal forces and ignore class conflict within and beyond the state. State and society are interdependent, and must be analyzed as such.
>
> (Gilbert and Howe, 1991, p.205; emphasis original)

In the discussion of East Asian development, there is a similar view stressing the *interdependence* of state and business. Weiss calls this the 'governed interdependence theory', premised on the proposition that 'the ability of East Asian firms and industry more generally to adapt quickly to economic change is based on a system that socializes risk and thereby co-ordinates change across a broad array of organizations – both public and private' (Weiss, 1995, p.594). Governed interdependence refers to a system of central co-ordination in which the government and industry co-operate and communicate to bring about innovation and realize competitive potentials. Again, this model has both analytical and policy implications, since it simultaneously generalizes about state–business co-ordination in East Asia and how this relationship has contributed to the economic success of the region.

This theory departs from the state-led model in its insistence that development policies cannot simply be *imposed* upon the private sector without compromising the effectiveness of such policies. The really effective policies are those formulated in consultation with the private sector and implemented with the willing co-operation of firms. 'Co-ordination' is the key to this system. Why is industrial co-ordination possible? Apart from the autonomy emphasized so much in the state-led models, Weiss attributes the institutional capacities for co-ordination to the proper kind of state–industry linkages. She argues that in Korea, Taiwan and Japan, elaborate matrices of institutional linkages have been established between state agencies and the private sector. Such 'policy networks' provide a vital mechanism for acquiring information and for co-ordinating agreement with the private sector' (Weiss, 1995, p.600). In Japan, for example, MITI benefits from the work of over 250 deliberative councils which enable the state to consult the private sector and to collect valuable information. Only by so doing can a strong ministry avoid formulating policies in isolation from the private sector and act in concert with industry. These policy networks are themselves vitally aided by the highly 'organized' nature of the Japanese enterprise system, based upon the *keiretsu* form of business group.

Keiretsu

Keiretsu is the name for the modern Japanese enterprise group. They comprise a collection of firms in various industries (themselves known as *kaisha*) which hold shares in one another's businesses, borrow from the same financial institution which serves all group members, and tend to behave strategically as a group. Some of these groups evolved from pre-Second World War industrial conglomerates knows as *zaibatsu*, which were broken up after the War. The six largest contemporary *keiretsu* are Mitsui, Mitsubishi, Sumitomo, Funo, Sanwa and Ikkan. The first three are former *zaibatsu*, while some well-known former *zaibatsu* joined together to form the Funo group, which includes companies such as the Nissan motor corporation. Other motor companies such as Daihatsu and Isuzu are members of the Sanwa and Ikkan groups respectively; Toyota is a member of the Mitsui group.

These groups are noted for their cross holding of shares, both between companies within the same group and between the groups themselves. The groups are often considered to be led by an important banking company. These relationships form the basis for the strong degree of 'group loyalty' and, to a lesser extent, industry loyalty, which typifies Japanese business activity. In addition to the 'bank-led' groups mentioned above, there are a further series of smaller non-bank, or 'independent', groups. A well-known example of this category is the Sony Corporation, which itself has over eighty subsidiary and affiliate companies in which it owns shares. Unlike the pre-war *zaibatsu*, there are no holding companies that dictate actions and determine strategy associated with any of these groups. They are groups of 'independent' decision-making companies who simply co-operate with each other.

Each of the ex-*zaibatsu* enterprise groups includes a large general trading company (*Sogo Shosha*) as part of its overall activity, and there are others attached to some of the other groups. These companies specialize in exporting and importing in a wide range of commodities, and help to organize domestic wholesale and retail activity. The top nine of these general trading companies accounted for about 50 per cent of Japanese exports and 65 per cent of imports in the later 1980s, giving them enormous power over foreign trade.

(Source: Ito, 1992)

(See Chapter 9 for further elaboration on the nature of these Japanese business groups.)

To facilitate public–private co-ordination, it is essential for industry to be organized in an *encompassing* fashion. Fragmentation in interest representation of the private sector will be inimical to co-ordination, while a highly centralized and active peak association among producers is essential. In the Japanese case, the *Keidanren* (federation of economic organizations) and industry-specific manufacturing trade associations provide a basis for co-ordination. In Korea, the highly centralized industrial structure dominated by the *chaebol* invariably facilitates public–private co-operation, and the state also fosters the growth of encompassing peak associations in the private sector. Taiwan is also characterized by the presence of such encompassing institutions as the Taiwan Textile Federation and the Taiwan Electrical Appliances Manufacturer Association (Weiss, 1995, pp.602–4).

Weiss's theory is in fact a more sophisticated formulation of earlier studies of Japanese state–business relations, and her contribution is also distinctive in attempting to generalize beyond the Japanese case. For example, in his study of energy policies in Japan, Samuels (1987) talks of 'the politics of reciprocal consent' to highlight the political interdependence of state and market. 'Reciprocal consent' is the mutual accommodation of state and market. It is an iterative process of reassurance among market players and public officials, one that works better where the parties to these negotiations are stable and where the institutions that guarantee their compacts are enduring' (Samuels, 1987, p.8). He points out that as a result of such 'reciprocal consent', the Japanese state pursues an energy policy that largely seeks to guarantee the stability of the private market rather than to compete or displace private entrepreneurship.

Similarly, Okimoto seeks to qualify the record of MITI's industrial policy as a history of unmixed state-led success. Rather than a simple imposition of public priorities over private impulses, he attributed the peculiar effectiveness of Japan's industrial policy to its particular role in consensus building:

It has served as the main instrument for consensus building, the vehicle for information exchange and public–private communication. Close government–business relations would be hard to imagine in its absence. Indeed the whole system of consensus, on which Japan's political economy relies, would be hard to maintain without industrial policy as an integrative mechanism.

(Okimoto, 1989, p.231)

Calder's study of industrial finance in Japan and his formulation of 'strategic capitalism' also stresses the existence of a hybrid public–private system, 'driven pre-eminently by market-oriented private-sector calculations, but with active public-sector involvement to encourage public spiritedness and long-range vision' (Calder, 1993, p.16).

While not dealing exclusively with East Asia, Evans also highlights the fact that successful development states could not simply be autonomous, they are also 'embedded in a concrete set of social ties that binds the state to society and provides institutionalized channels for the continual negotiation and re-negotiation of goals and policies' (Evans, 1995, p.12).

Criticisms of governed interdependence

As a set of policy prescriptions, the view outlined above has the promise of correcting the excesses of the state-led models. The simple moral of the story is that either too much or too little state, and too much or too little market, is no good for the long-term growth of the economy. Effective state co-ordination of economic change comes only when there is a proper balance of state and market. The focus on the institutional underpinning of effective policy is valuable. However, while we are sympathetic to the policy prescriptions of this new approach, we find Weiss's model, as an analytical approach, problematic on three counts.

First, by proposing that the governed interdependence model explains why some states are more efficient than others in co-ordinating economic growth, Weiss is, at the empirical level, simply trying to replace one general homogeneous imagery of East Asian growth with another one. Are state–business relations in Japan, Korea and Taiwan equally co-operative, and is the balance of state and business power the same across the three countries? If Japan can be characterized by a high level of public–private co-operation and a balance of bureaucratic autonomy and linkages with the private sector, can the same be said about the Korean case? Amsden has provided ample evidence of how the Korean state sought to change business behaviours in the light of public objectives. The variety of measures by the Korean state to solicit compliance from the private sector is also legendary, such as the use of tax investigations to rein in recalcitrant firms. Furthermore, how much can we attribute Taiwan's export success to public–private co-ordination? For one thing, Taiwan's export manufacturing is characterized by a multitude of small and medium-sized firms, which does not seem to be too conducive to the kind of centralized co-ordination that Weiss envisages. The political schism for most of the post-war years between the Mainlander Kuomintang (KMT) regime and the primarily Taiwanese small entrepreneurs also makes co-operation difficult.

Second, Weiss chides previous research as being static in scope, typically basing their conclusions on a snapshot view of government–industry relations frozen in time (Weiss, 1996, p.606). She maintains, quite rightly, that it is essential to capture the dynamic picture of state–business relations. It is unclear, however, what time frames her model is deemed applicable to. If governed interdependence is the primary factor explaining effective state 'intervention' in East Asian development, we should expect it to be able to help us make sense of the post-war industrial take-off. Yet Weiss also points out that government–business relations have been changed 'from a situation in which government (the economic bureaucracy) was largely making the big decisions – usually out of necessity, due to a destabilized or underdeveloped business sector – to a situation in which the private sector is being increasingly invited to take more initiatives' (Weiss, 1995, p.607). If this is true (and we basically agree that it is), the problem becomes whether Weiss thinks that past economic growth in Taiwan and Korea can be explained by public–private co-operation or not, since she acknowledges that state–business relations are undergoing a process of transformation in these two economies. Is she also guilty of over-generalizing from current experiences? For example, if the relationship between the KMT-controlled state and the Taiwanese bourgeoisie can be viewed as co-operative since the 1980s, the same certainly cannot be said for earlier decades.

Third, in generalizing the idea of governed interdependence to the case of Taiwan, Korea and Japan, Weiss is liable to mix explanations with prescriptions. Even if co-ordination, communication and co-operation between the public and private sector is the ideal pattern of relations between the two, Weiss's analysis still poses the question of whether this model adequately *explains* the economic success of the three economies. Prescribing public–private co-ordination is one thing; arguing this has actually happened and attributing past success to it are entirely different issues. If we could conceptualize, for example, a continuum of different degrees of state–business co-operation, an interesting question would be: what are the conditions responsible for co-operation, or, conversely, for non-co-operation? We would then see state–business relations as a result of the incessant negotiation, bargaining, and even conflicts and struggles between state agencies and private firms. Their interests may converge in certain countries, but diverge in others. Or public–private co-operation may be more possible in certain sectors within certain countries but not others. Seen in this light, we need to ascertain whether co-operation is really the case in a certain economy over a certain period, and then try to deduce the possible impact on economic performance. In other words, we need to separate prescription from explanation in the analysis of the role of the state in East Asian development, or even developmental processes in general. For example, while Evans (1995) also prescribes state–society co-ordination, he is careful to examine the conditions both for its presence and absence in different developing countries.

We are more inclined towards the view of the relationship between 'politics' and development expounded by Friedman (1988). He argues that statists such as Johnson often subscribe to a view of development which is inherently neo-classical. It is based on an apolitical conception of the relationship between state action and industrial change. The role of the state, in this view, is to implement rules or allocate resources which prompt private sector actors to adopt the most efficient 'best practices' of production. Friedman adds:

> Comparative research in political economy was often refined to the coding of different forms of state regulation and the attempt to show which practices best enhanced efficiency. The problem, however, and one that the Japanese case highlights, is that politics may be much more significant than the conventional research scheme admits. The Japanese case demonstrates that significant political events affecting industrial development may not involve the state at all, but rather are shaped by worker ideologies, interfirm co-operation, and the like. The political resolution of conflicts in these areas may often be of importance equal to or greater than that of state actions.
>
> (Friedman, 1988, p.209)

As we have delineated elsewhere, it is necessary to consider the organizational framework and wider institutional context in which industrial development occurs, rather than simply focusing on the role of the state (Chiu *et al.*, 1997). By placing 'politics' at the centre of the analysis, we are steadfastly committed to putting the empirical analysis of the complex roles of the state in development rather than simply generalizing on the best practice of state intervention. In some cases, it is undeniable that the role of the state is critical in orchestrating the institutional configurations of development. Even in these cases, however, it is important to recognize the wider political origins of state actions. Furthermore, as our comparison of Hong Kong and Singapore indicates, there may be no one single best practice for development. Different roles of the state, coupled with different institutional frameworks, may produce equally impressive economic growth but with divergent patterns and distributional consequences.

6.5   The many faces of the state in East Asia

A good way to re-orient our conceptualization of the role of the state in East Asian development is to re-examine the divergent experiences of state interventions in the post-war era. Without going into the merits of different sets of policy prescriptions, we believe that the market-led, state-led, and governed interdependence models are all unable to capture the empirical and historical complexity of the roles of the state in East Asian development. Simply put, we have seen not one single model, but *models* of East Asian development. Such a typology helps us address the region's diversity without lapsing into empiricism. Coming to grips with the different strategic roles played by the state in industrialization in Korea, Taiwan, Singapore and Hong Kong will help us decipher a major source of diversity in the region. Different courses of state action constitute the most marked difference among the industrialization patterns of the East Asian economies, and these, in their turn, exacerbate other differences.

If we set the case of Japan aside, there are indeed some outstanding similarities in the East Asian NIEs' developmental patterns. As discussed earlier, the East Asian NIEs shared remarkably similar timing in their industrial take-off and rates of economic growth. Also commonly acknowledged as important are export and industrial expansion for generating economic growth (Balassa, 1988; Chen, 1979). However, recent studies show growing sensitivity to the diversity in developmental experience within the East Asian region. For example, Haggard (1990) identifies two development trajectories among the East Asian NIEs: Korea and Taiwan share the same export-led growth strategy, while Hong Kong and Singapore share an entrepôt (transhipment) growth strategy. Cheng, on the other hand, seeks to account for the East Asian NIEs' industrial restructuring process in the 1970s. As he states:

> The four East Asian NI[E]s diverged in their responses to the identical challenges [of industrial restructuring] specified above. In rhetoric, all of the four NI[E]s in 1971 simultaneously announced their intent to restructure industry in order to adjust to new parameters in international economic systems. In reality, the four NIEs diverged in their approaches to industrial and economic changes, as manifested in the variation of their industrial policies, mechanisms that implement policies, and policy outcomes.
>
> (Cheng, 1987, p.15)

These studies represent a significant advance over previous studies that lumped the East Asian NIEs into a single model of development. Nevertheless, they still do not give sufficient attention to the diversities in the development trajectories and strategies of East Asian NIEs. While recognizing the differences among the NIEs in his concrete analysis, Haggard overlooks such differences in conceptualizing a typology of development strategies. According to his typology, all East Asian NIEs pursue an export-led growth strategy. The differences between Singapore and Hong Kong are also not captured by the so-called common entrepôt (transhipment) growth strategy. Cheng, on the other hand, recognizes the East Asian NIEs' divergent responses to industrial restructuring, but assumes a common developmental strategy among the four countries *before* their restructuring. 'While the four East Asian NIEs converged to initiate the ELI [export-led industrialization] and became the same crop of small and open economies, they part company with each other in the advanced stage of ELI' (Cheng, 1987, p.46). Building on these analyses, we will now briefly discuss the salient differences in the state's role among the East Asian economies.

If there are controversies over whether Japan is really a developmental state or whether the state had a major impact on the post-war 'miracle', there is no doubt about the archetypical status of the South Korean state as the strong developmental state in East Asia. If Japan could claim to have a relatively strong bourgeoisie after the Second World War, South Korea had only a minuscule business community at tFhe aftermath of independence.

The economy was in a real shambles in the early 1950s after the Korean War. The Korean state, especially after the assumption of power by Park Chung Hee, did indeed have a major impact on the course of development from the 1960s. We do not want to go into the hypothetical question of what would have happened had the state acted differently; this would not have been possible given the economic and political circumstances of the time. What we want to say is that the actions of the Korean state are inseparable from what we consider to be an economic success story, or at least inseparable from the specific *ways* in which the South Korean economy attained its current level of development. The state channelled large amount of foreign aid and credit into a selected group of large conglomerates, the *chaebol*, and helped them to grow into Fortune 500 calibre. It opened up the economy to foreign trade and pursued aggressively an active industrial policy to promote export-oriented production. Compared with Japan, the Korean state did all a developmental state is supposed to do, and more.

The case of Taiwan is different. While we agree that the Taiwanese state under the KMT has largely been active, playing a significant role in the course of post-war industrialization, we think that most proponents of a developmental state in Taiwan ignore an important fact about Taiwan's post-war development: the role of small and medium-sized enterprises (SMEs). These SMEs have been the backbone of Taiwan's manufacturing sector and have generated much of the export earnings. They are deeply inserted into the international division of labour and are important producers of a large variety of consumer and capital products, for example, auto parts, shoes and garments. Since the 1980s a new breed of high technology SMEs has emerged to produce electronics components and computer hardware.

Taiwanese SMEs have of course benefited from the relatively sound and stable monetary and fiscal policies, the export credit and tax rebates system, as well as the impressive investments in infrastructure and education. Nevertheless, the existing record suggests that the multitude of Taiwanese SMEs have been relatively untouched by government industrial policies (except perhaps the export credit system), at least during the hyper-growth period of the 1960s and '70s. There have always been complaints about government policy not benefiting the SMEs in Taiwan; for example, the state-owned commercial banks have been regarded as acting more like pawn shops (imposing strict collateral requirements) by many SME entrepreneurs, and it has been difficult for the latter to get credit from them. Instead, a bustling informal financial market has met most of the SMEs' credit needs. In contrast, the public enterprises benefit disproportionately from bank credits and foreign loans. The SMEs in Taiwan thrive largely on their flexibility and a dense network of collaborations among themselves.

The cases of the two East Asian city economies also pose interesting contrasts with the larger East Asian economies, and also diverge between themselves. They shared a similar colonial experience, were 'underdeveloped' and faced a similar set of 'external' pressures and constraints. We documented in an earlier work how Hong Kong and Singapore parted ways in the early post-war era from a common entrepôt and British colonial legacy (Chiu *et al.*, 1997).

In Singapore, the state played an active role in shaping post-war industrialization, but in ways markedly different from Taiwan, South Korea and Japan. All three of the large East Asian states have jealously guarded their domestic markets from foreign imports with a protectionist tariff and quota system. They have also restricted the inflow of foreign direct investments, although with substantial variations among the three in terms of the rigidity and scope of restrictions (with Taiwan less restrictive than the others). Singapore, on the other hand, has kept its economy open to foreign trade and investment. In fact, the basic tenor of the state's developmental strategy is to actively promote and attract foreign direct investment in Singapore's manufacturing sector. Since the 1960s, the Singaporean state under the ruling People's Action Party has installed a fiscal incentive system to various 'pioneer' industries and firms which substantially benefits foreign firms producing locally. The state tamed the once militant labour movement and built an industrial relations system based on tripartite co-operation between the state, management and trade unions. Government infrastructure constructions served an important role in facilitating the coming of foreign firms. State-invested enterprises also seek to induce foreign investments by forming strategic alliances with foreign partners, thus reducing significantly the risk of such undertakings.

Hong Kong, by contrast, has not pursued a selective industrial policy. Throughout the course of its post-war industrial development it has repeatedly rejected suggestions from its manufacturers for assistance schemes or incentives directed specifically towards manufacturing indus-tries. In the 1950s, for example, it refused to establish an industrial bank, commonplace in other East Asian economies, to provide long-term credits to industries. The Industry Department plays only a supportive role for manufacturers and the most salient areas of government assistance to industries have been in infrastructure and overseas promotions of domestic exports. The Hong Kong state has striven to maintain a universalist and non-selective approach towards economic development, rather than giving special favours to specific sectors. It has, however, played a major role in the provision of means of collective consumption which help keep the lid on wage increases. It has been the largest landlord in Hong Kong through its massive public housing programme; the education system, from primary to tertiary institutions, has largely been state funded; and the public health system provides the population with cheap medical services. The most visible role of the state in Hong Kong's development is, of course, in its renowned low and simple tax system, as well as the British legal framework that stresses the enforcement of contracts. While lately the state has moved to give more selective incentives to high technology industries, such efforts have been widely regarded as too little, too late.

6.6 Conclusion

The focus of this brief survey of the role of the state in East Asian development has been analytical. We have concentrated on the analytical value of different models; that is, have they been able to unearth the empirical and historical patterns of state actions in the post-war development of East Asia? Are their generalizations accurate in view of the available information, especially from the comparative vantage point? With these considerations in mind, we raised analytical doubts about the market-led, state-led and interdependence models of East Asian development, arguing that these models have not been able to capture adequately the empirical and historical diversities among Japan and the East Asian NIEs in terms of the role of the state in development. Neither the imageries of the free market, the strong development state, nor state–business co-operation have been able to describe the experiences of the East Asian economies.

We have not gone into great detail regarding the prescriptive side of these models, although our doubts about their analytical value should guide any interpretations of wholesale generalizations regarding the proper role of the state. Indeed, the East Asian economies followed very different kinds of prescriptions. Among those states commonly assumed to be strong, the South Korean state dominated business, in Japan the state and private business excel in co-ordination and communication, and in Taiwan the state combined a heavy-handed intervention through state enterprises with a benign neglect of small export enterprises, at least until the 1980s. Between the two alleged weaker states, the Singapore state developed strength from weakness and has become increasingly visible in economic affairs since independence, while the Hong Kong colonial state steadfastly resisted the temptation of active industrial policy, but involved itself deeply in other areas.

It is still possible, however, to make some more modest generalizations. From a broader comparative point of view, all five states exhibit what Evans (1995) call 'embedded autonomy', that is, combining an autonomous and strong state bureaucracy with an embeddedness in a network of ties with the private sector. In this view, the internal organization of these states approach a Weberian bureaucracy: meritocratic, coherent, and with a clear chain of command. At the same time, they also take into account inputs from the society when formulating policies and are not simply an insulated Leviathan sitting above the civil society (see Rueschemeyer and Evans, 1985). To (over)simplify Evans' argument, successful state intervention depends on a competent civil service and the willingness of the state elite to listen to opinions from the society. The opposite of these are the many African states, where the state is 'soft', personalistic, particularistic and patrimonial (Hyden, 1983).

Still, that does not mean that a strong state has to be an interventionist state, or that the intervention has to be of a particular kind. On this our position is more circumspect. The proper mix of public policies to promote economic development, as the East Asian experiences suggest, is probably contingent and hinged upon the concrete situation. In Hong Kong, where private entrepreneurship is dynamic, a more restrained state suffices. In post-war Japan, MITI gave the already well-developed private sector a push and offered administrative guidance regarding the direction of development. In South Korea and Singapore, the state intervened actively in the absence of a dynamic local bourgeoisie. In Taiwan, the Nationalists erected a huge edifice of state enterprises and kept a distance from indigenous Taiwanese enterprises, but local entrepreneurs sprang up to take advantage of the infrastructure and political stability generated by the state. The remarkable success of the East Asian economies suggests that these policies, ranging from *laissez-faire* to omnipresent intervention, are all effective to a certain extent, *relative to their particular national circumstances*. The relationship, however, between the concrete historical situations and the need for a specific kind of state action is clearly beyond the scope of the present discussion. More important, we argue that even if there is a need for a certain policy, or a policy is clearly counterproductive, there is no guarantee that the good policy will be implemented or the bad policy avoided. The *political determinants* of state development policies are, therefore, analytically as important as, if not prior to, the prescriptive question.

References

Amsden, A. (1985) 'The state and Taiwan's economic development' in Evans, P., Rueschemeyer, D. and Skocpol, T. (eds) *Bringing the State Back In*, Cambridge, Cambridge University Press.

Amsden, A. (1989) *Asia's Next Giant: South Korea and Late Industrialization*, New York, Oxford University Press.

Appelbaum, R. and Henderson, J. (eds) (1992) *States and Development in the Asian Pacific Rim*, Newbury Park, Sage.

Balassa, B. (1988) 'The lessons of East Asian development: an overview', *Economic Development and Cultural Change*, vol.36, no.3 (supplement), S273–90.

Balassa, B. *et al.* (1982) *Development Strategies in Semi-Industrial Economies*, Baltimore, Johns Hopkins University Press.

Bradford, C. (1986) 'East Asian "models": myths and lessons' in Lewis, J.P. and Kallab, V. (eds) *Development Strategies Reconsidered*, New Brunswick, Transaction Books.

Calder, K. (1993) *Strategic Capitalism: Private Business and Public Purpose in Japanese Industrial Finance*, Princeton, Princeton University Press.

Castells, M. (1992) 'Four Asian tigers with a dragon head: a comparative analysis of the state, economy and society in the Asian Pacific rim' in Appelbaum, R. and Henderson, J. (eds) *States and Development in the Asian Pacific Rim*, Newbury Park, Sage.

Chen, E.K.Y. (1979) *Hyper-Growth in Asian Economies: A Comparative Study of Hong Kong, Japan, Korea, Singapore and Taiwan*, London, Macmillan.

Cheng, Tun-Jen (1987) 'The politics of industrial transformation: the case of the East Asian NICs', PhD Dissertation, University of California, Berkeley.

Chiu, S.W.K., Ho, K-C. and Tai-lok Lui (1995) 'A tale of two cities rekindled: Hong Kong and Singapore's divergent paths to industrialism', *Journal of Developing Societies*, vol.11, pp.98–122.

Chiu, S.W.K., Ho, K-C. and Tai-Lok Lui (1997) *City-States in the Global Economy: Industrial Restructuring in Hong Kong and Singapore*, Boulder, CO, Westview.

Deyo, F. (ed.) (1987) *The Political Economy of East Asian Industrialism*, Ithaca, Cornell University Press.

The Economist (1996) 'In the shadow of the chaebol', 6 July, pp.57–8.

Evans, P. (1995) *Embedded Autonomy: States and Industrial Transformation*, Princeton, Princeton University Press.

Friedman, D. (1988) *The Misunderstood Miracle: Industrial Development and Political Change in Japan*, Ithaca, Cornell University Press.

Gerschenkron, A. (1962) *Economic Backwardness in Historical Perspective*, Cambridge, Mass, Harvard University Press.

Gilbert, J. and Howe, C. (1991) 'Beyond "state vs society": theories of the state and new deal agricultural policies', *American Sociological Review*, vol.56, no.2, pp.204–20.

Gold, T.B. (1986) *State and Society in the Taiwan Miracle*, Armonk, New York, M.E. Sharpe.

Haggard, S. (1990) *Pathways from the Periphery: The Politics of Growth in the Newly Industrializing Countries*, Ithaca, Cornell University Press.

Hyden, G. (1983) *No Shortcuts to Progress: African Development Management in Perspective*, Berkeley, University of California Press.

Ho, S.P.S. (1980) 'Small-scale enterprises in Korea and Taiwan', *World Bank Staff Working Paper No. 384*, Washington, World Bank.

Ito, T. (1992) *The Japanese Economy*, Cambridge, Mass, MIT Press.

Johnson, C. (1982) *MITI and the Japanese Miracle*, Stanford, Stanford University Press.

Johnson, C. (1987) 'Political institutions and economic performance: the government–business relationship in Japan, South Korea and Taiwan' in Deyo, F. (ed.) *The Political Economy of the New Asian Industrialism*, Ithaca, Cornell University Press.

Jones, L. (1994) 'Big business groups in South Korea: causation, growth and policies' in Lee-Jay Cho and Yoon Hyung Kim (eds) *Korea's Political Economy: An Institutional Perspective*, Boulder, CO, Westview.

Kuznets, P.W. (1988) 'An East Asian model of economic development: Japan, Taiwan, and South Korea', *Economic Development and Cultural Change*, vol.36, no.3 (supplement), pp.11–43.

Little, I.M.D. (1981) 'The experiences and causes of rapid labour-intensive development in Korea, Taiwan Province, Hong Kong and Singapore and the possibility of emulation' in Lee, E. (ed.) *Export led Industrialization and Development*, Bangkok, ILO-ARTEP.

Luedde-Neurath, R. (1986) *Import Control and Export-Oriented Development*, Boulder, CO, Westview.

Okimoto, D.I. (1989) *Between MITI and the Market*, Stanford, Stanford University Press.

Onis, Z. (1991) 'The logic of the developmental state', *Comparative Politics*, review article, vol.24, no.1, pp.109–26.

Rueschemeyer, D. and Evans, P. (1985) 'The state and economic transformation: toward an analysis of the conditions underlying effective intervention' in Evans, P., Rueschemeyer, D. and Skocpol, T. (eds) *Bringing the State Back In*, Cambridge, Cambridge University Press.

Samuels, R. (1987) *The Business of the Japanese State: Energy Markets in Comparative and Historical Perspective*, Ithaca, Cornell University Press.

Steers, R., Yoo Keun Shin and Ungson, G. (1989) *The Chaebol: Korea's New Industrial Might*, New York, Harper and Row.

Wade, R. (1988) 'State intervention in "outward-looking" development: neo-classical theory and Taiwanese practice' in White, G. (ed.) *Developmental States in East Asia*, London, Macmillan.

Wade, R. (1990) *Governing the Market: Economic Theory and the Role of Government in East Asian Industrialization*, Princeton, Princeton University Press.

Wade, R. (1992) 'East Asian economic success: conflicting perspectives, partial insight, shaky evidence', *World Politics*, review article, vol.44, no.2, pp.270–320.

Wade, R. (1993) 'Managing trade: Taiwan and South Korea as challenges to economics and political science', *Comparative Politics*, vol.25, no.2, pp.147–67.

Wade, R. (1996) 'Japan, the World Bank and the art of paradigm maintenance: *The East Asian Miracle* in political perspective', *New Left Review*, no.217, pp.3–36.

Wade, R. and White, G. (eds) (1984) 'Developmentalist states in East Asia', *Institute of Developmental Studies Bulletin*, special issue, Brighton, University of Sussex.

Weiss, L. (1995) 'Governed interdependence: rethinking the government–business relationship in East Asia', *The Pacific Review*, vol.8, no.4, pp.589–616.

Woo, Jun-en (1991) *Race to the Swift: State and Finance in Korean Industrialisation*, New York, Columbia University Press.

World Bank (1993) *The East Asian Miracle: Economic Growth and Public Policy*, New York, Oxford University Press.

PART 2

The Processes of Integration

Economic integration in the Asia-Pacific region

Ippei Yamazawa

7.1 Introduction

It seems to be a universal phenomenon that, while private firms expand their activities beyond national borders and become multinational companies, individual national governments – of both developing and developed countries alike – try to attract multinational firms to start up on their home territories in order to take advantage of their technology and capital for stimulating new industries and generating production and employment. This phenomenon has not taken place uniformly across the world, but more intensively in some geographical areas than in others. It is a process called 'regional economic integration'. The form regional integration takes ranges from the elimination of tariffs and non-tariff barriers to the harmonization of domestic regulations and policies, and even to the creation of a single currency area. Its most advanced form can be found in the European Union (EU), which has undertaken extensive integration for the past forty years, and now aims for monetary union and possibly political union sometime in the future. The North American Free Trade Agreement (NAFTA) is at a lower level of integration as it moves towards becoming a free trade area (FTA). These FTAs not only focus on the elimination of cross border measures that limit trade, but also introduce the harmonization of domestic commercial conditions to varying degrees.

In the Asia-Pacific region, a much looser form of integration has been going on since 1989 known as the Asia Pacific Economic Co-operation (APEC) forum. Although the extent of its integration remains at a lower level, its membership coverage and possible leadership role in the world economy attracts attention to its current developments. Why do the APEC countries prefer a loose form of integration? Can they achieve real integration of practical significance, which is different from that of the European Union or NAFTA? Can they prevent discrimination against non-members, or prevent co-operation with non-members? After analysing the major characteristics of APEC, I will examine two questions: how will APEC develop in the future? and second, will APEC liberalization be implemented

in a manner consistent with the multilateral regime that works under the auspices of the World Trade Organization (WTO)?

7.2   Emerging regional integration in the Asia-Pacific

The Asia-Pacific Economic Co-operation forum is an emerging regional group of eighteen member economies in the Asia-Pacific. In 1997 it comprised eleven Asian countries; six ASEAN members plus China, Hong Kong, Japan, South Korea, and Chinese Taipei; the three Oceania countries of Australia, New Zealand, and Papua New Guinea (PNG); and the four American countries of Canada, the USA, Mexico, and Chile. In the run up to its Subic meeting in the Philippines in November 1996, APEC member governments prepared detailed concrete programmes for regional co-operation. APEC has now become a major regional group, second only to the European Union in terms of its membership coverage. The combined share of its eighteen members in the world total GDP and export trade amounted to 47.8 per cent (in 1989) and 39.1 per cent (in 1990) respectively, which should be compared with 23.7 per cent and 40.9 per cent for EU12 in the same years.

APEC began in 1989 as a series of annual ministerial meetings. However, since 1993 the national leaders have met each year, and these meetings have been setting its future direction. In Seattle in November 1993, the APEC leaders envisioned APEC as 'a community of Asia Pacific economies', a flexible forum for promoting economic growth in the region, which is quite different from such tightly structured organizations as the European Union and the North American Free Trade Agreement.

In Bogor in November 1994, the leaders declared their political commitment to the idea that developed members should achieve free and open trade in the region by 2010 and the rest should achieve the same goal by 2020. In addition, trade 'facilitation' (enhancement) and development co-operation would be promoted as well. Trade liberalization in the region for the next 25 years will be slower than liberalization schemes elsewhere but it is supplemented by the facilitation and development co-operation processes (APEC, 1995a; APEC/EPG, 1994).

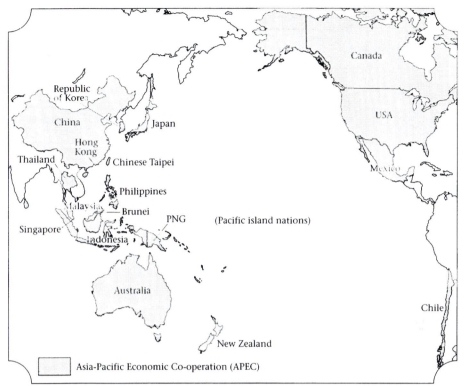

Figure 7.1 *Map of members of APEC*

In 1995 the Osaka Action Agenda provided a guideline for implementing the policy measures designed to reach these targets. In 1996 the APEC leaders adopted the Manila Action Plans for APEC (MAPA) in which all members submitted their individual action plans (IPAs) to be implemented from 1997 onwards.

It should be remembered that economic co-operation in the Pacific region was not something that arose just in the past few years. The movement for economic co-operation started in the middle of the 1960s and experienced three surges of growth. These developments in the Pacific had a close and observable connection to moves in the development of the European Community. The first proposal for Pacific economic co-operation was made by economists and businessmen in the 1960s, stimulated by the successful development of the European Common Market. Annual gatherings of businessmen, known as the Pacific Basin Economic Council (PBEC), started in 1967 and a gathering of economists, the Pacific Trade and Development conference (PAFTAD), began in 1968. Table 7.1 presents a history of those initiatives as well as of APEC.

Pacific co-operation activity decelerated during the oil crisis in the middle of the 1970s but revived toward the end of that decade, partly benefiting from the oil and resources boom in the ASEAN countries. The Japanese Prime Minister Masayoshi Ohira made a proposal for a 'Pacific community' in his inaugural speech in 1978. Coming from an influential politician, this proposal extended the discussion of Pacific co-operation

Table 7.1 *History of economic co-operation in Asia-Pacific*

Date	Initiative
1967	Association of South-East Asian Nations (ASEAN) started with five members
Late 1960s	Proposals for Pacific economic co-operation; PBEC (1967) and PAFTAD (1968)
1978	Proposal for Pacific Economic Community by Japanese PM (Ohira). Report of PEC Study Group (1979)
1980	The first Pacific Economic Co-operation Council (PECC) meeting (Canberra)
1989	Canada–USA Free Trade Agreement (CUSFTA)
1989	Asia Pacific Economic Co-operation (APEC) Ministerial meeting started in Canberra with 12 members
1990	APEC II (Singapore)
1991	APEC III (Seoul); three Chinas joined, Seoul Declaration
1992	APEC IV (Bangkok); Eminent Persons Group established
1993	CUSFTA expanded to NAFTA by including Mexico
1993	APEC V (Seattle); Informal Economic Leaders Meeting, Mexico joined
1994	APEC VI (Jakarta/Bogor); Bogor Declaration, PNG and Chile joined
1995	Vietnam joined ASEAN
1995	APEC VII (Osaka); Osaka Action Agenda adopted with Initial Actions announced
1996 March	Asia–Europe Summit Meeting (AESM) in Bangkok
1996 November	APEC VIII (Subic); action plans announced and implemented by individual members
1996 December	WTO Ministerial Meeting in Singapore
1997	APEC IX (Canada)
1998	APEC X (Malaysia)
1999	APEX XI (New Zealand)

beyond economists and businessmen to a wider circle of politicians, diplomats, academics in international relations, and the mass media. Subsequently, Prime Minister Ohira established a study group which prepared a report on Pacific co-operation in 1979. During his visit to Australia and New Zealand, Ohira showed his proposal to the prime ministers of the two countries who welcomed it. Australian Prime Minister Malcolm Fraser organized a seminar in Canberra in 1980 on economic co-operation which has continued as the Pacific Economic Co-operation Council (PECC) forum. It started with thirteen members, five developed countries (the liberal market economies of Australia, Canada, Japan, New Zealand and the USA), six ASEAN members, South Korea, and a Pacific island nations group; it added China and Chinese Taipei in 1986. It now comprises 21 members following the addition of Hong Kong, Mexico, Chile, Peru, Columbia and Russia, giving it a larger membership than the current APEC. The PECC has the unique tripartite participation of business, academia, and government, all acting in their private capacities. It has been providing a regular free exchange of views and extensive research in order to form a region wide consensus on various issues of economic co-operation in the Asia-Pacific.

In Europe during this period (the late 1970s) momentum toward integration slowed down, and European economies stagnated, an event that became known as the 'European crisis'. The stagnation continued into the early 1980s, when the European Community countries introduced their 'single European Market' programme. They were pushed along in this direction by the rapid industrialization of the Asia-Pacific countries and the increased export of Asian products to the European market. The EU also added three new members, Greece, Spain, and Portugal, bringing its membership to twelve. Deeper integration and an enlarged market stimulated European firms to increase their business activity and engage in an active mergers and acquisitions policy across national borders. This brought on a boom, often termed the 'European fever', in the latter half of the 1980s. The proposal for APEC, the first official inter-governmental forum on economic co-operation in the Asia-Pacific, came during this third surge in European integration in the late 1980s.

Reflecting its Asian members' preference, APEC started with a loose, informal structure, with no treaty like the Treaty of Rome or the Maastricht Treaty. But this informal structure has tended to mislead some writers encouraging them to underestimate its possible impacts. However, its membership coverage and current action agenda should assure any sceptics that APEC can take a joint initiative in managing the world economy together with the European Union (see also Chapter 13).

7.3   Co-operation from diversity

The following three key terms describe APEC's major characteristics:

- diversity among its members
- high growth potential
- informal structure.

A large diversity among members is the main feature of Asia-Pacific economies (see Chapter 2). This is more so than for any other regional economy in the world.

1   There is a difference in natural resource endowment and in size of geographical area.

2   There is a great difference in the stage of their economic development; some have already matured into advanced economies while others have only begun to take off over the past two decades, and still have a high growth potential.

3   They are divided into several groups on religious grounds, their cultural heritage, and in terms of their philosophical values and outlooks. Huntington (1993) contended that in the post-Cold War era the conflict between different ideologies would be replaced by a 'clash of

civilizations' between different groups of countries. However, the Asia-Pacific has so far avoided a severe clash of civilization.

4   They were divided into market and socialist economies in the Cold War era. Although some socialist economies are being transformed into market economies, it will take them many decades to complete their transformation.

5   Three sub-groups of free trade areas (FTAs) exist in the region promoting their own liberalization programmes: the North American Free Trade Agreement (NAFTA), the ASEAN Free Trade Area (AFTA), and the Australia–New Zealand Closer Economic Relations Agreement (ANZCER), all these having predated the formation of APEC. They have been active since the late 1980s, partly interacting with the APEC process (see Table 7.1).

6   In addition, several sub-regional informal economic zones (SREZs) have emerged. These are the 'Growth triangle', the Greater South China economic zone, the Yellow Sea economic zone, the Baht zone, and the Japan Sea economic zone, all shown in Figure 7.2 and defined in Table 7.2. Each of these is composed of neighbouring provinces in different

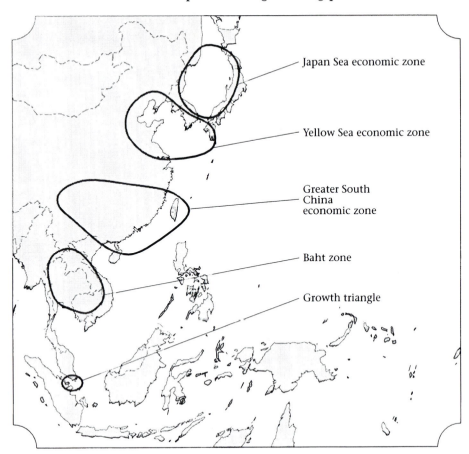

Figure 7.2 *Map of the sub-regional economic zones in East Asia*

countries closely interlinked through trade, investment, and personnel movement across national borders, and forming a unique base for rapid development in the Asia-Pacific.

Table 7.2 *Constituent members of the sub-regional economic zones in East Asia*

- *'Growth triangle'*: Singapore, Johore State of Malaysia, and Batam and Liau Islands
- *Baht zone*: Thailand, Laos, and Cambodia
- *Greater South China economic zone*: Hong Kong, China's Guangdong and Fujian provinces, and Taiwan
- *Yellow Sea economic zone*: coastal areas facing the Yellow Sea of North and North-East China, North and South Korea, and Japan
- *Japan Sea economic zone*: coastal areas of North-East China, Russian Far East, South and North Korea, and Japan.

Box 7.1 Sub-regional informal economic zones

Before we go on to analyse the APEC process further it is worthwhile examining the mechanism underlying the development of the East Asian SREZs (see also **Brook, 1998**). They are characterized as follows: first, each forms a natural economic territory across a national border, in which neighbourhood trade has been activated at some time or another. Second, there are both a centre and a periphery in each SREZ, where the growth of the centre tends to be constrained by its limited area and labour force. These pressures at the centre are transmitted to the periphery through trade, investment, and labour movement. Third, no formal agreements are made between the governments concerned. In some SREZs, free trade zones are established by local governments in the periphery in order to accelerate the transfer of industries from the centre. In the 'Growth triangle', Singapore and the adjacent Johore State of Malaysia have had long developed border trade, which was accelerated partly by the inflow of foreign direct investment in this area since the late 1980s, and partly by the limit on further development of Singapore's territory and its human resources (see Chapter 2). The development of Batam Island followed a tacit agreement in 1988 between President Suharto and Prime Minister Goh Chok Tong, the respective leaders of Indonesia and Singapore, but it has been stimulated by the same market mechanism, as in the case of Johore, and its management has been left to the private sectors of the two countries.

Fourth, all SREZs except for the 'growth triangle' are located along the borders between market and socialist economies. Formerly, trade and investment exchanges between both sides were severely restricted. With the end of the Cold War and the adoption of more open economic policies by the socialist countries, these border zones have begun to show signs of economic vitality, similar to other areas of the region, and cross-border movements of merchandise, investment, and even people have begun to thrive. In the case of the Greater South China zone and the Yellow Sea zone, it goes without saying that the development of cross-border economic activity in these regions owes much to the political acquiescence, and even encouragement, of the governments concerned. This has taken the form of, for example, Chinese leaders outlining the country's new open economic policy and a tacit acceptance of the situation by the governments of Taiwan and South Korea. As for the South China zone, confidence in its future is very much dependent on the general perception of conditions now that Hong Kong has been returned to China. However, these kinds of informal relations are different from the formal agreements governing relations among countries of the EU and NAFTA, since they involve no officially established mechanism for the management of the ongoing economic integration.

Finally, the region has never attempted any region-wide *formal* integration and thus it is often called a 'market-driven integration' of the Asia-Pacific *vis-à-vis* an 'institutional integration based on a treaty' as in the EU and NAFTA.

Returning to the diversity of the APEC countries, this has two aspects, one positive and the other negative. On the positive side, Asia-Pacific economies have taken advantage of their diversity and the resulting economic complementarity between them (see Chapter 2). A wide ranging disparity and different resource endowments have generated high economic complementarity within the region, which in turn has stimulated active trade and investment and enabled many developing members to achieve high growth rates – the 'East Asian miracle' (see Chapter 3). The developed economies could maintain their growth through export of resource products, technology products, and high value-added services and invest in the manufacturing activities of the developing economies. Thus Asia Pacific economies have achieved a strong interdependence and rapid development of the region. Intra-APEC trade increased from 56 per cent in 1980 to 66 per cent in 1990, which compares with an increase from 53 per cent to 63 per cent within the EC12. The main motivation for promoting APEC is to sustain high growth in the region which is shared by all members.

On the negative side, a result of this diversity is insufficient understanding of each member's position and interests, it requires more time to form a region-wide consensus and to take joint action by members. This diversity has made it difficult to start with any formal structures. Nevertheless, its market driven integration is now affected by persistent imbalances and frequent trade disputes between members (see Chapter 2). Bottlenecks caused by poor infrastructures in the member states with a developing economy impede further realization of their high growth potential. Asia-Pacific economies need to strengthen their co-operation in order to mitigate these impediments to further growth in the region.

Thus the three key terms of diversity, high growth potential and informal structures are interrelated and are all reflected in the Osaka Action Agenda. I will examine this now in greater detail.

7.4   Osaka Action Agenda and its implementation

The Osaka Action Agenda consists of two parts. Part One covers trade liberalization and facilitation (the reduction of the costs of doing business) and Part Two covers economic and technical co-operation (APEC, 1995b).

Trade liberalization and facilitation

The action agenda for trade liberalization and facilitation starts with nine general principles; comprehensiveness, WTO-consistency, comparability, non-discrimination, transparency, standstill, simultaneous start/continuous process/differentiated timetables, flexibility, and co-operation.

It has an extensive coverage of fifteen areas: tariffs, non-tariff measures, services, investment, standard and conformance, customs procedures, intellectual property rights, competition policy, government procurement, deregulation, rules of origin, dispute mediation, mobility of business people, implementation of the Uruguay Round outcomes, information gathering and analysis. The action agenda suggests a menu of actions by individual member governments and concerted actions by all members in individual areas.

Its new and particular modality – the way to implement liberalization and facilitation programmes – is the *concerted unilateral liberalization*. That is, individual member governments announce unilaterally their own liberalization and facilitation programmes and implement them in accordance with their own domestic rules. However, individual APEC members also closely watch each other's liberalization programme and its implementation. Pressures then build up on each member so that they feel obliged to submit a liberalization programme as extensive as those of their neighbours. They are also encouraged to implement the programmes they have committed themselves to so as not to lose face. The whole process relies upon a 'peer pressure' among APEC members to urge all members to join the liberalization programme. This is the essence of concerted unilateral liberalization.

This modality is often criticized as non-assertive in comparison with the Western approaches to negotiating, as demonstrated by the GATT and WTO liberalization agreements. These are legally binding on the signatories. This means they can be punished and sanctioned if they fail to implement their commitments. At such an initial stage this legalistic approach to negotiations cannot be accepted by the Asian members of APEC in particular. However, this should not be understood as Asian members' hesitance to commit to liberalization. Asian members have so far implemented trade and investment liberalization unilaterally, and have realized that their recent high growth has been based on their open economic policy and continued efforts to liberalize their trade and investment regimes. This the leaders recognize as indispensable for further growth, which is reflected in their commitment to the Bogor Declaration. This new modality is based on such past experience and calls for the unilateral liberalization in a concerted manner within the Osaka Action

Agenda framework. This is a practical way of promoting liberalization without losing momentum for the liberalization process enhanced by the Bogor Declaration. It would take several more years of negotiation if there was an attempt to try to change APEC into a negotiating body like the GATT or WTO.

Economic and technical co-operation

Part two of the Osaka Action Agenda covers thirteen areas of economic and technical co-operation: human resource development, industrial science and technology, small and medium sized enterprises, economic infrastructure, energy, transportation, telecommunication and information, tourism, trade and investment data, trade promotion, marine resource conservation, fisheries, and agricultural technology (see also Chapter 10). Environmental protection is mentioned in relation to several areas but is not included as an independent area.

Co-operation programmes are needed within APEC to fill gaps in the technology levels, managerial and administrative capabilities, public infrastructure, and so on, resulting from the diversity of its members. Both bilateral and multilateral development co-operation programmes have so far been implemented to resolve these deficiencies and they are likely to continue. However, new elements have evolved in these areas and new types of co-operation programmes are now being developed.

The Osaka Action Agenda sets a new modality for APEC co-operation. It emphasizes the departure from the conventional modality of distinct donor-recipient relationships. Member governments contribute the resources they think they have available on a voluntary basis, such as financial funds, technology, and human skills, and they feel all will gain from this type of co-operation programme. Consistency with market mechanism is emphasized and the participation of the private sector is encouraged. Economic co-operation has so far attracted less attention but it will provide a variety of business opportunities in the region.

It still needs to be explained how co-operation programmes organized along these guidelines are to be implemented. Three hundred and twenty projects have been proposed under the APEC Work Projects initiative. But these remain to be studied and discussed, so have yet to be implemented. Up to 1997 there had been no visible achievements. A Japanese proposal in 1997 for Partners for Progress (PFP) aimed to make a breakthrough in the hesitation associated with the actual implementation of projects, pushing beyond mere studies and seminars. It made a cautious start with technical co-operation in training customs officials, improving administrative capability of intellectual property rights (IPR), standard and conformance (S&C), and competition policy. These are very necessary for successful implementation of liberalization and facilitation and could be easily agreed upon. Japan has also taken the initiative to establish a new task force to tackle such medium- and long-term issues as population, environment, energy and foodstuffs.

7.5 Liberalization and facilitation in progress

In 1996, the leaders adopted the Manila Action Plans for APEC in which individual APEC members announced their Individual Action Plans (IAPs) of liberalization and facilitation to be implemented from 1997 onwards (APEC, 1996). The crucial question is, are they big enough to achieve their Bogor target?

First, all APEC members submitted their IAPs in spite of prior speculation to the contrary. It is thus something that they will start to implement just two years after the Bogor Declaration.

Second, however, the commitments differ greatly between members, partly because of their nature as unilateral announcements. The chair country provided a common format of IAPs in a matrix of fifteen areas times three different time frames (short, intermediate, and long term). Three types of responses were identified: (1) some members committed concrete measures within a clear time frame; (2) some stated an intent that they would make efforts to achieve the Bogor target; (3) others said they would examine their current measures for possible amendment. By and large many members committed to (1) for their short-term measures, while (2) and (3) tended to prevail for intermediate and long-term measures. Indeed detailed implementation plans covering 15 to 25 years cannot be expected immediately.

Third, the comparison of the IAPs between countries is never easy because of different levels of current impediments and different target dates. While they are assessed against the common format, the positive list of liberalization announced in IAPs needs to be compared with existing impediments in order to find out how much still remains to be done (Yamazawa, 1997).

How many impediments still remain to trade and investment in the Asia-Pacific region? APEC has commissioned studies by the PECC's Trade Policy Forum to undertake the first region-wide survey of these impediments (APEC, 1995c). The studies covered tariffs and non-tariff barriers on commodity trade, and regulations on services, trades, foreign investment, and intellectual property rights. The level and structure of impediments to trade and investment differ greatly among APEC member economies reflecting their different resource endowments and stages of industrial development.

However, the studies found that numerous impediments are common to members throughout the region:

1 Tariff levels differ greatly between members. Developed economy members have tariffs of around 5 per cent on many items. Developing economy members have tariffs of 10–20 per cent, while a few have levels of over 30 per cent on many items. In both developed and developing members, higher tariffs still remain on textiles, leather goods, and wood products (15–20 per cent in developed economy members and 25–60 per cent in developing economy members). Figure

7.3 shows the average tariff for all APEC countries in 1993 arranged on an industry by industry basis.

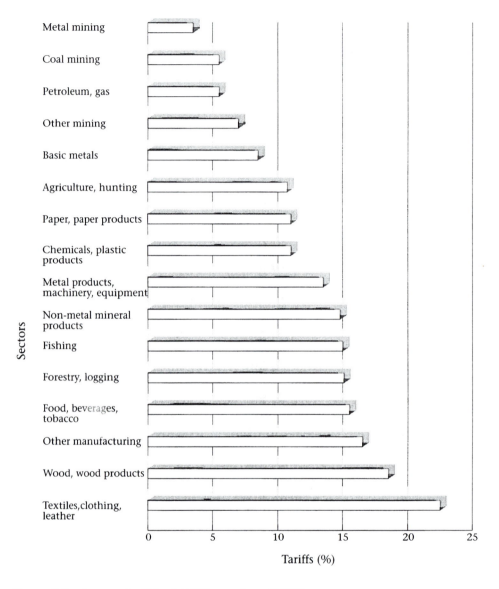

Figure 7.3 *Average tariffs of APEC members (1993)*
Source: APEC (1995)

2   NTBs (non-tariff barriers) are imposed on agriculture, labour-intensive manufactures, steel and automobiles by many members. Including the NTB elements, tariff equivalent rates (excess of domestic prices over import prices) reach very high levels, especially for agricultural products.

3   The services trade accounts for a third of APEC's commodity trade. However, many trade sectors are regulated and some are completely closed. Figure 7.4 shows the frequency of impediments to full liberalization of service sectors amongst the APEC countries. Moreover, among members there is considerable variation in the regulations they still maintain. Developed economy members have a score of 100 in three to seven areas, while developing economy members have the same score in more than half of the areas.

4   FDI (foreign direct investment) is still restricted in market access and national treatment and is subject to fiscal incentives (subsidies and tax exemptions) and performance requirements (local content requirements, export requirements, and foreign exchange balancing conditions).

5   Most members have made changes in existing domestic legal structures to put in place substantive protection of intellectual property rights. Despite these initiatives there still remains a substantial variance in this protection, and many developing members have some distance to travel to meet their Trade Related Intellectual Property (TRIP) obligations under the WTO agreement.

These remaining impediments, as clarified by the PECC's studies, suggest that we should anticipate strong resistance to liberalization and deregulation from vested interest groups in those sectors. Generally speaking, two broad types of arguments can be anticipated. One is the argument by developing country members for infant industry protection. They are in the process of 'catching-up industrialization' and may claim infant industry protection for new technology industries and high value-added services (see Chapter 2).

The second argument concerns the protection of such older industries as agriculture and labour-intensive manufactures. At present the developed members are calling for this protection, but it will also start coming from developing members as they reach higher income levels. These industries cause another type of adjustment difficulty. APEC senior officials discussed until the last minutes before the end of the Osaka meeting whether agriculture could be excluded from the liberalization agenda. At those discussions the exclusion was supported by only four members: Japan, South Korea, Chinese Taipei, and China. However, agricultural protection will likely become a concern of the ASEAN countries and Mexico in the near future as their economies develop further and income disparity widens between agriculture and other industries. Agricultural protection can be easily politicized which frequently prevents rational economic solutions. Increased budgetary burdens at home and international commitments to the WTO and APEC for liberalization are likely to be the only means for breaking through these arguments.

Labour-intensive industries such as textiles and footwear share the same difficulty as agriculture, although with less extensive protection and political distortion. Currently only developed countries complain of

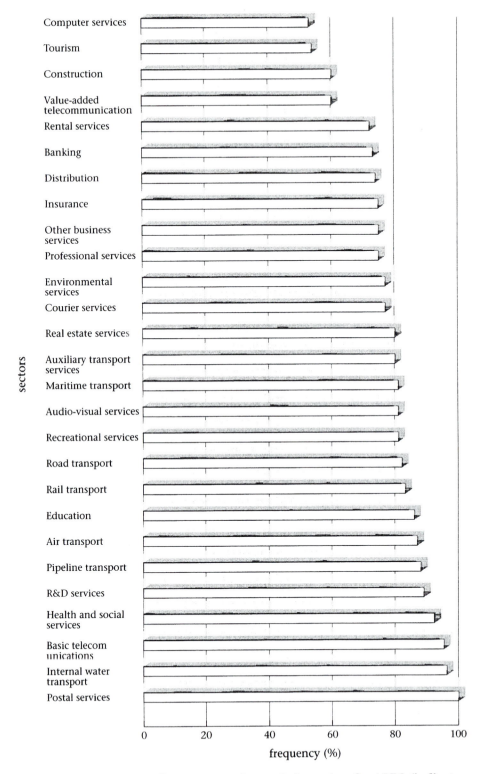

Figure 7.4 *Average impediments to service trade by sectors for APEC (indicators of the absence of commitments as a percentage)*

Source: APEC (1995)

increasing imports from low-income economies, but the developing members of APEC currently exporting these products also maintain high tariffs on their import of these products. The latter members will soon be importers of these products as their income levels increase, and they can restrict imports from lower-income countries. It is important for all of APEC's members not to exclude these difficult sectors from their liberalization agendas.

The best test of the commitments of APEC to liberalization is to look at what has been proposed for *tariff reduction.* Most members indicated their plans for tariff reduction over the next few years. Some members attach time schedules for reducing these to zero or in terms of sectoral details. Generally speaking, while developed members committed themselves to a tariff reduction of 'UR plus a small alpha' (Uruguay Round plus a small difference) but still short of achieving the Bogor target (a zero tariff by 2010), some developing members committed to a 'UR plus a large alpha' (Uruguay Round plus a larger difference) and sufficient for achieving their Bogor target (a zero tariff by 2020). This can be illustrated in the schematic diagram Figure 7.5. The dotted lines show linear tariff reduction over 15 and 25 years, while the solid lines show 'actual reduction (up to 1995) plus IAP commitment (from 1996 to 2000)'.

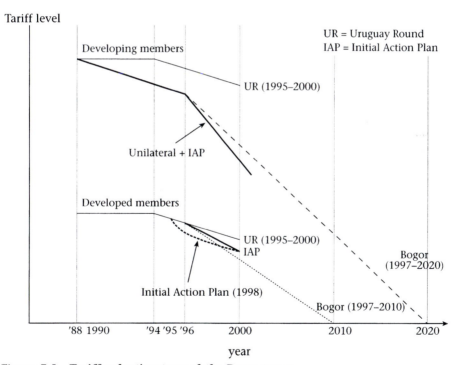

Figure 7.5 *Tariff reduction toward the Bogor target*

I will now clarify the relationship between Uruguay Round commitments, Bogor targets and APEC/IAP (as well as unilateral reduction and Initial Actions) in both their time scale and tariff levels. This will help assess individual member's IAP commitments within this complicated context of tariff reductions. It also shows the two track approach by APEC.

As regards *non-tariff measures* (NTMs), developed members, plus Chile, Hong Kong, and Singapore claimed that they had no NTMs inconsistent with WTO guidelines. Nevertheless, Canada and the USA stated that they would phase out the multifibre agreement (MFA – a specific international tariff and quota agreement dealing with textile and other fibre trade) quota restrictions by 2004. Japan, South Korea, and Philippines excepted rice from their liberalization package. South Korea committed itself to eliminate most of the current NTMs by 2001. Some developing members did not refer to any specific NTMs but stated that they would study and review their NTMs and gradually reduce the number.

As regards *services*, all members seem to be more cautious here partly because the services trade is more regulated than is the commodity trade by many members, and partly because some services trade is now being negotiated at the WTO. Some members outlined a clear commitment to the liberalization in many services, while many members referred to selected sectors such as telecommunications, transport, tourism, financial services, and business services. However, the submission of IAPs urges APEC members to get more committed to liberalization in this area, which helps the WTO with its liberalization process.

As far as *investment* is concerned, developed members have already achieved liberalization beyond APEC's non-binding investment principles and they are ready to adopt the Multilateral Agreement on Investment established by the Organization for Economic Co-operation and Development (OECD). However, developing members are still cautious about improving their investment regimes. Since FDI has been a prime motivator of the continued growth of the Asia-Pacific economies, the investment liberalization needs to proceed liberalization in other areas. Slow liberalization over 25 years, as suggested by some developing members, may mean a failure on their part to attract sufficient FDI needed for their development programmes.

A further eleven areas are grouped under the heading of *facilitation* measures, which are concerned with 'reducing the cost of doing business' in the Asia-Pacific, an equally important task in the APEC process. These measures are similar to the Single European Market programme. However, while EU members have already implemented over 90 per cent of the harmonization of nearly 300 physical, technical and fiscal measures among themselves, APEC has just started in this direction. Facilitation measures are implemented jointly as Collective Action Plans (CAPs) as well as individually by member countries. However, as yet no agreed check list of progress has been established and a straightforward comparison between different countries' efforts is difficult. Nevertheless the 'nugget' of the APEC liberalization process may be found in these areas. Member governments have to: (1) establish domestic rules or legal frameworks; (2) give sufficient information and make them transparent to both local and foreign firms; and (3) either mutually recognize each other's rules and frameworks or adjust their own to international rules and frameworks. Developed members have already completed phase (1) and are committed to phase (2), and express their intention to proceed to (3). However, many developing members have yet to achieve phase (1) and will take time to proceed to (3). Individual IAPs in these areas reflect this difference in their current preparedness.

Prospects differ between different facilitation measures. Clear progress has been made in establishing common customs procedures, in clarifying standards and conformance criteria, and in securing agreement on the mobility of business persons. These are to be followed by protocols on intellectual property rights, rules of origin, and government purchases. Competition policy and deregulation cannot proceed beyond level (2). The availability of facilitation and technical co-operation measures supporting liberalization measures organized along those lines is certainly an advantage that APEC has over the WTO.

To conclude, APEC's unilateral liberalization process has made a good start. It could induce tariff reduction of 'UR plus' from most members and help to maintain the current momentum for liberalization in NTMs, services, and investment. However, the IAPs of most members have so far only assured progress over the next few years. This needs to be encouraged so that its momentum will be maintained to enable all members to reach their established goals.

APEC has already introduced two mechanisms to encourage this. One is the 'rolling plan formula' and the other is to incorporate the business sectors into the APEC process. The current IAPs are not the final versions but they will continue to be improved every year. Ministers have invited business leaders to jointly monitor and review the progress of APEC liberalization. As the third mechanism we might add 'independent analysis by academia', which will help to publicize APEC progress and attract support from the private sector.

With its basic philosophy of consensus and voluntarism the APEC process cannot be fast track. But both the Bogor Declaration and the Osaka Action Agenda have shown the future direction of changes in Asia-Pacific economic order.

7.6   A new model of regional integration

APEC's informal style often leads observers into levelling criticism at it. Some argue that APEC is ineffective because of the diversity of its members. Others argue that East Asia will continue its rapid economic development even without an institution like APEC. Some critics also complain that nothing concrete was decided at either Bogor or Osaka.

All of these criticisms are based on applying an EU – or NAFTA– type model to APEC. A much better model is that of the Open Economic Association (OEA), a much looser regional integration than either the EU or NAFTA. An OEA is:

- open in that its structure and its policies do not lead to discrimination against trade and investment with the rest of the world;
- economic in its primary policy focus;
- a voluntary association in that its members do not cede sovereignty to any supranational regional institution (Yamazawa, 1992 and 1996).

Recognizing the increasingly sophisticated nature of international economic transactions, the scope of an OEA goes well beyond traditional FTAs. The tempo of trade liberalization may be less rapid than in traditional FTAs, but liberalization will be applied both to members and non-members alike on a most favoured nation (MFN) basis. (MFN refers to the principle that whatever favourable conditions are agreed for trade between any two nations should be extended to others on a non-discriminatory and similar basis.) In addition, the gradual liberalization of trade in goods and services will be supplemented by facilitation to dismantle all impediments to international economic transactions as well as to development co-operation. This balanced programme reflects the vast differences in stages of development, current level of impediments to trade and investment, and preparedness for reform among members.

An OEA is a departure from the textbook typology of regional integration, which is derived from the five stages proposed by Bela Balassa (1961). The five stages comprise of a 'free trade area (FTA)', a 'customs union', a 'common market', an 'economic union', and a 'complete economic union', with development taking place in roughly this order. Balassa's typology was developed by 'focusing on the elimination of discriminatory practices within a particular region'. Two problems arise when we apply this concept to the Asia-Pacific. First, the FTA as the first stage tends to be accompanied by discrimination against non members. Second, we need a concept with a lower degree of integration, incorporating non-discrimination against non members and supplementing partial liberalization with facilitation and co-operation programmes. This is closer to the APEC model.

Balassa himself acknowledged the potential for international economic co-operation of various kinds, extending beyond the simple elimination of discriminatory practices. The EU Common Agricultural Policy (CAP) has been in place since 1967, while co-operation in the steel and energy industries has been a feature of European life since before the founding of the EC itself. The momentum for regional integration calls not only for the abolition of discriminatory practices, but also for a large measure of policy and institutional co-operation and co-ordination. There is a fair degree of success in policy co-ordination and economic co-operation among the members of any regional integration.

The highly inter-dependent, private-sector driven growth of the Asia-Pacific economies has been generated by active trade and investment in spite of the remaining tariffs and NTMs. It is not necessary to further strengthen this market driven integration but sufficient to have a gradual trade liberalization, facilitating trade and investment, and economic co-operation in order to create a steady trade and investment expansion in the region.

With this realistic concept of an OEA to hand, we can address the criticisms of APEC noted above. OEA is feasible within the vast diversity of the Asia-Pacific. OEA is needed in order to continue the current high growth rates of the region. At Bogor, the leaders committed themselves to an Asia-Pacific OEA. The Osaka Agenda made it clear that they aimed at an Asia-Pacific OEA.

This is APEC's vision of 'a community of Asia-Pacific economies'. If countries share an objective of sustaining the regional growth and co-operate with each other, the region will be worthy of the title 'community'. There is an evolving sense of community in the Asia-Pacific region. The feeling of community will enhance the certainty and stability of the region, thereby attracting the private enterprises of members and non members alike.

7.7   APEC's consistency with multilateral trading regime

Regional integration has often been criticized in the past as inconsistent with multilateral liberalization. But it has recently become widely agreed that regional integration and multilateral liberalization can be consistent and have actually evolved together in many ways. A recent report by the OECD (1995) surveyed the existing regional integrations such as the EU, EFTA, CUSFTA, and NAFTA and came to the conclusion that some aspects of regional integration, such as preferential tariff reductions and strict rules of origin, can by nature discriminate against non members and indeed be contradictory to multilateral liberalization. However, the regional integration groups have also implemented measures such as harmonization of rules and standards, investment principles, services trade policy, intellectual property rights, and environmental protection and industrial co-operation. These measures do not discriminate against others but serve as a laboratory, a halfway house, in the effort to move from national standards to a multilateral standard.

This new concept of regional integration is consistent with the 'open regionalism' often mentioned in regard to APEC. 'Open regionalism' or 'open regional co-operation' implies the promotion of regional co-operation in a way consistent with multilateral rules. This two pronged thrust of 'open regionalism' has become an important aspect of the APEC process. It conveys a positive image of 'good regional integration' in distinction to the notion of a 'Fortress Europe' often mentioned in respect to the European Community in the 1980s.

Because of the long-term interdependence of trade and investment links beyond the region, Asia-Pacific economies have shown a great interest in global trade liberalization and have participated actively in the Uruguay Round negotiations. The Osaka Action Agenda confirmed 'consistency with multilateral liberalization' as one of its general principles and suggested accelerated implementation of the liberalization commitments of the Uruguay Round. Like other GATT/WTO commitments, it is likely to be ruled by the most favoured nation's (MFN) treatment of GATT Article 1. Many APEC members will extend their APEC liberalization to members and non members alike on a MFN basis. The implementation of these liberalization packages will be monitored and reviewed jointly for the continued attention of all members, and the mutual encouragement between them.

But APEC members have not yet agreed upon whether to apply the MFN treatment to non-APEC members. A majority of APEC members are supportive of non-discrimination to non-members, while a minority have objections to it on the ground that it will allow the EU unfair benefits, and insists that the APEC liberalization should be applied to the EU only if the EU implements a matching liberalization on the MFN basis. This reciprocal application of the APEC liberalization departs from the OEA model, but can still be referred to as 'open regionalism'. Of course this causes some ambiguity in the term, which invites criticism by non-APEC economists. This difference in philosophy has yet to be resolved.

However, it is unlikely that this difference will lead immediately to the APEC liberalization programmes discriminating against non members. The facilitation part of the programme, as well as the investment liberalization, is unlikely to lead to discrimination against non-members. Indeed there are likely to be some sensitive areas for which unilateral liberalization is difficult to achieve, which, however, will be left to multilateral negotiation at a later stage.

Multilateral liberalization is the best but we cannot be optimistic about its speedy progress. All cautious observers realize that multilateral liberalization will not move forward unless certain key players work together. The APEC group as well as the EU are supposed to be its prime movers. APEC governments have started to talk to the EU to encourage it to join in a similar accelerated implementation of the Uruguay Round outcome (see Chapter 13). At a later stage, APEC could call for a joint initiative for a new WTO round of global liberalization.

APEC and the EU share the same adjustment difficulty in agriculture and textiles and they will need a wider stage for co-ordination and negotiation for these difficult sectors than their own regional groups. If APEC and the EU take a joint initiative in launching the new WTO round of multilateral liberalization, the possibility of a 'free-rider' problem arising (one side taking advantage of the other) will be dissolved, and the momentum for multilateral liberalization will increase significantly.

7.8   APEC and Europe

Let me summarize this analysis of APEC by reference to its relationship to the European Union.

Regional approaches to trade and investment liberalization has been widely adopted in recent years. This represents a 'pragmatic approach by individual nation-states' in response to the 'globalization of business firm activity'. Nation-states responsible for maintaining economic growth and employment have to encourage both domestic and foreign firms to operate actively within their territories. To this end the elimination of the impediments to cross-border transactions and deregulation of various restrictive domestic measures are the ones being resorted to instead of direct tax incentives to firms. The recently inaugurated World Trade Organization (WTO) also aims in this same direction, but takes a longer time to reach agreement because it has 127 members. Many members of the WTO jump ahead of this with a quicker and more manageable solution by combining with their like-minded neighbours.

Both the EU and APEC have adopted pragmatic regional approaches but they represent different models for regional co-operation. The EU is a successful 'role model' of regional integration. For the past 40 years it has achieved liberalization of trade, investment and personnel movement, elimination of a substantial part of physical, technical, and fiscal impediments, and is now attempting a monetary union by 2000. APEC only started in 1989 and has now launched an action programme characterized as the Manila Action Plan. Its facilitation programmes aim at a similar economic outcome as the Single European Market programme, but this is still at its initial stage. APEC will remain similar to a Pacific OECD (the discussion forum of the older advanced countries) just sufficient to promote liberalization, facilitation, and economic and technical co-operation, but will never aim at a political union. APEC is a different 'role model' of regional co-operation. The EU model may be applicable only to Europe, though the APEC model might be applicable to regional groups with diverse members in other parts of the world (Shand and Kalirajan, 1997).

Its open regionalism is a function of its wide range of trading partners and its diverse membership, but it is consistent with the WTO regime. The APEC liberalization will be made more effective through linking it with the WTO liberalization. APEC has good reasons for co-operating closely with the EU, another major actor in the WTO regime in promoting global liberalization.

The Asia–Europe Summit Meeting (AESM) becomes important in this context. The AESM began in Bangkok in March 1996 in order to strengthen the weakest link in the triad of Asia, America and Europe. It represents another attempt of inter-regional co-operation (see Chapter 13). Unlike APEC, AESM was started with a meeting of 26 leaders, ten Asian (seven ASEAN plus Japan, China and South Korea) and 16 EU leaders (including the Chairman of the European Commission) but it has now extended its activity so as to promote the inter-regional business at ministerial meetings, and collaborative business fora (see also **Smith, 1998**).

The AESM is another APEC type model for inter-regional co-operation. It contains diverse members, Asians and Europeans. Concrete programmes for liberalization, facilitation, and economic and technical co-operation could be modelled after those in APEC, and voluntarism and flexibility need to be observed in implementing these programmes.

References

APEC/EPG (1994) *Achieving the APEC Vision: Free and Open Trade in the Asia Pacific*, Singapore, APEC Secretariat.

APEC (1995a) *Selected APEC Documents: 1989–1994*, Singapore, APEC Secretariat.

APEC (1995b) *The Osaka Action Agenda: Implementation of the Bogor Declaration*, Osaka, APEC Secretariat.

APEC (1995c) *Survey of Impediments to Trade and Investment in the APEC Region*, Singapore, APEC Secretariat.

APEC (1996) *Manila Action Plans for APEC*, Manila, APEC Secretariat.

Balassa, B. (1961) *The Theory of Economic Integration*, Homewood, Richard D. Irwin.

Brook, C. (1998) 'Regionalism and globalism' in McGrew, A. and Brook, C. (eds).

Huntington, S.P. (1993) 'The clash of civilizations?', *Foreign Affairs*, vol.72, no.3.

McGrew, A. and Brook, C. (eds) (1998) *Asia-Pacific in the New World Order*, London, Routledge in association with The Open University.

Organization for Economic Co-operation and Development (1995) *Regional Integration Agreements and the Multilateral Trading System: Are They Compatible?* TD/TC (93) 15, Paris, OECD.

Shand, R. and Kalirajan, K.P. (1997) 'Yamazawa's open economic association: an Indian Ocean grouping for economic co-operation', *The Developing Economies*, vol.XXXVI, no.1, pp.3–27.

Smith, M. (1998) 'The European Union and the Asia-Pacific' in McGrew, A. and Brook, C. (eds).

Yamazawa, I. (1992) 'On Pacific economic integration', *The Economic Journal*, vol.102, no.415, pp.1519–29.

Yamazawa, I. (1996) 'APEC's new development and its implications for non member developing countries', *The Developing Economies*, vol.XXXIV, no.2, pp.113–37.

Yamazawa, I. (1997) 'APEC's liberalization and WTO', *The Australian Economic Review*, vol.30, no.1.

CHAPTER 8

Measuring the size of foreign multinationals in the Asia-Pacific

Eric Ramstetter

8.1 The problem

The primary focus of this chapter is a very simple question: have foreign multinational corporations (MNCs) become more important in host economies in the Asia-Pacific region in recent years? This issue, though important, is somewhat narrower in scope than those taken up by other chapters in this book. A key question to ask of the Asia-Pacific region is whether MNCs have become increasingly important agents of regional integration. However, this chapter argues that because of the lack of data it is impossible to provide an accurate answer to that question. For example, there is no information from home country sources on MNCs from Hong Kong, only limited information on MNCs from Korea, Singapore and Taiwan, and while there are a lot of data on Japanese MNCs, much of the data are highly unreliable in some respect or another (Ramstetter, 1996a). It is also impossible to assemble consistent and comprehensive information on foreign MNCs classified by country of origin from host economy sources. Thus, there are literally no comprehensive and reliable data on the economic activity of MNCs (for example, foreign direct investment flows or stocks, employment, production, trade) classified by source economy and recipient economy in the Asia-Pacific region (and most other regions). This makes it difficult to show how MNCs have contributed to regional integration.

Of course there are empirical studies that attempt to analyse the contribution of MNCs to regional integration. But these studies are highly speculative, due in large part to the lack of meaningful data on which to base their analyses (see, for example, Bora, 1996). Other studies have a sounder analytical basis, but typically focus heavily on Japanese and/or US MNCs because the data for these MNCs are relatively abundant (Kreinin *et al.*, 1997; Petri and Plummer, 1995). This chapter attempts to widen the focus somewhat to the activities of foreign MNCs in eleven host economies in the Asia-Pacific. Although only indirectly related to issues of economic integration, this focus has the advantage of facilitating a simple, yet reasonably sound analysis of trends in MNCs in a large number of the major host economies in the region.

Economists often face measurement problems, but these problems can be particularly severe when it comes to analysing MNCs. For example, it is much easier to analyse aspects of economic integration related to international trade because there are data on trade flows classified by source economy and recipient economy (as well as by industry). As indicated above, corresponding data do not exist for the economic activities of MNCs. Indeed, only one economic activity of MNCs is measured in a manner that is even vaguely standardized internationally: foreign direct investment (FDI) flows as reported in balance of payments data. However, even here there are important holes in the data as Hong Kong, a major investing and host economy, does not publish data on outward FDI, and no consistent breakdowns by host/recipient country and/ or industry are available.

As will be detailed below, in the aggregate, both inward FDI flows and stocks (that is, cumulative flows) have increased very rapidly in the Asia-Pacific region since the mid 1980s. Correspondingly, it is commonly believed that MNCs have become more important. However, there are two important reasons why even this seemingly straightforward conclusion may not be correct.

First, FDI is a financial flow, the stock of FDI being one item, and often a relatively small item, on the liability side of a corporate balance sheet. More precisely, FDI refers to international investment from one economy to another, where the foreign ownership share exceeds a certain threshold. These thresholds differ across reporting economies, the most common threshold in recent years being ten per cent. FDI consists of equity, loans from related companies, and reinvested earnings, though a number of economies do not report data on reinvested earnings. In addition, official publications from some economies (for example, Japan and Taiwan) often use data on reported or approved FDI, instead of data on FDI actually remitted and reported in the balance of payments. However, even when measured correctly, changes in FDI may simply reflect a restructuring of a firm's liabilities and have little or no relationship to changes in production or other related activities in MNCs, such as employment and trade. Moreover, except in cases where issues related to the balance of payments or corporate finance are the primary concern, production and related variables are usually thought to provide more meaningful measures of MNC activities.

Second, there is no counterpart to FDI for non-MNCs and it is thus very difficult to measure the size of MNCs relative to all firms in an economy in terms of FDI. Two kinds of measures, ratios of FDI to gross domestic product (GDP) or ratios of FDI to total investment or fixed investment are often used as proxies in this regard. However, they both have distinct drawbacks. On the other hand, production (for example, GDP) and related indicators (for example, employment, trade) can be measured in the same way for both MNCs and non-MNCs. Thus it is a rather straightforward exercise to measure the shares of MNCs in terms of production or related indicators.

This chapter examines changes in the level of foreign MNC presence in Asia-Pacific economies since 1970 by comparing trends in ratios of inward FDI *flows* to GDP, and inward FDI *stocks* to GDP, and with foreign MNC *shares* of production (= GDP). Due to the lack of production data for multinational parents in key investing economies (Hong Kong, Korea, Singapore and Taiwan), this comparison is limited to host economies, that is to the comparison of measures based on inward FDI and measures based on the production of foreign MNCs. In order to put this comparison in context, the chapter first looks at why economists are interested in measuring the activities of MNCs and the various uses of such measures (Section 8.2). Section 8.3 describes indicators used to measure foreign MNC presence and the statistical tools used to examine trends in those indicators. In Section 8.4 these indicators and tools are used to examine foreign MNC presence in eleven Asia-Pacific economies, and some of the major factors thought to underlie the trends observed are indicated. Finally, in Section 8.5, the major conclusions of the analysis are summarized. The chapter is based heavily on Lipsey *et al.* (1995) and Ramstetter (1996b).

8.2 Why and how to measure the activities of MNCs

The first step here is to clearly define what is meant by a multinational corporation. For the purposes of this chapter an MNC is defined as a firm with operations in two or more countries. A foreign MNC is then a firm that has a foreign ownership share above a certain cut-off. This definition can be ambiguous in important respects. For example, as with FDI flows, ownership cut-offs differ among reporting economies and even among different data sources for one reporting economy. More importantly, when joint ventures (firms with more than one owner) are involved, especially when no one owner has majority control, any ownership criterion can become ambiguous, especially when trying to distinguish among groups of foreign owners. In addition, some firms classified as foreign MNCs in this chapter may actually be better classified as local firms, as their only operations may be in the local economy (for example, a Taiwanese factory transplanted to Thailand where the owner remains in Taiwan).

Moreover, this definition of an MNC does not distinguish between types of MNCs, nor does it encompass the vast array of non-ownership based international relationships (for example, international sub-contracting of various types) that exist among firms (see Chapters 10 and 14). There may also be important distinctions between affiliates of MNCs established through mergers and acquisitions and affiliates arising from the formation of new affiliates, between investments in expanding the operation of previously existing affiliates and investments in the establishment of new affiliates, or between wholly foreign owned affiliates and joint ventures. It is important to note that the analysis here says nothing about these differences. In short, what is of most interest here, and what is of most fundamental importance to the economic analysis of MNCs, is the distinction between whether a firm has operations in one economy or in two or more economies.

Correspondingly, the economic theory of the multinational corporation focuses first and foremost on the question of why a firm chooses to become a multinational and incur costs of cross-border operations not incurred by non-MNCs. Very simply put, this question is commonly answered by identifying the advantages that MNCs have that allow them to overcome the disadvantages of the additional costs of operating across international borders. The interested reader is encouraged to see more comprehensive surveys of this literature (Caves, 1996; Dunning, 1993), but here I summarize the three sets of advantages that are often hypothesized in this regard.

The first set consists of advantages accruing from exploitation of assets that belong to a given firm. These assets are often called *firm-specific assets* and advantages accruing from the possession of such assets are called ownership advantages. Important examples of such firm-specific assets are patents, in-house research capability, and exclusive marketing networks. The intangible nature of such assets is often emphasized in comparison to the tangible nature of fixed assets (for example, buildings, machinery).

The second set of advantages are those accruing from the internalization of economic transactions within a single firm unit. These advantages are called *internalization advantages*. For example, when uncertainty makes inter-firm transactions risky and thus costly, a firm can often reduce costs by arranging to carry out that transaction or an equivalent activity within the firm. Suppose, for example, a firm develops a very advanced semiconductor that can greatly improve the performance of a personal computer. In such a case there is likely to be a problem of asymmetric information – namely, that the firm developing the semiconductor will know far more about its capabilities than any prospective buyer. This will lead to a tendency for the buyer to undervalue the semiconductor (from the perspective of the developer) and will thus create a motive for the developer to produce its own personal computers, using the semiconductor, in an attempt to extract (what the developer perceives as) the full value from its development efforts.

Another example is when quality is very important to a final goods producer (for example, a personal computer company). Such a producer will be very reluctant to purchase from an intermediate goods supplier (for example, a subcontractor), unless they are assured that concerns about quality control will be addressed by the supplier. Moreover, the firm producing the intermediate goods may have a smaller incentive to emphasize quality than the final goods producer. If this is the case, the final goods producer may have to produce the intermediate goods itself rather than buying it from a supplier. Both of these are examples where transactions that would take place in arm's length markets may end up internalized within a single firm. The existence of such internalization advantages is often thought to be a major reason for the existence of MNCs.

The third set consists of advantages accrued from operating in a specific location or *locational advantages*. Traditional examples of locational advantages are reductions in the costs of serving markets when firms are faced with high levels of trade protection in the target market, and reductions in production costs afforded by increased access to lower cost factors of production (for example, labour and natural resources).

Together, these three elements comprise Dunning's OLI (ownership–location–internalization) paradigm (see Dunning, 1993). There is an extensive theoretical debate over whether all of these advantages are a necessary condition for a firm to become a multinational (and thus for FDI to occur), with some arguing that internalization advantages alone are sufficient to explain the existence of the multinational firm (see Buckley and Casson, 1991; Rugman, 1985). However, from an empirical point of view the general agreement that MNCs tend to possess a distinctive set of firm-specific, intangible assets is important, whether or not such assets are necessary for a firm to become a multinational. The possession of distinctive firm-specific, intangible assets is important because it implies that the behaviour of MNCs differs systematically from the behaviour of non-MNCs. More specifically, there are at least three interrelated sets of firm-specific, intangible assets that MNCs are thought to possess in relatively large amounts: production technology, marketing networks, and management know-how.

The possession of superior production technology (and superior management know-how) implies that MNCs tend to be more efficient than non-MNCs. One simple example lending support to this proposition is the casual observation that foreign MNC shares of host country production tend to be larger than corresponding shares of employment. In other words, the average product of labour (= production per worker) often tends to be relatively high in foreign MNCs. However, it is also important to note that there is often very large *variation* in productivity differentials between MNCs and non-MNCs (see Ramstetter, 1994, 1995a, 1996c). As a result, there is a relatively high statistical probability (greater than five per cent) that one would be wrong if one concluded that there are productivity differentials between MNCs and non-MNCs in many cases.

In addition, the relatively sophisticated marketing networks of MNCs, particularly those related to international trade, also lead to the expectation that MNCs will be more dependent on trade than non-MNCs. This proposition is again supported by the casual observation that foreign MNC shares of host country exports tend to be much larger than shares of production and employment, or, in other words, that trade propensities (for example, export–sales ratios or ratios of imports to total inputs) are higher in MNCs than non-MNCs. It is also important that the variation of differentials between MNCs and non-MNCs tends to be much smaller in terms of trade propensities than in terms of average labour productivity (Ramstetter, 1994, 1995a, 1996c). Thus, there is a relatively low statistical probability (less than five per cent) of being wrong if one concludes that differentials between MNCs and non-MNCs exist in terms of trade propensities.

In some contrast to the focus on differences between MNCs and non-MNCs discussed above, this chapter is concerned with the more basic questions of:

1   How important are foreign MNCs in Asia-Pacific production?

2   How has the importance of foreign MNCs changed over time in the Asia-Pacific?

The answers to these questions are, however, closely related to the discussion above, because the relative size of MNCs differs dramatically depending on the activity measured. For example, if one were to focus on the relatively low shares of foreign MNCs in employment, one would likely conclude that foreign MNCs are generally unimportant in the Asia-Pacific. At the other extreme, if one were to focus on the large foreign MNC shares of exports, one would likely conclude that MNCs are very important. Furthermore, a focus on production would lead one to the conclusion that MNCs are of intermediate importance.

As explained in the introduction, FDI is the only indicator of economic activity in MNCs that is even vaguely standardized internationally – and measures of this have been used extensively in other chapters. It should also be emphasized that data on FDI are available far more often and far more quickly than data on production and related variables. As a result, FDI flows or stocks are often used as a general proxy for the level of economic activities in MNCs. For example, to quote from the United Nations:

> World-wide foreign-direct-investment (FDI) flows quadrupled between 1980 and 1990 ... This rapid growth is an indication of the growing importance of FDI as an instrument of international economic integration.
>
> (United Nations Transnational Corporations and Management Division,
> 1993, p.1)

> The principal measure of annual changes in the cross-border investment activities of TNCs [transnational corporations] is FDI flows. As long as such flows remain positive, even if they decline from year to year, they mark the expansion of TNC activities.
>
> (United Nations Conference on Trade and Development, 1994, p.9)

These statements are somewhat vague on a very important point, that is whether 'the growing importance of FDI' and 'the expansion of TNC activities' refer to financial activities of MNCs only, or whether they also refer to production and related activities in these firms. Nonetheless, these works, and dozens more like them, imply that FDI is a proxy for the activities of MNCs in general, not just for activities related to international finance.

8.3 A simple methodology for evaluating foreign MNC presence

As indicated above, increases in FDI are often cited as evidence that MNCs have been much more important in the Asia-Pacific region since the 1970s. In contrast, I believe that this assertion is so often incorrect that it constitutes a myth. However, it is important to recognize that those who make this claim are wrong not because they lack empirical evidence to support the assertion. Rather, my argument is that they err in relying on FDI-based indicators that are not robust for evaluating the relative size of foreign MNCs or foreign MNC presence. One may think that this is just nit-picking because FDI flows and FDI stocks, though not definitionally correlated with the production of MNCs and related indicators, are in fact correlated with them empirically. To some extent this viewpoint is probably valid. On the other hand, the evidence below suggests that trends in FDI flows and FDI stocks, even when averaged over relatively long periods of time, are, in a number of cases, poor proxies for trends in production.

More specifically, FDI flows and stocks often display trends that differ markedly from trends in MNCs, and trends in FDI flows and FDI stocks are often subject to far more variation than trends in MNC production. These points are examined in some detail below. To the extent that data are available, trends in the following four indicators are compared for the 1970–95 period:

1   ratios of inward FDI flows to gross domestic product (GDP);

2   ratios of inward FDI stocks (defined as cumulative FDI flows from the first year for which data are available, usually 1970) to GDP;

3   shares of foreign MNCs in production (usually measured as GDP=value added) in all industries;

4   shares of foreign MNCs in manufacturing production (again, usually measured as GDP=value added).

These indicators are examined in two steps. First, the trends in each indicator are plotted against time so that trends can be examined visually. Second, two basic statistical properties of each measure, mean ratios and a measure of the variation in mean ratios, the coefficients of variation, are calculated for each indicator for three sub-periods, 1970–78, 1979–86 and 1987–95. The mean ratio is simply the average of the ratio in question for the period in question. The coeffecient of variation is the ratio of the standard deviation of the mean ratio to the mean ratio itself for the period in question, where the standard deviation is a measure of the average difference between annual ratios and the mean ratio for the period in question. For example, in a sample of nine observations (the largest sample used here) the mean ratio can be said to display a very large degree of variation if the associated coefficient of variation is greater than 0.54, because if one concludes that the mean ratio is greater than zero in such a case, there is a relatively large statistical probability (greater than five per cent) that even this very weak conclusion would be incorrect.

A large number of statistical difficulties and caveats arise in any comparison of economic activity across countries. As already mentioned, definitions differ, coverage is often inconsistent and patchy, and methodologies for data collection and presentation are far from uniform. All these remain very important in the case of the FDI and production indicators which are being dealt with here. However, what follows is the most consistent set of comparative statistics I could construct given the limitations of the data. (The sources of these data are given in the appendix to this chapter.)

8.4 The relative size of multinationals in selected Asia-Pacific economies

This section will attempt to answer two questions. Do FDI-based measures and MNC shares of production:

1 display similar trends over time?

2 display similar levels of variation or volatility over time?

For simplicity, the data will be presented country by country. In addition to examining the patterns observed from the data, an attempt will be made to describe some of the more important factors underlying the patterns observed. It should be noted, however, that discussions of underlying factors are not comprehensive, but only suggestive in nature.

Canada

In Canada, ratios of inward FDI flows or stocks to GDP were rather low in the 1970s, decreased markedly in 1980 to 1982, and then rose to a rather higher level thereafter (see Figure 8.1). Correspondingly, mean ratios of FDI flows to GDP decreased between 1970–78 and 1979–86, but then increased rather dramatically in 1987–95 (see Table 8.1).

In marked contrast, foreign MNC shares of production (that is, ratios of production by foreign MNCs to GDP), both in all industries and in manufacturing, rose between 1970 and 1974 but tended to decline thereafter. Moreover, foreign MNC shares moved in a much narrower range than did FDI-based measures, as indicated by relatively low coefficients of variation. Here, it is important to note that the low frequency of data on foreign MNC shares of production means that comparisons of variation are not as meaningful statistically as corresponding comparisons for countries with more observations. Nonetheless, the contrast between the two types of measures is stark, with FDI-based measures indicating that MNCs have become much more important in Canada since the mid 1980s, while foreign MNC shares of production tended to decline and moved in a much narrower range.

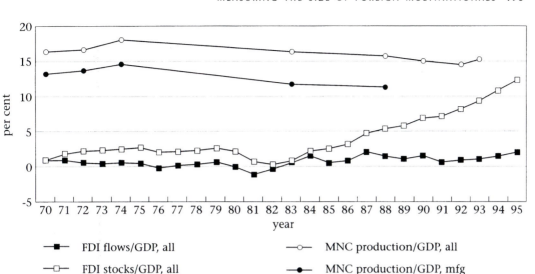

Figure 8.1 *Foreign MNC presence in Canada*

Table 8.1 *Foreign MNC presence in Canada, mean and variation*

Measure, industry	Mean ratios (per cent)			Coefficients of variation		
	1970–78	1979–86	1987–95	1970–78	1979–86	1987–95
FDI flows/GDP, all	0.44	0.22	1.21	0.91	3.69	0.41
FDI stocks/GDP, all	2.06	1.66	7.67	0.24	0.65	0.33
MNC production/GDP, all	16.97	16.20	14.95	0.05	NA	0.04
MNC production/GDP, mfg	13.77	NA	11.10	0.05	NA	NA

Note: all calculations exclude years for which data are not available; NA = no data are available for the period

These trends are probably closely related to the fact that the United States is by far the largest investor in Canada, and that US MNCs have had a large presence in Canada for the entire period under study. In other words, assuming that trends in US MNCs dominate trends in foreign MNCs in Canada, these data indicate that US investors have greatly increased the foreign liabilities of their Canadian affiliates, but that increases in production by US affiliates in Canada have been much more moderate.

Japan

Japan contrasts with other developed economies (for example, Canada and the United States) in that foreign MNCs are apparently relatively unimportant by any measure (see Figure 8.2 and Table 8.2). Moreover, the importance of foreign MNCs has apparently declined over time, with ratios of FDI flows to GDP and foreign MNC shares of production all showing downward trends. However, although ratios of FDI flows to GDP and foreign MNC shares of production show similar downward trends, foreign MNC shares declined much more than FDI-based measures.

in the value of the US dollar in 1978 and again in 1985 (which in turn led to large decreases in the prices of US assets and production costs when measured in foreign currency).

Hong Kong

The data on Hong Kong refer only to FDI from Organization for Economic Co-operation and Development (OECD) economies as this is all that could be reasonably estimated. Substantial FDI from China and other non-OECD economies in Asia (for example, Korea, Taiwan, Singapore) is excluded. Moreover, foreign MNC shares of production can be calculated for manufacturing only and for the post 1983 period only. Since the vast majority of inward FDI in Hong Kong is in non-manufacturing, this means that there are large definitional differences between FDI-based measures and foreign MNC shares of production. Nonetheless, both the FDI-based measures and foreign MNC shares indicate a substantial increase in foreign presence between 1979–86 and 1987–95 (see Figure 8.4 and Table 8.4). However, here again, the FDI-based measures tend to fluctuate in a much wider range as indicated by relatively large coefficients of variation for these measures.

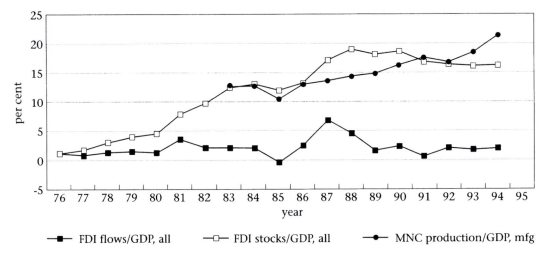

Figure 8.4 *Foreign MNC presence in Hong Kong*

Table 8.4 *Foreign MNC presence in Hong Kong, mean and variation*

Measure, industry	Mean ratios (per cent)			Coefficients of variation		
	1970–78	1979–86	1987–95	1970–78	1979–86	1987–95
FDI flows/GDP, all	1.17	1.83	2.70	0.20	0.62	0.72
FDI stocks/GDP, all	2.05	9.47	17.24	0.45	0.39	0.07
MNC production/GDP, mfg	NA	12.30	16.64	NA	0.09	0.16

Note: all calculations exclude years for which data are not available; NA = no data are available for the period

Additional notes and sources: see Appendix A

With regard to investment in Hong Kong, two factors are particularly important. First, Hong Kong has always been very open to foreign trade and FDI, and has maintained very low corporate tax rates. It has always provided an attractive policy environment for foreign MNCs seeking to invest in East Asia, and it is very unlikely that the recent increase in foreign presence in Hong Kong is due to changes in Hong Kong's economic policies. Second, Hong Kong is an entrepôt and a large portion of foreign MNC presence there is focused on providing goods and services for third markets – for example, China, Japan, the United States, and South-East Asia. Moreover, Hong Kong is a key financial and co-ordinating centre for MNCs in the region, and a very large portion (about half or more) of its large outward flows of FDI originate from affiliates of foreign MNCs operating there (Low *et al.*, 1996). Assuming that China itself does not experience substantial economic or political difficulties, these characteristics are also powerful reasons to expect that Hong Kong's reversion to Chinese sovereignty may have little effect on foreign MNC presence.

Korea

Korea, like Japan, has very low ratios of FDI flows and stocks to GDP (see Figure 8.5 and Table 8.5). These ratios declined between 1970–78 and 1979–86 and then increased again in 1987–95. Average foreign MNC shares of production also declined between 1974–78 and 1984–86, the only years for which such ratios can be calculated. As in the Canadian case, it is not very meaningful to compare variation in FDI-based measures of foreign MNC shares of production due to the lack of data. However, the comparisons that can be made reveal that variation of foreign MNC shares is much larger relative to the variation in FDI-based measures than in most of the other economies studied in this chapter. In other words, the limited data that exists in the Korean case differs from most of the other cases studied here in revealing relatively little difference in the variation of trends of FDI-based measures and the variation of trends in foreign shares of production.

As in Japan, foreign MNC presence is very limited in Korea. Moreover, like Japan in the 1960s, the low level of foreign MNC presence can be attributed to restrictions on foreign MNCs, several of which remain today. In Korea, restrictions on Japanese MNCs are particularly strict. For example, sales of Japanese cars under Japanese labels are forbidden in Korea, though the Japanese do manufacture and sell a large number of cars in joint ventures with Korean firms. Moreover, despite these restrictions, Japanese MNCs are among the leading investors in Korea and are likely to continue to be important in this respect in the future. It is also of some interest that, despite the fact that Korean restrictions on foreign MNCs are probably far stricter than corresponding Japanese restrictions have ever been, foreign MNC shares of production are apparently substantially larger in Korea than in Japan.

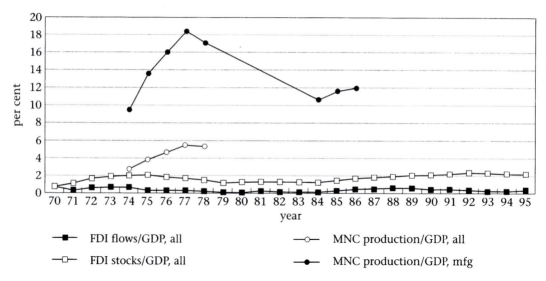

Figure 8.5 *Foreign MNC presence in Korea*

Table 8.5 *Foreign MNC presence in Korea, mean and variation*

Measure, industry	Mean ratios (per cent)			Coefficients of variation		
	1970–78	*1979–86*	*1987–95*	*1970–78*	*1979–86*	*1987–95*
FDI flows/GDP, all	0.46	0.15	0.36	0.48	0.90	0.37
FDI stocks/GDP, all	1.61	1.28	2.14	0.28	0.13	0.10
MNC production/GDP, all	4.42	NA	NA	0.26	NA	NA
MNC production/GDP, mfg	14.92	11.41	NA	0.23	0.06	NA

Note: all calculations exclude years for which data are not available; NA = no data are available for the period

Additional notes and sources: see Appendix A

Singapore

Relative to the size of the host economy, foreign MNCs are far larger in Singapore than in any other economy in East Asia, and perhaps in the world. An indication of this is very high ratios of FDI stocks to GDP in recent years (70 per cent in 1987–95, see Figure 8.6 and Table 8.6). Moreover, there have been very large increases in FDI flows and stocks in recent years and commensurate increases in ratios of these variables to GDP. As in Hong Kong, foreign MNC shares of production are only available for manufacturing, and because foreign FDI non-manufacturing is extremely important, comparisons of FDI-based measures and foreign MNC shares are imprecise in this case as well. However, it is also important that, as in the United States, the increase in foreign MNC shares of manufacturing production is much smaller than increases in FDI-based measures. Part of the reason for this is the extremely high level – over 60 per cent – of foreign MNC shares in manufacturing. Here again, fluctuations in foreign MNC shares are much smaller than corresponding fluctuations in FDI-based measures.

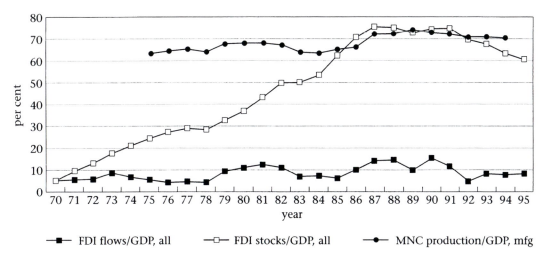

Figure 8.6 *Foreign MNC presence in Singapore*

Table 8.6 *Foreign MNC presence in Singapore, mean and variation*

Measure, industry	Mean ratios (per cent)			Coefficients of variation		
	1970–78	1979–86	1987–95	1970–78	1979–86	1987–95
FDI flows/GDP, all	5.34	8.84	10.21	0.27	0.25	0.35
FDI stocks/GDP, all	19.13	49.40	70.30	0.45	0.26	0.08
MNC production/GDP, mfg	63.86	65.75	71.73	0.02	0.03	0.02

Note: all calculations exclude years for which data are not available

Additional notes and sources: see Appendix A

The contrast between the very large foreign presence of MNCs in Singapore and the much more moderate presence in Hong Kong is of some interest, given that these economies share several important characteristics. Both economies are very open to foreign MNCs and international trade, are entrepôts for their respective regions, and are important outward investors with large portions of that outward investment coming from foreign MNCs in each respective economy (Low *et al.*, 1996). Given these important similarities, it is somewhat puzzling that foreign MNC shares of manufacturing production are four to five times larger in Singapore than in Hong Kong. Three possible explanations for this are that:

1   Hong Kong is a much larger economy (about twofold);

2   high wages in the public sector in Singapore have tended to encourage the best workers to seek employment in the public sector;

3   policies in Singapore have tended to favour foreign MNCs and public corporations compared to local entrepreneurs.

However, there are also important reasons to expect that foreign MNC presence should actually be larger in Hong Kong than in Singapore. Namely, the policy environment is probably less friendly to foreign MNCs in Singapore because:

1   the government tends to intervene more in the economy, especially in labour and capital markets, than in Hong Kong;

2   corporate tax rates are higher in Singapore;

3   restrictions related to social policy tend to be stricter in Singapore.

In short, the much larger foreign MNC presence in Singapore seems paradoxical in many respects. Furthermore, the low foreign MNC shares of manufacturing production in Hong Kong also seems paradoxical when it is realized that corresponding shares tended to be somewhat higher in Taiwan and Indonesia (see below), two economies which have restricted the access of foreign MNCs to a much greater extent than Hong Kong or Singapore.

Taiwan

Taiwan is another economy where ratios of FDI flows and stocks to GDP have generally been very low (see Figure 8.7 and Table 8.7). As in Korea, ratios of FDI flows to GDP fell between 1970–78 and 1979–86 before rising in 1987–95. However, in contrast to Korea, ratios of FDI stocks to GDP rose more continuously over these three periods, with the largest increase between the second and third periods. In all industries, foreign MNC shares of production changed very little between the first two periods but then rose substantially in the later one. In manufacturing, foreign MNC shares fell slightly between the first and second periods, rising somewhat in the later period. However, mean ratios were relatively constant in the 17 to 20 per cent range. In the first two periods, fluctuations in ratios of FDI flows to GDP were much larger than fluctuations in foreign MNC shares of production, but of similar magnitude in the third period, and fluctuations in ratios of FDI stocks to GDP were the smallest of any indicator in the later two periods. Thus, Taiwan is an example where FDI-related indicators and foreign MNC shares display similar trends and, in the later period, similarly high levels of variation. However, it should be noted that the surveys from which MNC shares are taken are not mandatory and are subject to wide variation in sample coverage. In short, variations in survey coverage may be one reason why relatively large variation is observed for foreign MNC shares in Taiwan.

Data for Taiwan are suggestive in at least two other important respects. First, as in Korea, foreign MNC shares of production are larger than might be expected given the low level of FDI in the economy relative to GDP. Indeed, the fact that foreign MNCs have accounted for an average of about one fifth of manufacturing production in Taiwan would seem to suggest that low levels of FDI may not necessarily imply low levels of MNC presence. Second, on the other hand, it also seems clear that recent policy reforms, notably the liberalization of capital markets and restrictions on foreign MNCs in service industries in the late 1980s, have resulted in increases in foreign MNC shares of production, as well as increases in FDI-related indicators. This fact suggests that a similar process may have occurred in Korea, where policy restrictions were also relaxed in the 1980s and FDI–GDP ratios have been rising thereafter.

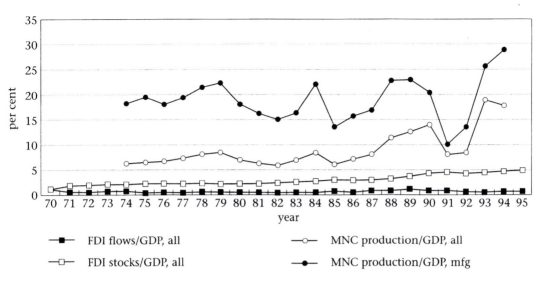

Figure 8.7 *Foreign MNC presence in Taiwan*

Table 8.7 *Foreign MNC presence in Taiwan, mean and variation*

Measure, industry	Mean ratios (per cent)			Coefficients of variation		
	1970–78	1979–86	1987–95	1970–78	1979–86	1987–95
FDI flows/GDP, all	0.52	0.36	0.68	0.55	0.51	0.18
FDI stocks/GDP, all	1.86	2.37	4.03	0.17	0.05	0.02
MNC production/GDP, all	6.84	6.91	12.34	0.11	0.13	0.07
MNC production/GDP, mfg	19.10	17.24	20.05	0.07	0.10	0.10

Note: all calculations exclude years for which data are not available

Additional notes and sources: see Appendix A

Indonesia

The data for Indonesia display patterns that are similar to those observed in the Taiwanese data in two important respects (see Figure 8.8 and Table 8.8). First, FDI flow–GDP ratios fell between 1970–78 and 1979–86 but then rose again in 1987–95. Second, ratios of FDI stocks to GDP rose continuously over these three periods, with by far the largest increase between the second and third periods. However, the data on foreign MNC shares of manufacturing production contrast with Taiwanese data and FDI-related indicators for Indonesia in suggesting that foreign MNC presence tended to fall over the three periods. Moreover, the Indonesian data follow a general pattern observed in this sample of countries, with foreign MNC shares of production fluctuating less that FDI-related indicators.

Indonesia has always been rather receptive to FDI by foreign MNCs, but it also tended to severely restrict the activities of those foreign MNCs, as well as local private firms, until the late 1980s. In this respect, the fact that Indonesia had among the highest levels of import protection in the region prior to 1986 is particularly important, and the liberalization of trade begun

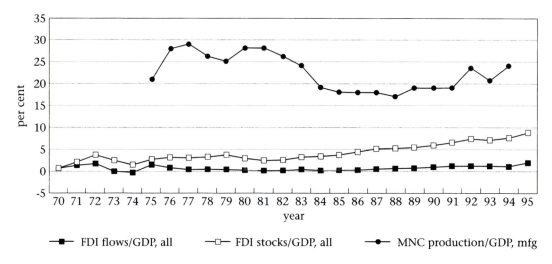

Figure 8.8 *Foreign MNC presence in Indonesia*

Table 8.8 *Foreign MNC presence in Indonesia, mean and variation*

Measure, industry	Mean ratios (per cent)			Coefficients of variation		
	1970–78	*1979–86*	*1987–95*	*1970–78*	*1979–86*	*1987–95*
FDI flows/GDP, all	0.86	0.29	1.14	0.81	0.31	0.43
FDI stocks/GDP, all	2.68	3.35	6.69	0.35	0.20	0.19
MNC production/GDP, mfg	26.00	23.25	20.07	0.14	0.18	0.13

Note: all calculations exclude years for which data are not available

Additional notes and sources: see Appendix A

in 1986 has been the major cause of the extremely large changes in the Indonesian economy in subsequent years. Increases in inward FDI are often pointed to as one of the favourable effects resulting from the liberalization of trade and the relaxation of other restrictions on private business. However, as in Canada, it is interesting that the large increase of FDI-related measures were not accompanied by increases in foreign MNC shares, despite the fact that manufacturing apparently accounted for a large portion of the increase in FDI after 1992. (These data are from unpublished mimeos of the Investment Co-ordinating Board and refer to realized FDI stocks outside of oil and banking.)

Malaysia

Like Singapore, Malaysia is distinguished by an extremely large presence of foreign MNCs compared to other countries in this sample, with the ratio of FDI stocks to GDP approaching 50 per cent in recent years (see Figure 8.9 and Table 8.9). Moreover, again like Singapore, FDI-based indicators have increased over the three periods identified, with the largest increases coming between 1979–86 and 1987–95. In marked contrast to Singapore, however, foreign MNC shares of production fell between 1970–78 and

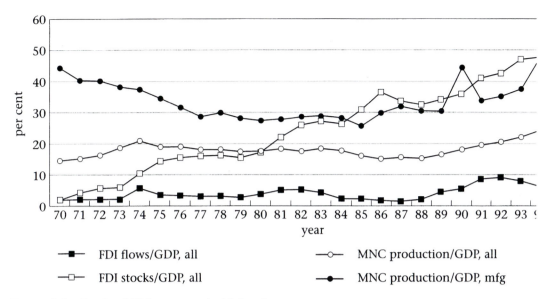

Figure 8.9 *Foreign MNC presence in Malaysia*

Table 8.9 *Foreign MNC presence in Malaysia, mean and variation*

Measure, industry	Mean ratios (per cent)			Coefficients of variation		
	1970–78	1979–86	1987–95	1970–78	1979–86	1987–95
FDI flows/GDP, all	3.05	3.41	5.52	0.38	0.39	0.49
FDI stocks/GDP, all	10.14	25.05	39.74	0.55	0.28	0.15
MNC production/GDP, all	17.77	17.17	18.97	0.11	0.07	0.17
MNC production/GDP, mfg	36.05	27.91	36.34	0.15	0.04	0.18

Note: all calculations exclude years for which data are not available

Additional notes and sources: see Appendix A

1979–86 but then rose afterwards. In all industries, mean shares changed very little, staying in the 17 to 19 per cent range. This is, in a sense, the opposite of patterns observed in Korea and Taiwan in that foreign MNC shares of production are below what they might be expected to be given the high level of FDI stock to GDP ratios. In manufacturing, the decline in the middle period was more pronounced than in all industries, but the pattern was similar in that foreign MNC shares of production were of similar magnitude in the earlier and later periods. Moreover, as in most other economies in this sample, foreign MNC shares of production tended to fluctuate less than FDI-related measures, the exception being the FDI stock to GDP ratio in the later period.

In contrast to Hong Kong, where the level of foreign MNC presence may be considered paradoxically low, it may be considered paradoxically high in both Malaysia and Singapore, particularly in manufacturing. Part of the reason for this is the importance of the electrical and electronic machinery industry in these economies and the almost total domination of this industry by foreign MNCs. For example, data from the Malaysian Industrial Development Authority (1996) indicate that electrical and electronic machinery accounted for 18 per cent of the fixed assets in all manufacturing in 1994 and that foreign MNCs account for 88 per cent of all the fixed assets in electrical and electronic machinery. Data from the Singapore Economic Development Board (1996) indicate that these shares were also large – 28 per cent and 86 per cent respectively – in that country in 1994. As illustrated by Plummer and Ramstetter (1991), in Asia MNCs tend to be present in industries where knowledge-based intangible assets such as technologies generated by research and development and marketing networks (terminology from Markusen, 1991) are relatively important.

Although significant, this is certainly only one of the factors underlying the large foreign MNC presence in these economies. For example, it also seems to be no coincidence that both Singapore and Malaysia have a similar geography and history, though it is very difficult to interpret the role of these factors in economic terms. Indeed, it may be a failure to appreciate the importance of these factors that leads me to consider the high level of foreign multinational presence in Malaysia and Singapore as somewhat paradoxical.

Thailand

In Thailand, ratios of FDI flows to GDP remained rather constant throughout the 1970–78 and 1979–86 periods, but then increased a good deal in 1987–95, while ratios of FDI stocks to GDP increased steadily over the three periods (see Figure 8.10 and Table 8.10). Here again, however, fluctuations in ratios of FDI flows to GDP are quite pronounced, with coefficients of variation being rather large (0.4 to 0.5). Data on foreign MNC shares of production are very sparse and the figures used here refer only to foreign MNCs that are accorded promoted status and responded to surveys by the Board of Investment. These figures indicate that foreign MNC shares were rather steady in the 13 to 16 per cent range in 1974, 1986 and 1990. More comprehensive estimates for 1990 (from Ramstetter, 1994, 1996b) indicate that the share of all foreign MNCs, including non-promoted MNCs and promoted MNCs that did not respond to the aforementioned survey, in manufacturing value added was roughly twice this level (about 31 per cent).

The Thai case combines elements observed in other South-East Asian economies. First, there has been very rapid growth in manufacturing in recent years, especially in electrical and electronic machinery as well as the car industries. As described above, foreign MNCs dominate the former industry and have a very large presence in the latter industry as well. Second, like Indonesia, Thailand previously had relatively high levels of import protection but these barriers have gradually liberalized, especially in recent years. Third, another important factor not yet mentioned with respect to Asian economies is the role of macroeconomic fluctuations.

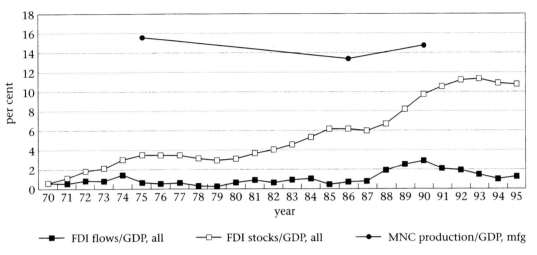

Figure 8.10 *Foreign MNC presence in Thailand*

Table 8.10 *Foreign MNC presence in Thailand, mean and variation*

Measure, industry	Mean ratios (per cent)			Coefficients of variation		
	1970–78	1979–86	1987–95	1970–78	1979–86	1987–95
FDI flows/GDP, all	0.65	0.63	1.71	0.49	0.41	0.41
FDI stocks/GDP, all	2.45	4.47	9.45	0.44	0.29	0.22
MNC production/GDP, mfg	15.53	13.32	14.76	NA	NA	NA

Note: all calculations exclude years for which data are not available; NA = no data are available for the period

Additional notes and sources: see Appendix A

Thailand, like Indonesia, Malaysia, and Singapore, experienced a marked economic slowdown in the early to mid 1980s. Moreover, due in large part to austere macroeconomic policies during these difficult years, a robust recovery and economic boom followed in the late 1980s. The fact that this recovery coincided with the large appreciations of the yen and the New Taiwan dollar is also thought to be significant by some. Other studies have shown that variation in macroeconomic variables can explain a very large portion of FDI fluctuations in Thailand and in Malaysia (Ramstetter, 1995b,c). In short, it is no coincidence that the rapid growth of FDI followed closely behind the macroeconomic boom of the late 1980s in these economies.

China

Like the United States, China is a large economy that has, by any measure, experienced significant increases in foreign MNC presence in the 1980s and 1990s (see Figure 8.11 and Table 8.11).

China differs a great deal from the other economies studied here, both developed and developing, in that it was a centrally planned economy until 1978 and only began the transition to a market-based economy thereafter. There are two important characteristics of this transition. First, although

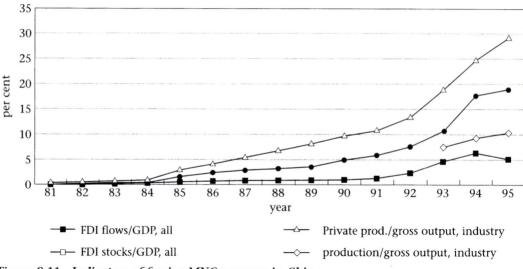

Figure 8.11 *Indicators of foreign MNC presence in China*

Table 8.11 *Indicators of foreign MNC presence in China, mean and variation*

Measure, industry	Mean ratios (per cent)		Coefficients of variation	
	1981–86	1987–95	1981–86	1987–95
FDI flows/GDP, all	0.39	2.50	0.52	0.88
FDI stocks/GDP, all	1.00	8.20	0.75	0.75
Private prod./gross output, industry	1.79	14.27	0.83	0.59
MNC production/gross output, industry	NA	9.07	NA	0.17

Note: all calculations exclude years for which data are not available; NA = no data are available for the period

Additional notes and sources: see Appendix A

there were virtually no foreign MNCs active in China before this transition, China quickly opened up to foreign MNCs. Moreover, although China instituted severe restrictions on the activities of foreign MNCs, the lure of what is potentially the largest national economy in the world led to a large increase in foreign MNC presence. Indeed, China became among the largest Asian recipients of FDI flows by the late 1980s and became the second largest recipient worldwide, behind the United States, in the mid 1990s (International Monetary Fund, 1997). Accordingly, ratios of FDI flows and stocks to GDP rose rapidly throughout the post-1978 period. Moreover, due in large part to the fact that these ratios increased extremely rapidly, the variation in these ratios within sub-periods was also quite large.

Second, there were virtually no private firms in China before the 1978 transition, and the growth of foreign MNCs was a major element of the rapid growth of the private business sector. On a national level it is impossible to measure foreign MNC shares of production directly for 1992 and earlier. However, because the growth of MNCs and private business in general have been closely related in China, it is instructive to look at trends in the shares of private enterprises (that is, firms that are not state owned or collective owned) in the gross output of all industry (that is, value added plus intermediate inputs in manufacturing, plus mining, construction, and electricity, gas and water). This share represents an upper limit on the shares of foreign MNCs in gross output. In a manner very similar to FDI flows and stocks, the private share of industrial production grew rapidly, with large variations within sub-periods that are, again, a direct result of the rapid rates of growth. Since 1993 it is possible to get estimates of gross output for foreign MNCs with independent accounting systems. These MNCs accounted for 7 to 10 per cent of all gross output of all industrial enterprises in 1993–95, compared to 19 to 29 per cent for all private firms. In short, as China has liberalized, foreign MNCs have apparently seized a substantial portion of the opportunities that China's economic reforms have allowed private business to pursue.

8.5   Conclusion

The evidence presented above suggests at least three very simple conclusions. First, trends in foreign MNC shares of production in the eleven economies studied suggest that foreign MNCs have become more important in recent years in a number of economies in the region, and probably the region as a whole. For example, these ratios rose very rapidly in China, rather rapidly in Hong Kong and the United States, and more modestly in Singapore, Taiwan and Malaysia. Moreover, it is fairly clear that these increases far outweigh the moderate decreases in Canada, Japan and Indonesia, mainly due to the relatively big increases in the large US and Chinese economies. A similar conclusion can be reached about foreign MNC shares worldwide (see Lipsey *et al.*, 1995). However, it is also important to emphasize that the region-wide increase was heavily concentrated in two economies, China and the United States.

Second, if one interprets FDI-based measures as a proxy for foreign MNC presence, one gets the impression that the increase in foreign MNC presence was much greater than if one focuses on foreign MNC shares of production. For example, FDI-based measures were higher in 1987–95 than in 1970–78 or 1979–86 in a wide range of Asia-Pacific economies – Canada, the United States, Hong Kong, Singapore, Taiwan, Indonesia, Malaysia and Thailand. However, foreign MNC shares of production increased very little, or actually declined, in most of the economies studied – Canada, Singapore, Taiwan, Indonesia, Malaysia and Thailand. Furthermore, although both FDI-based measures and foreign MNCs shares of production increased appreciably in Hong Kong and the United States, the rate at which foreign MNC shares of production increased was much lower than the rate at which FDI-related indicators increased. In short, only one economy, China, experienced similarly high rates of growth in foreign MNC shares of production and FDI-related indicators.

Third, if one evaluates foreign MNC presence from FDI-based indicators, one would conclude from the large variation over time that it is extremely volatile. However, if one evaluates on the basis of foreign MNC shares of production, foreign MNC presence appears to be much less volatile, with variation in these shares tending to be a good deal lower than variation in FDI-based indicators in Canada, Japan, the United States, Hong Kong, Singapore, Indonesia and Malaysia. Only in Korea, Taiwan in the later period, and China is variation of a similar magnitude for both measures of foreign MNC presence.

In addition to describing the evidence leading to these three simple conclusions, the chapter also tried to point out some of the major causes for the trends observed. These causes are numerous, and the relationships involved are very complex, making it impossible for this chapter to draw clear and comprehensive conclusions. Indeed, it would take at least a book, including a lot of statistical analysis that has not yet been performed, to accomplish that task. However, it is possible to indicate several factors that such an analysis would probably reveal to be important.

First, macroeconomic trends, for example interrelated trends in economic growth rates, inflation rates, interest rates, and exchange rates, as well as related policies, were thought to be important. Second, policies towards foreign MNCs are of obvious importance in some cases. Third, other policies, for example those towards international trade, international capital flows, taxation, and private business in general were also thought to be significant. Fourth, industrial structure was also thought to be important, as MNCs tend to be concentrated in industries with specific characteristics.

To return to the three simple conclusions outlined above, it is worth emphasizing two important implications that follow from the second and third of them. The second finding, namely that FDI-based indicators and foreign MNC shares of production often display very different trends, strongly suggests that FDI-based indicators are rather poor indicators of foreign MNC presence. More specifically, since foreign MNC shares of production are clearly a more accurate measure of foreign MNC presence, focusing on FDI-related measures apparently leads to significant over estimation of the extent to which foreign MNC presence has grown in the Asia-Pacific region since the 1970s. In this respect, however, it is also important to acknowledge that this chapter has presented estimates of foreign shares in terms of one indicator only, that is production. Similar calculations of foreign shares of other economic activities (for example, foreign MNC shares of employment and exports) might reveal trends that differ in important respects from those in foreign MNC shares of production. Thus, the reader should understand that this chapter analyses limited aspects of foreign MNC presence only and that more comprehensive descriptions remain an item on the agenda for future research.

The third conclusion described above, that foreign MNC shares of production tend to vary less over time than FDI-related indicators, has perhaps an even more important implication. Namely, economic activities of foreign MNCs have often been viewed as highly volatile by host economy policymakers, a view that is reinforced if one focuses on the large variation of FDI-related indicators. On the other hand, the relatively low variation in foreign MNC shares of production suggests that this view may be incorrect. In other words, although FDI may be a relatively volatile and hence unreliable source of balance of payments' finance, the production of foreign MNCs is generally much less volatile and hence more reliable.

Finally, if this chapter has one message to communicate to its readers, it is to reiterate the need for close attention to data issues when analysing MNCs in the Asia-Pacific region (or elsewhere). Correspondingly, it is wise to be highly sceptical of any analyst, economist or otherwise, pretending to know more than the data can tell one.

References

Asian Development Bank (various years a) *Key Indicators of Developing Member Countries*, vol.15–16 (April issues, 1984–85), vol.17–21 (July issues, 1986–90), Manila, Asian Development Bank.

Asian Development Bank (various years b) *Key Indicators of Developing Asian and Pacific Countries*, vol.22–27, (1991–96 issues), Manila, Oxford University Press.

Bora, B. (1996) 'Foreign direct investment' in Bora, B. and Findlay, C. (eds) *Regional Integration and the Asia-Pacific*, Melbourne, Oxford University Press.

Buckley, P.J. and Casson, M. (1991) *The Future of the Multinational Enterprise*, 2nd edn, London, Macmillan.

Caves, R.E. (1996) *Multinational Enterprise and Economic Analysis*, 2nd edn, Cambridge, Cambridge University Press.

Dunning, J.H. (1993) *Multinational Enterprises and the Global Economy*, Workingham, Addison-Wesley.

Encarnation, D. (1992) *Rivals Beyond Trade: America versus Japan in Global Competition*, Ithaca, Cornell University Press.

Fahim-Nader, M. and Zeile, W.J. (1997) 'Foreign direct investment in the United States: new investment in 1996, affiliate operations in 1995', *Survey of Current Business*, June, pp.42–69.

Hong Kong, Census and Statistics Department (various years) *Survey of Industrial Production*, 1992–94 issues, Hong Kong, Census and Statistics Department.

Indonesia, Biro Pusat Statistik (various years) diskettes with data from *Statistik Industri*, 1990–94, Jakarta, Biro Pusat Statistik.

International Monetary Fund (1997) *International Financial Statistics*, March, CD-ROM, Washington, DC, International Monetary Fund.

Japan, Ministry of Finance (various years) *Hojin Kigyou Toukei Shiho (Corporation Statistics Quarterly)*, April–June issues 1994–96.

Japan, Ministry of International Trade and Industry (1995) *Gaishikei Kigyou no Doukou (Trends in Foreign-Owned Firms)*, no.27, Tokyo, Ministry of Finance Printing Bureau.

Kreinin, M.E., Plummer, M.G. and Abe, S. (1997) 'Export and direct foreign investment links: a three country comparison', paper presented at International

Conference on 'International Economic Links and Policy Formations: Where do we go from here?', Kobe University, Kobe, Japan, June 12–13.

Lipsey, R.E., Blomström, M. and Ramstetter, E.D. (1995) 'Internationalized production in world output', *NBER Working Paper 5385*, Cambridge, Mass.

Low, L., Ramstetter, E.D. and Yeung, H.W-C. (1996) 'Accounting for outward direct investment from Hong Kong and Singapore: who controls what?', *NBER Working Paper 5858*, Cambridge, Mass.

Malaysia, Department of Statistics (various years) *Report on the Financial Survey of Limited Companies*, 1992–94 issues, Kuala Lumpur, Department of Statistics.

Malaysia Industrial Development Authority (1996) *Statistics on the Manufacturing Sector 1991–1995*, Kuala Lumpur, Malaysia Industrial Development Authority.

Markusen, J.R. (1991) 'The theory of the multinational enterprise: a common analytical framework' in Ramstetter, E.D. (ed.) *Direct Foreign Investment in Asia's Developing Economies and Structural Change in the Asia-Pacific Region*, Boulder, CO, Westview Press.

Organisation for Economic Co-operation and Development (OECD) (various years) *Geographical Distribution of Financial Flows to Developing Countries*, 1990–93, 1991–94 issues, Paris, OECD.

People's Republic of China, State Statistical Bureau (various years) *China Statistical Yearbook*, 1994–96 issues, Beijing, State Statistical Bureau.

Petri, P.A. and Plummer, M.G. (1995) 'The determinants of US direct investment abroad: evidence of trade–investment linkages', paper presented at International Conference on Economic Development and Co-operation in the Pacific Basin, University of California at Berkeley, Berkeley, CA, 30 June–1 July.

Plummer, M.G. and Ramstetter, E.D. (1991) 'Multinational affiliates and the changing division of labor in the Asia-Pacific region' in Ramstetter, E.D. (ed.) *Direct Foreign Investment in Asia's Developing Economies and Structural Change in the Asia-Pacific Region*, Boulder, CO, Westview Press.

Ramstetter, E.D. (1994) 'Comparisons of Japanese multinationals and other firms in Thailand's non-oil manufacturing industries', *ASEAN Economic Bulletin*, vol.11, no.1, pp.36–58.

Ramstetter, E.D. (1995a) 'Characteristics of multinational firms in Malaysia: a time series perspective' in Toida, M. and Hiratsuka, D. (eds) *Ajia Kogyoken no Keizai Bunseki to Yosoku (IV)*, (*Projections for Asian Industrializing Region (IV)*), Tokyo, Institute of Developing Economies.

Ramstetter, E.D. (1995b) 'Sectoral flows of foreign direct investment in Malaysia' in Economic and Social Commission for Asia and the Pacific, *Sectoral Studies of Foreign Direct Investment in Asia and the Pacific*, ST/ESCAP/1501, New York, United Nations.

Ramstetter, E.D. (1995c) 'Sectoral flows of foreign direct investment in Thailand' in Economic and Social Commission for Asia and the Pacific, *Sectoral Studies of Foreign Direct Investment in Asia and the Pacific*, ST/ESCAP/1501, New York, United Nations.

Ramstetter, E.D. (1996a) 'Estimating economic activities by Japanese transnational corporations: how to make sense of the data?', *Transnational Corporations*, vol.5, no.2, pp.107–43.

Ramstetter, E.D. (1996b) 'Trends in production in foreign multinational firms in Asian economies: a note on an economic myth related to poor measurement', *Kansai University Review of Economics and Business*, vol.24, no.1–2, pp.49–107.

Ramstetter, E.D. (1996c) 'Characteristics of Singapore's manufacturing establishments by nationality of ownership' in Toida, M. and Hiratsuka, D. (eds) *Ajia Kogyoken no Keizai Bunseki to Yosoku (V) (Projections for Asian Industrializing Region (V))*, Tokyo, Institute of Developing Economies.

Ramstetter, E.D. and James, W.E. (1993) 'Multinationals, Japan–US economic relations, and economic policy: the uncomfortable reality', *Transnational Corporations*, vol.2, no.3, pp.68–96.

Republic of China, Investment Commission (various years) *A Survey of Overseas Chinese and Foreign Firms and Their Effects on National Economic Development*, 1992–94 issues, Taipei, Investment Commission (in Chinese).

Republic of China, Central Bank of China (1997) 'Balance of payments, Taiwan District, The Republic of China', March issue, Taipei, The Central Bank of China.

Rugman, A.M. (1985) 'Internalization is still a general theory of foreign direct investment', *Weltwirtschaftliches Archiv*, Band 121, Heft 3, pp.570–5.

Singapore Economic Development Board (1996) mimeos of unpublished data from the Census on Industrial Production, September 1996, December 1996.

STAT-USA (1997) Internet-based collection of US government statistics, accessed June 1997.

United Nations Conference on Trade and Development (1994) *World Investment Report 1994, Transnational Corporations, Employment and the Workplace*, New York and Geneva, United Nations (Sales No.E94.II.A.14).

United Nations Transnational Corporations and Management Division (1993) *World Investment Directory, Volume III: Developed Countries*, New York, United Nations (Sales No.E.93.II.A.9).

World Bank (1995) *World Data 1995*, CD-ROM, Washington, DC, World Bank.

World Bank (1997) *World Development Indicators 1997*, CD-ROM, Washington, DC, World Bank.

Appendix A   Notes on the data and their sources

The following notes and sources are summarized by indicator and country.

1 Foreign direct investment (FDI)
Notes: Reinvested earnings are not included for Japan, Singapore, Indonesia, Malaysia, Thailand and China. For Hong Kong, FDI data refer to FDI from OECD economies only, as reported by OECD economies. For all other economies data are taken from balance of payments statistics. Original data are reported in US dollars or special drawing rights (SDRs) and translated to US dollars using annual average exchange rates. Stocks are cumulative flows calculated from US dollar figures.

Sources: International Monetary Fund (1997); Ramstetter (1996b); Republic of China, Central Bank of China (1997).

2 Gross domestic product (GDP)
Notes: Data reported in local currency and translated to US dollars using annual average exchange rates.

Sources: Asian Development Bank (various years a, b), International Monetary Fund (1997), Ramstetter (1996b); World Bank (1995, 1997).

3 MNC production and foreign MNC shares

For detailed notes on these data sources see Lipsey *et al.* (1995) and Ramstetter (1996b). Data for 1991, 1992, or 1993 (depending on the country) are generally taken from these sources. Updates are from the additional sources summarized below.

Japan: data for 1993 from Japan, Ministry of Finance (various years) and Japan, Ministry of International Trade and Industry (1995).

United States: foreign MNC production for 1990–95 are from Fahim-Nader and Zeile (1997) and shares are calculated with GDP data from the sources noted above and STAT-USA (1997).

Hong Kong: data for 1993–94 from Hong Kong, Census and Statistics Department (various issues). All data refer to gross value added of firms with majority- or wholly-foreign plants as a share of all gross value added in manufacturing.

Singapore: data for 1993–1994 from Singapore Economic Development Board (1996). All data refer to gross value added of firms with majority- or wholly-foreign plants as a share of all gross value added in manufacturing.

Taiwan: data for 1992–94 are taken from Republic of China, Investment Commission (various years). All data refer to published MNC shares of production.

Indonesia: data for 1991–94 are extrapolations based on the series in Ramstetter (1996b) and Indonesia, Biro Pusat Statistik (various years). Extrapolations are used because the 1975–90 estimates are from the backcast series which is adjusted for plants not responding to the industrial survey, while the 1991–94 data are from raw data not adjusted in this manner.

Malaysia: data for 1992–94 are from Malaysia, Department of Statistics (various years). All data refer to production of foreign limited companies as shares of GDP.

East-Asian and Anglo-American business systems

Richard Whitley

9.1 Introduction

The post-war success of Japanese firms in Western markets has been accompanied by the widespread recognition that they behave in quite different ways from many Western ones, especially US and British companies. The more recent growth and export success of firms in South Korea (henceforth Korea), Taiwan, Hong Kong and Singapore – the four 'little dragons' – has also highlighted the considerable success and variety of economic systems in East Asia. Firms and markets in these economies not only differ greatly from those in Anglo-American capitalism – including Australia – but also vary considerably among themselves. The post-war Japanese *kaisha* (corporation) is quite different in many important respects from the Korean *chaebol* (conglomerate), and from the Chinese family business (CFB) that dominates the export industries of Taiwan and Hong Kong (see Chapter 6). Additionally, the ways in which these firms deal with each other also differ such that they constitute distinctive business systems, or forms of capitalism (Whitley, 1992a).

These different types of capitalism reflect variations in processes of industrialization – which in turn partly reflect differences in the nature of pre-industrial Japan, Korea and China – and continuing differences in the nature of dominant institutions in these societies. The ways in which the political, financial and labour systems have developed during the twentieth century vary considerably across East Asia and have led to contrasting kinds of firms and market relations becoming established. Continuing differences between these societies mean that these contrasts will remain significant despite the growing interdependence of their economies and firms.

This chapter describes the main characteristics of these varieties of capitalism as distinct business systems. First, the key components and characteristics of business systems as particular forms of economic organization are described. Then a brief section outlines the main features of the Anglo-American business system, which typifies to varying degrees the USA, Australia and New Zealand in the Asia-Pacific region. The main body of the chapter summarizes in turn the central characteristics of the Japanese, Korean and Taiwanese business systems as they have developed over the past four decades or so. Comparisons with the dominant features of Anglo-American business systems are drawn where appropriate. These business systems are treated in a very generalized way in this chapter. The Anglo-American one, in particular, displays considerable variation between the countries and regions in which it operates, and between different sectors. The picture presented here is something of a stereotype which can act as a benchmark against which the distinguishing features of the other systems are compared.

9.2   Components of business systems

In comparing and contrasting the organization of market economies, it is useful to summarize their major characteristics as aspects of particular *business systems*. Business systems are distinctive configurations of firms and markets which have become established in particular institutional contexts as the dominant ways of structuring economic activities (Whitley, 1992b). These contexts are usually national because of the critical role of the nation state in establishing and maintaining property rights and managing economic development and other key institutional arenas such as the labour system. There are three basic components of business systems that vary in particular ways to constitute distinct forms of economic organization. They are:

- the nature of economic agents;
- the nature of market relations;
- the nature of the work co-ordination and control system.

The nature of economic agents

The first basic component of a business system is the nature of the economic agent, or 'firm'. Is it, for instance, the diversified, divisionalized Anglo-American corporation, or the small family business of the Italian industrial districts and overseas Chinese communities (Redding, 1990)? It is important to note here that the privately owned resource-controlling and allocating unit is the object of analysis, not necessarily the individual 'firm' which may be only part of a larger grouping.

Four critical aspects of economic agents that vary between business systems are:

1   The diversity of activities controlled and the capabilities developed, from being narrowly specialized in a single production process, through to some integration of complementary activities in a production chain, to a high degree of vertical and horizontal diversification.

2   The degree and rate of change in central, or 'core', activities, from Western holding companies buying and selling businesses as items in

an investment portfolio to firms committed to particular skills and industries.

3   The extent of owner involvement in, and control over, the management of firms. Portfolio investors in Western, especially Anglo-American, capital markets, for example, typically have little interest in the affairs of any individual firm, as they focus on financial returns from holding particular assets. Banks and other large owners who are locked into the destinies of specific clients, on the other hand, have to take a much greater interest in their success and often share risks with them in undertaking new developments. Personal and family owners, of course, are usually highly involved in the management of their firms.

4   The nature of risk management and growth strategies differ significantly across countries in terms of the degree of internalization of risks and restriction of commitments, and the focus on internal growth as distinct from external acquisitions.

Market organization

The second component of business systems concerns the nature of market relationships between firms. Are they, for example, mostly short term, *ad hoc* and impersonal, as in many commodity markets and Anglo-American industries, or are they more particularistic with longer-term commitments being common between specific firms? And are relations between firms co-ordinated, vertically and/or horizontally, by powerful intermediaries, such as the Japanese general trading companies, or are they highly competitive and predatory with outcomes largely determined by short-term price movements? In general terms, market economies vary considerably in the importance and stability of networks and commitments, and obligations between firms, as is exemplified by the analysis of business groups and networks in East Asia in comparison with Western economies (Hamilton and Biggart, 1988; Orru *et al.*, 1991). Two key aspects of market organization concern:

1   The extent of vertical co-ordination, which refers to the degree to which exchange relationships between suppliers and customers within an industry are repeated and based upon mutual commitments with some knowledge and risk sharing, as well as involving third parties such as banks or trading companies.

2   Horizontal collaboration, which refers to the extent to which agents co-operate in setting standards, lobbying state agencies, negotiating with labour organizations, establishing and monitoring training programmes, etc. within industries, and share information, resources and developments across industries.

Work co-ordination and control

The third component of business systems is the dominant pattern of work co-ordination and control, employment relations and management. Economies clearly differ in the ways in which work is divided, allocated and co-ordinated in major economic agents, and these variations are closely connected to differences in dominant institutions, especially those governing the generation and availability of skilled labour power. This component is not just a matter of bureaucratization and centralization, but rather includes broader considerations of authority relations and personnel policies as part of the general pattern of work organization which has become established in particular market economies. It is the overall way in which economic agents manage their resources and activities that is the focus here, not so much the particular variations in formal organizational structures. Key dimensions here are:

1   the centralization of decision making and control, which concerns the delegation of operational and strategic control to non-owning managers and to lower levels of the hierarchy within organizations;

2   employer–employee interdependence, which refers to the extent to which both employers and employees are locked into each other's destinies and cannot easily change these commitments;

3   manager–worker distance, which concerns the separation between managerial staff and manual workers in terms of their education and skills, conditions of employment and reward systems;

4   discretion over how work is performed varies greatly between business systems with some institutionalizing strong supervisor control while others delegate substantial control to workers, either in groups or individually;

5   specialization, which likewise varies considerably between the rigid, inflexible specification of tasks, jobs and roles characteristic of 'scientific management' principles and the more fluid and diffuse approaches of many Asian firms.

These dimensions of the three basic components of business systems are listed in summary form in Box 9.1 and will be applied to the post-war business systems of Japan, Korea and Taiwan after a brief discussion of the Anglo-American business system.

Box 9.1   Business system components and their key characteristics

The nature of economic agents

1   Diversity of economic activities and capabilities co-ordinated by owners and/or managers.

2   Degree and rate of change of economic activities and capabilities.

3   Extent of owner involvement in, and control over, firm management.

4   Prevalent growth and risk management strategies.

Market organization

1   Extent of vertical co-ordination of inputs and outputs and risk sharing between economic agents in production chains.

2   Extent of horizontal collaboration between firms within an industry and between firms across industries.

Work co-ordination and control

1   Centralization of decision making and control.

2   Extent of employer–employee mutual dependence and commitment.

3   Manager–worker differentiation and separation.

4   Supervisor control of work processes and work organization.

5   Task and role specialization

9.3   The Anglo-American business system in summary

Bearing in mind the general characteristics of a business system outlined in the previous section, how can we characterize the system that typifies the Anglo-American countries? Using the headings in Box 9.1 as a guide, Box 9.2 summarizes the main features of this particular system (Chandler, 1990; Hollingsworth, 1991).

Box 9.2   Characteristics of the Anglo-American business system

Nature of economic agents

1   Diversified and divisionalized firms. Conglomerate operations common.

2   High rate of company formation and death. Take-over and mergers the common means for company expansion.

3   Diversified and arm's length share ownership. Owners see their share holding as a portfolio, with little interest in the direct management of firms. Financial returns stressed. Low levels of small and medium sized firms with family ownership.

4   Low degree of organic internal growth; external acquisition levels high. Risks are internalized rather than shared.

Market organization

1   *Ad hoc* and impersonal market relations; little close networking with suppliers; any vertical integration is 'internal' to firms rather than through external relations.

2   Low levels of horizontal collaboration. Little cross company share holding. Low commitment to industry or sector-wide information exchange, training or lobbying.

Work co-ordination and control

1   Highly centralized strategic decision making and control by managers. Financial targets and control tight and paramount.

2 Frequent job changes for both shop floor and managerial personnel. Reliance on external labour market. Frequent lay-offs.

3 High separation of managers' and workers' reward structures and benefits systems. Inflexible and job-specific compensation schemes.

4 Strong supervision and control of workers, little worker autonomy, low levels of team work and 'trust'.

5 High individual specification of tasks. Little generalized skill competencies. Worker organizations reinforce demarcation structures.

As mentioned in the introductory remarks, the summary in Box 9.2 represents something of a stereotypical view of the Anglo-American system. In fact, there are significant variations between countries and sectors, and the system is subject to dynamic changes that have altered its typical characteristics over the years. But the summary can act as a convenient benchmark for comparisons. Before that is done, however, it is worth going through the features of the system in a little more detail.

The nature of economic agents

As far as the nature of economic agents in the Anglo-American system is concerned, the typical leading firm has been a large diversified corporation, particularly in the 1970s and 1980s. These operate in a range of product markets where there is no necessary connection between the different branches of the business. Firms thus tend to be operated as divisionalized units, with a relatively separated structure of functions within them (marketing, finance, R&D, production units). One feature of this system is the high rate of company formation and extinction. This is partly because of the turbulent nature of the economies in which the firms exist, booms and slumps leading to high birth and death rates for companies as the business cycle takes its course. But it is also due to an endemic feature of the financial systems in these countries, which encourages take-over and merger activity by companies. Company expansion tends to be through the absorption of other companies as much as through internally-generated growth.

The form of the financial systems in Anglo-American economies is a crucial element in the way their business systems work. 'Outside' ownership is prevalent, where individuals and, more importantly, specialist financial institutions own and manage a share portfolio of company assets. There is little direct cross-holding of shares between companies, or ownership by commercial banks. The direct management of companies is left to the managerial 'insiders' who run them, whilst the owners tend to look upon their share holding as a financial asset from which they derive an income. This is often argued to lead to a short-term outlook by the managers of companies, whose main objective is to provide a steady income stream from dividends for their shareholders and to enhance shareholder value. Thus they can often neglect the longer-term productive and innovative development of their companies. One consequence of this has been the relatively low proportions of small and medium sized firms in these systems.

Market organization

The market structure in these systems tends to be organized on an arm's length basis. Separate firms contract between themselves for specific inputs and outputs as discrete organizations. Supply chains are a discrete set of stages, organized via price relationships on a one-to-one competitive basis. Long-term close relationships between suppliers and main firms, seen as part of an extended network of co-operative operations, are relatively rare. Traditionally, the organization of production has relied upon an internal vertical relationship between different stages in a single production process within the firm, though this may be breaking down somewhat as more and more functions are externalized into specialized units. Managerial integration of relatively distinct but related aspects of business activity within the same firm is rather weak. The separation and independent nature of the business units has meant that there is traditionally a low level of commitment to industry-wide bodies which provide technological intelligence, common training and skill development programmes, information on market developments, and the like, and which represent the branch or industry politically at the level of lobbying and bargaining.

Work co-ordination and control

It is when we move to the area of work organization that the main differences amongst the Anglo-American business systems in the Asia-Pacific region emerge. These have traditionally arisen because of different degrees of worker organization. The US economy, for instance, has usually displayed low levels of organized labour, which has had to operate in a generally hostile commercial environment. Australia, on the other hand, has traditionally had high levels of unionized labour, which for long periods was explicitly incorporated, as a kind of 'partner', into many economic and business management decision-making processes. However, bearing these differences in mind, there are some broad common features in the way that work has tended to be organized.

Managerial prerogatives are strongly represented and defended. Strategic decision making is centralized within firms, particularly in the case of financial controls and targets. This is seen as the main way that diversified and divisionalized firms can be monitored and controlled. A second feature is that changing jobs can be common, particularly for top managers, who regularly move in and out of different companies. Further down the job hierarchy, security of tenure is low as lay-offs and redundancies are common. There tends to be a two-tiered labour market, where first resort is to an internal, sometimes informal, recruitment procedure, followed by a resort to the external labour market for outside recruitment. The labour force and the labour market are seen as highly differentiated and discriminating, however. Job demarcation is strong, payment systems discriminate between job grades, and benefit systems within the firm are often highly differentiated and inflexible. 'Social systems' within the firm are hierarchical, with little autonomy granted to workers. Team work is not common, so supervision is strong and ubiquitous.

Where there is strong independent worker organization, the demarcation of work tasks is often high. 'Them and us' attitudes have prevailed, with conflictual relations between management and worker organizations. Generalized skill competencies and flexibility in work organization tend to be low.

This description sums up the main features of the Anglo-American business system. Of course it has developed over the twentieth century and is not static, and, as suggested earlier, there is a lot of variation. An important feature of the system is the way in which it is incorporating elements of the East-Asian, and particularly the Japanese, system as these countries set up businesses within the USA and other Anglo-American economies (especially the UK).

9.4   The Japanese business system

The nature of economic agents

The major locus of authoritative resources control and co-ordination in post-war Japan is the large, industrially specialized corporation, or *kaisha*, run by internally promoted university educated managers with considerable autonomy from shareholders (Abegglen and Stalk, 1985, p.177; Clark, 1979, pp.55–64; Odagiri, 1992; see also Chapter 6). These corporations are enmeshed in extensive networks of mutual obligation and trust which both provide support and constrain strategic choices (Gerlach, 1992).

Considering first their diversity, Japanese companies are relatively specialized in two ways. First, they tend not to incorporate all the production and allied processes required to manufacture particular products into the managerial hierarchy in the way that large corporations do in North America. Second, they tend to restrict their major fields of economic activity to a single industrial sector and diversify within it. Thus, unrelated diversification is lower in Japan than in North America (Kagono *et al.*, 1985, pp.25–49).

Japanese companies concentrate much more on the particular skills and competencies which distinguish them as successful competitors than is common in Anglo-American firms. While the latter typically co-ordinate a considerable variety of activities and functional skills through the authority system, Japanese firms prefer to subcontract many activities which, although essential to their products and services, are basically complementary to their main activity. According to Friedman, 'about 70 per cent of all companies with more than thirty employees subcontract for a proportion of their production needs' (1988, p.146). Subcontracting is often focused on activities which can be relatively easily measured and assessed, such as the production of standardized parts and services. As Clark suggests, while production in America and Britain is a matter of organizing people within companies, in Japan it is a matter of organizing companies and their interconnections (1979, p.64).

This focus on specialized, similar activities relying on the same set of capabilities is echoed by a preference for specializing in a single industry and sector. While diversification into new fields of activity does occur quite often in Japan, this tends to be related to current capabilities, such as Honda moving from motor cycles to cars and Komatsu from construction equipment to forklift vehicles. Furthermore, once established as successful growing companies, these subsidiaries are usually hived off as separate, independent companies. Thus Toyota set up a specialized steel factory in 1935 because they could not find a supplier in Japan who could produce steel of the required quality, but then spun it off as an independent firm, Aichi Steel, in 1940 (Cusumano, 1985, p.63). Similarly, Fujitsu separated itself from its fast growing numerical controlled machine tool and robotics division, Fanuc, in 1972 (Abegglen and Stalk, 1985, p.180). This separation tends to be more thoroughgoing in Japan than in the West, with former subsidiaries developing their own networks and alliances and establishing their own enterprise union (Clark, 1979, p.61; Odagiri, 1992, pp.144–51).

The extensive reliance of large Japanese *kaisha* on subcontracting is closely connected to another significant feature of the Japanese business system: the continued importance of small and medium sized firms. The significance of small firms in Japan, especially in manufacturing, has often been seen as the key to large firm success there because many are tied to large assembly firms who can squeeze them when demand declines. However, this dual structure appears less widespread in the 1960s and 1970s than it was in the 1950s, especially in the machinery industry, and many small firms are less dependent on a single large customer than was once thought (Aoki, 1988, pp.219–23).

A further important characteristic of large firms in Japan is the considerable autonomy their managers have from property rights' holders. Although family share holdings were significant sources of co-ordination and power in the pre-war *zaibatsu* – the diversified holding companies which dominated the Japanese economy up to the Second World War – salaried, college educated managers were relied upon to run them throughout the twentieth century. Since the US occupation, which broke up the *zaibatsu* and prohibited large holding companies, the owner controlled business has largely disappeared from the ranks of large Japanese firms and the separation of ownership from control has become considerable. As Abegglen and Stalk put it, 'the common stock shareholder in the Japanese company is more in the position of a preferred shareholder in a Western company' and has little, if any, voice in corporate affairs (1985, p.184; see also Aoki, 1988, pp.120–7).

These characteristics of large firms in Japan have major implications for the ways in which strategic choices are made and firms develop. The close relationships with suppliers and customers enable them to share risks with business partners but also restrict firms' choices and limit their ability to take major breaks from previous activities. Radical changes in the nature of business activities undertaken by firms are also restricted by the long-term commitment to the current 'core' workforce and its skills that is characteristic of post-war *kaisha*. Kagono *et al.* found that top managers in Japanese firms felt much more constrained in seeking new markets and changing direction by their relations with distributors, customers, suppliers and competitors than did those in US firms in the same industries (1985, p.26).

Additionally, specialization plus extensive subcontracting plus internal promotions to the board of directors and autonomy from outside shareholders encourages incremental decision making rather than long-term grand designs. Change in large Japanese firms is more a process of continual improvement to current operations and developing internal resources than major shifts in direction involving the acquisition of new and different resources. Pressures for short-term financial results are weaker than in the USA and growth goals dominate (Abegglen and Stalk, 1985).

Market organization

The Japanese business system is characterized by high levels of market organization and dominated by strong inter-firm mutual obligation networks, some of which constitute large business groups, such as those formed by the Mitsui, Mitsubishi and Sumitomo associated companies (Hamilton and Biggart, 1988; see also Chapter 6). The relatively specialized nature of many *kaisha* means that transactions which would be co-ordinated internally in most Western societies occur across firms' boundaries in Japan. As a result, the volume of wholesale trade in Japan is four times the volume of retail trade, compared to a ratio of less than two in many Western countries (Dore, 1986, p.80). These transactions are typically organized around relatively long-term commitments between particular firms which range over a variety of exchanges. Networks of such commitments link firms within and across industrial sectors to a much greater extent than is common among Western companies (Clark, 1979, pp.221–2) and facilitate information exchange, joint technical development and risk sharing. While some of these networks are based on share swaps and joint ownership of other companies' shares, firms are also connected through joint financing of new ventures, joint production agreements and the development of common distribution channels.

Because firms tend to trade with a relatively small number of specific partners on a long-term basis, they compete for partnerships covering many transactions with customers rather than for individual, one-off sales. Thus, market exchanges in Japan are more specific to, and reciprocal with, particular economic actors than in many Western countries. They are more organized in the sense that they typically occur repeatedly between specific firms and incorporate a number of transactions. They also tend to be linked to broad obligation and trust relations (Sako, 1992).

A particularly important feature of these quasi-contractual networks is the emergence of stable business groups which collectively dominate the Japanese economy. These groups consist of quite large numbers of independent firms which are linked by a number of means, such as mutual share holdings, sharing information, managers and sometimes investments, on a long-term basis (Gerlach, 1992; Orru et al., 1991; Westney, 1996). Two major kinds of business groups can be distinguished: vertically organized *keiretsu* and horizontally connected inter-market groups, or *kigyo shudan* (Odagiri, 1992, pp.167–88). The former, such as those co-ordinated by the major car assemblers Toyota and Nissan, co-ordinate flows within a particular sector or industry, while the latter, such as Mitsui and Mitsubishi, link activities in different sectors, including financial services and international trade. Whereas the former tend to be dominated by a single large prime contractor, the latter groups are less hierarchically organized and there is not usually a central co-ordinating agency.

The sixteen largest business groups of both kinds contained 65 of the largest 100 firms in Japan in 1980, controlled 26 per cent of the total paid up capital of all non-financial enterprises, sold 33 per cent of all manufactured goods by value and employed a fifth of the total manufacturing workforce (Orru et al., 1991). Collectively they dominate the financial services and manufacturing sectors, especially in transportation equipment, chemicals, electronics, basic metals and petroleum. While not integrated through formal authority structures, these extensive and cohesive networks of reciprocal share holdings, joint ventures and information sharing co-ordinate a wide variety of economic activities in Japan.

The largest vertically linked business groups grew out of the networks of subcontractors already described. Thus among the ten largest 'independent' and 'semi-independent' groups are those organized by Nissan, Hitachi, Matsushita and Toshiba-IHI. They include their major subcontractors as well as successful subsidiaries that have been set up as separate companies. Additionally, two large, more diversified groups have formed around the Tokai Bank and the Industrial Bank of Japan (Orru et al., 1991). These latter groups, and others based upon department stores and railway companies, tend to be less integrated and cohesive than the vertically linked networks dominated by a single large parent company, or the six largest inter-market groups.

Work co-ordination and control

Turning now to consider how work is organized and controlled inside large Japanese firms in the post-war period, the most marked contrasts with US corporations concern the division of labour, together with differences in the work group discretion and performance assessment, and employment policies. Essentially, jobs and responsibilities are less individually specific and separate in Japanese firms and roles often overlap (Kagono *et al.*, 1985, pp.112–21; Koike, 1987). Such overlap is easier to manage when employers and core employees are highly dependent upon each other and expect to be working together for a long time, as in the Japanese organization-based employment system (Dore, 1986). The dominant unit of work performance and assessment is the work group rather than the individual and, despite elaborate work manuals, these groups have considerable latitude in deciding how tasks are to be carried out (Lincoln and Kalleberg, 1990, pp.85–9).

Responsibilities for making decisions are also shared and collective to a much greater extent in Japan than in many Western firms. The *ringi* system of circulating proposals and suggestions for approval by all interested parties before final approval by top management ensures widespread commitment before decisions are made and diffuses responsibility for it. As Clark puts it: 'In Japan [decision making] is presented as collective until it is worth someone's while to claim a decision as his own' (1979, p.130). In general, individual authority to commit resources is highly constrained and restricted so that managers usually have to obtain the support of colleagues for any substantial project and cannot make decisions independently. Thus, departments and sections are not regarded as 'belonging' to their heads in the way some Western managers consider they have the right to control 'their' organizational unit. Because of overlapping responsibilities and limited individual authority, ownership is shared and collective rather than specific to the individual manager (Clark, 1979, pp.126–34).

The considerable reliance on 'bottom up' ways of initiating change in Japanese firms, exemplified by the *ringi* system, suggests that decision making is less centralized in practice than purely formal measures of the source of ultimate authorization would suggest (Lincoln and Kalleberg, 1990, pp.206–10). While top management often has to agree to proposals, in many cases this is largely a formality once the circulation of the *ringi* has produced widespread support. Furthermore, where top management suggests changes which are not wholeheartedly supported by middle management groups, they may not be carried through.

This strong role of middle managers in large Japanese firms is linked to the distinctive nature of their employment policies. The institutionalization of long-term employment commitments to the 'core' workforce – which has been extended to most male manual workers in large companies since the war (Koike, 1987; 1994) – together with a correspondingly high dependence of employees on their particular employer, has facilitated the development of trust and common commitments among different groups of managers and workers. Delegation of significant influence to middle managers is obviously easier when nearly all male employees have spent their working lives in the same firm and are dependent on its success.

The long-term employment system in large Japanese companies excludes most women, who typically leave upon marriage or the birth of their first child, as well as 'temporary' workers (Clark, 1979). It thus applies to male high school and university graduates who work until they are 55 or 60 for the same employer and are effectively locked into its fate through seniority-based reward systems, bonus payments, corporate welfare programmes and the high social status associated with membership of a large and successful company. Movement to another firm is usually regarded as a sign of failure and disloyalty, and can often result in large salary reductions as well as loss of ancillary benefits.

This high level of dependence upon the 'permanent' core workforce of large Japanese firms means that managers rely on skill flexibility and intra-firm mobility between tasks and roles to deal with economic change and have to generate considerable commitment to corporate objectives among employees (Aoki, 1988, pp.50–71). Since enforced redundancy of core employees is often taken as a sign of managerial incompetence among large employers, and sometimes a cause for top managers to resign (Dore, 1986, pp.88–119), competitive pressures require extensive on-the-job retraining and skill development, together with frequent job changes and, sometimes, mobility between work sites. The high rate of successful technological change in Japanese factories reflects, and requires, worker acceptance of the need for role flexibility which, in turn, is based on relatively high levels of mutual trust (Abegglen and Stalk, 1985, pp.130–2), in addition to increasing competition for promotion (Koike, 1994; Odagiri, 1992, pp.50–76). Because employment for the core workforce is a long-term commitment on both sides of the labour 'contract', high levels of flexibility and willingness to change tasks are easier to develop than in firms where the dominant reaction to reductions in demand is enforced redundancies. Essentially, the rigidity of external labour markets for large Japanese firms is counterbalanced by the considerable internal flexibility of employees, while the reverse tends to be the case in the Anglo-American economies.

An important characteristic of the post-war Japanese employment system which encourages employee commitment is the organization of unions on an enterprise basis. Although craft-based and industry-based unions had developed during the process of industrialization in Japan (Dore, 1973, pp.388–403), the dominant pattern in many industries today is one of enterprise unions. Supported by the state and banks, many large firms established these 'second' unions in the early 1950s as a replacement for the more radical industry-wide unions which had developed during the US occupation (Cusumano, 1985, pp.149–74; Dore, 1973, pp.327–9), sometimes after a bitter strike such as that at Nissan in 1953.

In general, the level of unionization of the workforce increases with firm size and unions form an integral part of the managerial system in larger firms. Senior union officials sometimes come from the ranks of middle management and, in some firms, taking on such roles is seen as a useful career move. As Cusumano puts it: 'the union's labour affairs department and the company's personnel department [at Nissan] co-ordinated their activities to the point where, to an outside observer, they seemed almost indistinguishable' (1985, p.171). Union leaders had considerable influence on managerial promotions and managers, in turn, ensured that the union was supported by the workforce. However, Koike (1987) points out that not all enterprise unions are simply creatures of top management in Japan, and strikes and disputes are quite common. Overall, although many unions are members of industry federations which negotiate on annual basic wage increases, there seems little doubt that the enterprise unions are the most important representative unit in the regulation of work and the total reward system and their interests are more tied to the growth and success of the individual firm than are craft- or industry-based unions elsewhere.

The characteristics of the post-war Japanese business system are summarized in Box 9.3.

Box 9.3   Characteristics of the post-war Japanese business system

The nature of economic agents

1   Diversification limited to technologically and/or market related activities.

2   Low rate of change of core activities and capabilities.

3   Low involvement of shareholders in management, but substantial corporate cross share holdings to cement business relationships and limit take-over threats.

4   Growth preferred to short-term profits, risks shared with business partners.

Market organization

1   High degree of vertical co-ordination through customer–supplier networks, trading companies and banks.

2   Strong intra- and inter-industry collaboration through trade associations, inter-market groups, etc.

Work co-ordination and control

1   Strong role of middle management limits centralization in practice.

2   High employer–male employee interdependence in large firms.

3   Low manager–male employee differentiation.

4   Considerable work group discretion over work processes with supervisor involvement.

5   Low individual specialization of tasks and roles.

9.5 The Korean business system

The nature of economic agents

The dominant economic actors in post-Second World War Korea are the fast growing, diversified 'financial cliques', or *chaebol* (see Chapter 6). They dominate the heavy manufacturing and chemical industries sector, with most fields of economic activity being divided between three or four *chaebol*. Even more striking is the domination of the largest five and ten *chaebol*. In 1991, the sales of the top five accounted for just under 50 per cent of Korea's GNP (Fields, 1995, p.7). These also exhibited the greatest growth and diversification rates in the 1970s. As well as dominating many manufacturing industries, the *chaebol* also dominate significant parts of the service sector. In addition, the construction industry has become a favoured route to diversification and many *chaebol* are also active in transport services, insurance and related financial services. Finally, seven large general trading companies which are members of the largest ten *chaebol* have come to dominate Korea's export trade.

These large conglomerates are recent creations. Seventeen of the largest 20 *chaebol* in 1986 were founded after the end of the Japanese colonial period in 1945, and seven were established between 1955 and 1967 (Fields, 1995, p.33). Furthermore, even when the original company was a pre-1945 product, most *chaebol* only developed into diversified firms in the 1960s and 1970s (Kim, 1991). This rapid expansion and diversification was largely directed and underwritten by the state, especially the massive shift into the heavy manufacturing and chemical industries in the 1970s which transformed the *chaebol* into widely diversified conglomerates (Woo, 1991, pp.128–46). As a result, by 1983 'the average *chaebol* had firms operating in five different manufacturing industries' and a 'quarter of its manufacturing workforce employed in industries altogether unrelated to its primary manufacturing activity' (Zeile, 1991, p.307). Furthermore, the top *chaebol* were even more diversified, with their average diversification indices being 'one and a half to two times as large as the averages for the top fifty *chaebol*' (ibid.).

The dominant firms in the Korean economy, then, are fast growing and highly diversified, with an ability to move into totally new fields of activity quickly and successfully under state direction and patronage. It is important to note, though, that the *chaebol* are usually quite vertically integrated, and horizontal diversification typically came after such integration, so that they are not identical to the unrelatedly diversified conglomerates which developed in many Anglo-American economies in the 1980s.

The high level of diversity of economic resources and activities controlled by the *chaebol* since the 1960s provides considerable self-sufficiency and, in general, they perform many more activities 'in-house' rather than relying on subcontractors like the Japanese. For example, the Hyundai Motor Company subcontracts only 40 per cent of the value added in its cars, and most of that is to firms within the Hyundai group (Amsden, 1989, p.184). However, this self-sufficiency refers only to relations with other firms. As already pointed out, the *chaebol* became established under the aegis of the Korean state and remain highly dependent on state supplied and subsidized credit (Woo, 1991, pp.148–75). They have demonstrated this dependence by responding rapidly to state policies promoting new industries and, in particular, exports (Kim, 1991). Thus the *chaebol* are not as isolated from state agencies as the large diversified Anglo-American corporations and are able to rely on the state to share investment risks.

The *chaebol* remain largely family owned and controlled, despite their rapid growth and state pressure to sell shares on the stock market (Kim, 1991). Most of their expansion was funded by state subsidized debt, and so did not dilute family share holdings, and where shares have been publicly issued many were bought back by family-controlled subsidies (Orru *et al.*, 1991; Woo, 1991, p.175). Family ownership here continues to mean largely family control, with most of the leading posts held by family members and/or trusted colleagues from the same region or high school as the founding entrepreneur (Janelli, 1993; Kim, 1991). Ownership and control are thus closely linked in the Korean *chaebol*.

As already indicated, the *chaebol* have grown extremely quickly, and usually at the expense of profitability. Although there are considerable difficulties in relying on the public financial statements of Korean companies (Janelli, 1993, pp.124–9), detailed analyses of the *chaebol* suggest that 'the objective of the firms of the large *chaebol* is not to maximize profits but to maximize sales' (quoted in Janelli, 1993, p.91). Janelli's own analysis of the *chaebol* he studied suggested that 'since 1970, its profits have barely kept pace with its dividends' (1993, p.94). This is because ownership rights are held for control purposes more than for income, and growth has been financed by state provided and subsidized credit rather than out of retained profits. Also critical, of course, is the extra influence with the state that large size can provide and the fierce competition between the *chaebol* for being the largest enterprise group (Kim, 1991).

Market organization

The large size and self-sufficiency of the Korean *chaebol* mean that they exhibit low interdependence with suppliers and customers and are able to dominate small and medium sized firms. Because their dependence on suppliers is lower than in Japan, managers do not have to be so concerned about linkages with them. However, transactions between enterprises in Korea are more personal and particularistic than they are in the USA, and formal details of contracts appear to be less critical in determining a firm's behaviour when unforeseen circumstances arise. According to Janelli's respondents, reputations for fair dealing and showing sensitivity to the needs and circumstances of exchange partners were important aspects of market relations, although it is not clear how much this attitude affected dealings with small firms as opposed to those with other large enterprises (1993, pp.187–92). In general, legal details are less significant in governing inter-firm transactions in Korea than in the USA, but probably more so than in Chinese communities (Kao, 1991; Silin, 1976).

Relations between the *chaebol* tend to be fiercely competitive, with considerable reluctance to co-operate over joint projects such as complementary R&D programmes (Wade, 1990, pp.315–16). New industries are often the site of intense competition for dominance, and the major driving force behind many new investments often appears to be corporate rivalry for the leading position, as in the recent expansion of the petrochemical industry. This high degree of competition between the leading *chaebol*, which has been fuelled by the state's policy of selecting entrants to new industries and opportunities on the basis of competitive success, has severely limited the development of sector-based organizations in Korea (Amsden, 1989, pp.64–76; Wade, 1990). With the exception of the cotton spinning industry in the 1950s and 1960s, there have been few if any industry-wide trade associations or similar bodies promoting co-operation between firms and collectively lobbying the state. Additionally, since the dominant economic actors are highly diversified, their interests in any one sector are less important than they would be in economies where firms are more focused on particular industries, and so the incentives to develop strong sector-based collectivities are correspondingly lower.

Work co-ordination and control

The significance of family ownership and control of the *chaebol* is reflected in the importance of personal authority and the patriarchal management style of the chief executive. In the largest *chaebol*, especially those concentrated in heavy manufacturing industries, there is greater emphasis on formal rules and procedures, but personal discretion over how these are interpreted and applied remains high and it is clear that authority is much more personally focused than in large Japanese corporations (Bae, 1987; Chung *et al.*, 1988). An example of how formal procedures are often less significant than they might at first appear is given by Bae's account of recruitment at Hyundai's car factory in Ulsan (1987, pp.44–9). Although there was a formal requirement for new workers to pass an entrance examination, Bae concludes by saying: 'Despite everything, recruitment of workers at Hyundai is based more on recommendation than on any other consideration' (1987, p.48). Similar practices were observed by Kim (1991) and Janelli (1993) in their studies of large firms, and the use of personal recommendations seems to have become even more marked since the severe labour unrest of the late 1980s, when university students and others joined the *chaebol* as manual workers and became involved in organizing protests and strikes.

The importance of personal authority and avowal of a paternalistic ideology are accompanied by a largely authoritarian, not to say militaristic, management style. Generally, the Korean management system is characterized by top-down decision making, enforcement of vertical hierarchical relationships, low levels of consultation with subordinates, and low levels of trust, both horizontally and vertically (Bae, 1987; Chung *et al.*, 1988). Superiors tend to be seen as remote and less interested in subordinates' concerns or their ability to contribute than in their obedience. As Janelli puts it: 'subordinates advanced the view that the company was like the army' (1993, p.223) and 'in many ways my military experience served as a better guide to behaviour in the office than my understanding of American bureaucracies or South Korean villages and universities' (ibid., p.226). Similarly, Kim describes relations between supervisors and subordinates as 'formal, distant, and authoritarian' (1991, p.150) and cites some of the workers in Poongsan Corporation as viewing hierarchical relations as being worse than in the military.

This remoteness and emphasis on personal authority are echoed by the highly centralized nature of decision making and co-ordination of diverse activities in the Korean *chaebol*. Major decisions are taken personally by the chairman of each group and the top managers of subsidiary companies are clearly subordinated to him. In particular, all senior management positions in the entire group of firms are controlled by the chairman and he often moves managers between subsidiaries. As Amsden puts it: 'The personnel function in general, and the labour relations function in particular, are almost non-existent as a staff responsibility, whether at the group or subsidiary level' (1989, p.325). Managerial careers and rewards are thus directly controlled by the owner and his family, and depend greatly upon personal relationships with them.

The high level of centralization encourages considerable integration of economic activities, as capital, technology and personnel can be centrally allocated and moved between subsidiaries (Kim, 1991). An important role in this central direction and co-ordination of the *chaebol* is played by the secretariat, or planning group, which is the key corporate staff unit under the direct control of the chairman. This group allocates and analyses information from subsidiaries, and elsewhere, evaluates performance and prepares proposals for new ventures and shifting resources. It is largely responsible for co-ordinating plans and mobilizing resources across the whole *chaebol*, so that these diversified conglomerates are in fact managed as cohesive economic entities with a unified group culture focused on the *chaebol* owner. In this respect they are quite different from those Anglo-American conglomerate holding companies in which the central office functions more like a bank than as an integrated planning and control agency, and subsidiaries are simply set annual financial targets as separate, discrete entities.

Turning to consider employment policies, the level of employer–employee commitment is limited for most manual workers in the *chaebol*. Although seniority does appear to be important in affecting wage rates, and employers do provide accommodation and other fringe benefits in the newer industries, Korean firms are reluctant to make the sorts of long-term commitments to their workforce that many large Japanese ones do (Amsden, 1989; Bae, 1987). Mobility between firms, both enforced and voluntary, is considerably greater for manual workers – and some non-manual – than is common in Japan. Annual labour turnover rates of between 52 per cent and 72 per cent were quite usual in the 1970s in Korea, and were especially high in manufacturing industries (Michell, 1988, p.109).

Additionally, leading firms in Korea sometimes poach skilled workers from competitors rather than invest in training programmes (Amsden, 1989, pp.275–87; Janelli, 1993, p.139). Even where workers do not leave very often, this is more because they are locked into their current employer through high levels of overtime pay than because they feel committed to the firm (Bae, 1987), as was demonstrated by the wave of strikes and protests in 1987 and 1988 (Wilkinson, 1994). White collar employees are more favoured and tend to remain with large employers, not least because their pay and conditions are usually substantially better than they could obtain by moving (Janelli, 1993, p.153).

Personnel and reward policies are highly segmented in Korea, especially by gender, education and sector of employment. Women are paid around half of the average male wage and typically work in light, labour-intensive industries such as textiles, apparel, rubber and word processing (Amsden, 1989; Deyo, 1989; Michell, 1988). Men are more concentrated in heavy industry, where they tend to be more highly skilled and where employers take more pains to keep them. Relatedly, the level of formal education strongly affects wage rates, with college graduates being paid around three times the wages of primary school graduates and one and a half times as much as high school graduates. It is very difficult to become a manager in the leading *chaebol* without a college degree, and the differential between managers and production workers is over twice as great in Korea as in the USA (Amsden, 1989, pp.230–1). Employers have thus been able to follow quite different labour management policies according to market conditions, especially in the export-oriented manufacturing sector (Deyo, 1989).

Finally, the organization and control of tasks in the *chaebol* varies between sections of the workforce. The specialization of roles, skills and authority, in particular, is greater for unskilled manual workers than for other employees. According to Bae, 90 per cent of the manual workforce at Hyundai Motors remained at their initial job level and were not systematically upgraded (1987, p.60). Unskilled workers continued to carry out relatively narrow tasks without much movement between jobs and skill categories. Similarly, Kim found a considerable degree of worker specialization at Poongsan Corporation, with only 20 per cent having changed jobs more than once, and then nearly always in the same speciality (1991, p.209). However, more skilled and non-manual workers do appear to be moved between tasks and sections, and sometimes develop more varied skills, in the larger and more diversified *chaebol*. Because of the importance of personal authority in the Korean *chaebol*, jobs and responsibilities are more determined by superiors' wishes than by formal rules. Supervisory discretion means that the division of labour is less formally prescribed in the *chaebol* than in more rule-governed work systems. Overall, then, the degree of specialization is mixed, combining task flexibility and variety for some employees with considerable rigidity and narrowness for unskilled manual workers.

This emphasis on personal authority and control, together with the prevalent ideology of paternalism in most Korean companies, encourages close supervision of task performance. Frequently, the physical layout of office furniture and work space in general is carefully arranged so as to maximize supervisor surveillance of work processes (Janelli, 1993, p.164). Section chiefs and department heads also ensure control by narrowly circumscribing subordinates' tasks and carefully monitoring all messages coming into the work unit and work outputs. Subordinates in general were seen as children, needing firm guidance and direction. As mentioned above, these aspects of the *chaebol* were also related to considerable social distance between superiors and subordinates and permitted considerable personal discretion to supervisors in evaluating the performance and worth of their juniors.

The characteristics of the Korean business system are summarized in Box 9.4.

Box 9.4   Characteristics of the post-war Korean business system

The nature of economic agents

1   High diversification of activities within and across industries.

2   Considerable change in core activities, from light industry in the 1950s to heavy industry in the 1980s, as well as to service sector activities.

3   Strong owner involvement in, and control of, management.

4   Growth goals dominate, with risks shared with the state and state-controlled banks.

Market organization

1   Weak co-ordination of inputs and outputs outside *chaebol* boundaries.

2   Low horizontal collaboration outside *chaebol* boundaries.

Work co-ordination and control

1   High degree of centralization.

2   Low employer–manual worker interdependence and commitment.

3   High manager–manual worker differentiation and distance.

4   Low work-group autonomy and discretion; strong managerial control of work processes.

5   Specialized division of labour for unskilled and semi-skilled manual workers; flexibility expected of skilled and non-manual workers.

9.6 The Taiwanese business system

The nature of economic agents

In Taiwan there are two major types of enterprise: the large state owned firms, which are mostly in the capital-intensive sector, and the small to medium sized family owned and controlled firms in the export sector. As Wade points out: 'From the early 1950s onward Taiwan has had one of the biggest public enterprise sectors outside the communist bloc and Sub-Saharan Africa' (1990, p.176), and public enterprises contributed about twice as much to GDP as their equivalents in Korea in the 1970s. Similarly, their share of gross fixed capital formation was well over 30 per cent in that decade when Korea's was under a quarter and Japan's under an eighth. Indeed, the only Asian countries with a comparable public sector contribution to capital investment were India and Burma. In 1980 the Taiwanese Ministry of Economic Affairs owned firms in the power, petroleum, mining, aluminium, phosphates, alkali, sugar, chemicals, fertilizers, petrochemicals, steel, shipbuilding, engineering and machinery industries, while the Ministry of Finance owned four banks and eight insurance companies (Wade, 1990, p.178). These public enterprises were very large by comparison with privately owned ones and often dominated, if not monopolized, their sectors. Thus the state has retained ownership and control of the 'commanding heights' of the economy in Taiwan, especially the upstream capital intensive sectors.

The private sector does have some large enterprises, often established with state support, such as Nanya Plastics, but it is much less concentrated than its Korean equivalent. In 1990 those in the private sector employing under 300 people employed 70 per cent of the labour force and produced 60 per cent of Taiwan's exports (Fields, 1995, p.64). Furthermore, while the number of manufacturing firms increased 250 per cent between 1966 and 1976, the number of employees per firm grew by only 29 per cent, in strong contrast to Korea where the employment total per firm doubled in the same period. These smaller companies dominate the export trade; those with under 300 employees accounted for 65 per cent of manufactured exports in 1985 (Wade, 1990, p.70). It should, however, be borne in mind that many of these smaller firms are members of socially linked business groups, of which the largest 100 generated sales amounting to 34 per cent of Taiwan's GNP, and in 1991 the ten largest employed 12.6 per cent of the total workforce (Fields, 1995, pp.64–5; Hamilton and Biggart, 1988; Hamilton and Kao, 1990). These groups are not, though, nearly as tightly integrated and controlled as the Korean *chaebol*, but are more akin to personally connected networks. Furthermore, many larger private manufacturing enterprises remain single unit firms and do not form business groups. Overall, then, the Taiwanese economy is dualistic, with the large state enterprises dominating the inputs of the many smaller firms in the export sector.

Vertical integration is weak in privately-owned Taiwanese firms and they are rarely self-sufficient in terms of combining the management of key processes and activities in one organization. Instead, they are usually highly interdependent with other enterprises for inputs and for distributing their outputs, and form fluid sub-contracting networks (Hamilton and Kao, 1990; Redding, 1990). However, this interdependence is not usually accompanied by a willingness to share long-term risks with suppliers and buyers. Instead, more restricted and limited connections are preferred.

Diversification of a horizontal nature – 'opportunistic' in Hamilton and Kao's (1990) terms – is, though, more widespread in private firms, especially those forming business groups of associated companies. While by no means all successful firms develop into highly diversified business groups, including some of the largest, those that do diversify tend to move into a variety of sectors in a seemingly *ad hoc* and idiosyncratic way, often as the result of personal requests or obligations. Additionally, they appear able to switch products and markets quite readily in response to changing patterns of demand (Redding, 1990).

An important point about such diversification and growth is that it is not usually associated with managerial integration, but rather is achieved by setting up legally separate firms linked through common ownership and family management. Diversification is thus informal and, typically, personal. Each firm, in the sense of a formal management structure, tends to be quite specialized in its resources and spheres of economic activities, but families may well invest in and control a variety of businesses. While leading managers of each firm in a business group may well be members of the same family, they are not usually structured into a distinct hierarchy of authority relations. Overall, then, managerial diversification is limited in Chinese family businesses (CFBs), although entrepreneurial diversification can be much greater.

These firms are nearly all owned and controlled by families, as indeed are most Chinese businesses throughout South-East Asia (Redding, 1990). Owners are highly involved in the running of their firms and there are strong connections between ownership and direction of economic activities. Wong (1988, pp.170–2) has characterized the pervasive economic ethos generating this strong drive towards autonomy and proprietorship in Chinese communities as 'entrepreneurial familism' which has led to high rates of new firm formation in Taiwan, Hong Kong and elsewhere as families seek to be in control of their own businesses (see Gates, 1987; Greenhalgh, 1984). This emphasis on family ownership and control means that the dominant goal is the acquisition and growth of family wealth rather than the growth of the firm as a separate entity. The pursuit of large size irrespective of profitability is not the dominant objective in these firms, especially if it could lead to the loss of personal control or to being considered a threat to the interests of the family firm. It also discourages risk sharing and long-term mutual commitments between firms.

Market organization

The specialization and interdependence of Taiwanese family businesses mean that they have to rely on each other to obtain inputs for their products and services and to distribute and market them. Thus multiple market connections between firms are crucial to their operation. However, these are not necessarily long term or based on mutual obligations. Rather, inter-firm links are often managed in such a way as to reduce risks, and so commitments to other economic actors are restricted. Exchange partners may, then, be numerous and selected on the basis of their personal reputations for competence and reliability, but do not usually form networks of long-term trust and reciprocal loyalty (Redding, 1990). Sub-contracting, for instance, may involve a number of firms without any long-term commitment to continued orders being implied. Similarly, trading companies may select a particular supplier to fulfil an order without any obligation to do so for successive orders. Market relations can thus change rapidly and are quite fluid, flexibility being emphasized over long-term risk sharing (Hamilton and Kao, 1990).

Business partnerships, on the other hand, often do involve long-term reciprocal commitments and can lead to the development of elaborate networks of personal obligation which structure strategic decisions and new ventures (Kao, 1991). Where significant resources are involved and firms need to undertake activities jointly, connections are highly personal and dependent on trust between the owners. Without high levels of personal trust, such partnerships cannot be formed successfully in Taiwan and, as a result, many medium sized firms do not grow into large enterprises because they are unable to find partners they can rely on. While straightforward trading relationships, then, are quite limited in their mutual commitment, more substantial alliances and joint activities involve considerable personal obligations, often on a long-term basis. Even here, though, flexibility is valued, and families will often prefer to establish new ventures with a number of different partners rather than expand existing ones with their current associates (Hamilton and Kao, 1990).

Inter-firm connections are, then, highly personal, and form extensive networks of mutual, albeit often asymmetric, obligations, without developing into the sorts of long-term, wide-ranging inter-organizational linkages found in the Japanese inter-market groups (Hamilton and Biggart, 1988; Orru et al., 1991). Indeed, when the Taiwanese state did try to encourage the formation of Japanese style sub-contracting arrangements, they failed (Hamilton and Biggart, 1988). Equally, attempts to establish trading companies as long-term co-ordinating agencies in Taiwan have been less successful than in Korea, and there are few major intermediaries performing similar functions to the Japanese *sogo shosha* or German banks (Wade, 1990, pp.160–5).

Sectoral organizations are also limited by this concern with personal control, as well as being restricted by the state's intolerance of independent intermediary organizations, particularly those dominated by Taiwanese (Wade, 1990). Additionally, given the flexibility of most CFBs and their unwillingness to commit major resources to any single industry or activity for a long time, stable associations of industry-specific enterprises are difficult to maintain. However, the high population density in Taiwan – and of course in Hong Kong too – combined with considerable cultural homogeneity among the Taiwanese, has encouraged a strong reliance on reputation as the primary means of ensuring compliance with exchange commitments in the absence of an independent and reliable legal system (Gates, 1987; Greenhalgh, 1984; Silin, 1976).

Work co-ordination and control

One of the most significant characteristics of CFBs is the highly personal nature of authority relationships and the concentration of authority in the paternalistic owner (Deyo, 1989; Kao, 1991; Redding, 1990; Silin, 1976). Formal rules and procedures do exist in the larger firms, but these are less important in controlling activities than the personal decisions of owners, and formal status in the managerial hierarchy is often less significant than a manager's personal ties to the owner. As Silin suggests, 'the primary goal of the executive is then to secure and increase the respect of the boss, that is, to increase personal interaction with him' (1976, p.67). Despite the growing tendency for owner-managers to have been educated in Western universities and business schools, and increasing claims that they follow 'modern' management methods, there is little evidence to suggest that the highly personal nature of authority in Chinese firms has diminished (Redding, 1990).

As well as being personal, authority is also quite remote and distant in Chinese businesses. According to Silin, leadership is typically seen as a moral quality of individuals rather than as a technical skill which can be modified or taught (1976, pp.57–66). This emphasis on moral superiority means that the owner is sharply distinguished from employees, including managers, and is the source of the business 'wisdom' which guides decisions. As a result, the morally inferior cannot legitimately question his choices and are rarely called upon to contribute to the decision-making process. Centralization is thus high in CFBs, especially for financial, marketing and personnel decisions, which are usually made by the owner (Redding, 1990, pp.174–5). Even when there is a formal hierarchy, middle managers are often bypassed because of a lack of trust in formal accounting systems and subordinates and a strong preference for personal contact (Silin, 1976, pp.74–85).

This centralization of control within firms ensures that activities are tightly integrated, but the diverse and often unconnected nature of activities in many business groups in Taiwan mean that their formal co-ordination is weak. However, the strong personal ties between subsidiary heads and the owning family – often the same people – enable close collaboration and control to be maintained. This is especially true for entrepreneurial as distinct from operational management issues. While, then, the actual operations of each sub-unit may not be very closely integrated – and certainly not as much as in the Korean *chaebol* or Japanese corporations – they are by no means run as discrete entities under the umbrella of a relatively remote holding company. Rather, key resources may be switched between them and strategic choices are made by the group owner through direct personal links.

The personal nature of authority relations in Chinese family firms and the strong ideology of paternalism encourage considerable expectations of reciprocity in employment policies and practices. However, these are mitigated when there is little prior basis for personal commitments and employees were previously strangers. In practice, obligations become more attenuated as connections become more distant from the basic family unit. Thus, the strongest ties and sense of commitment occur between family members, somewhat weaker ones between schoolmates, neighbours and more distant kin, and the weakest ones between those who were strangers before employment. Long-term commitments and seniority-based promotion practices tend to be reserved for those workers with strong personal ties to the owner, while previously unknown staff hired through impersonal channels neither expect nor receive such commitments. In particular, young, female, semi-skilled, non-family workers in the light manufacturing export sector are expected to stay for a short time only and are rarely trained for more demanding posts (Deyo, 1989; Gates, 1987). As in Korea, women in general tend to be worse off than men, and white-collar staff are better treated than many manual workers, though these differences do not seem so rigid and sharply institutionalized in Taiwanese firms (Gates, 1987; Silin, 1976). In general, the segmentation of labour markets by gender and qualification is less strong here than in Korea and Japan (see Chapter 5).

Because senior managerial posts are restricted to family members or those who have family-like connections to the owner, many skilled workers and managers prefer to leave and start up their own businesses once they have acquired business skills and some capital (Greenhalgh, 1984; Wong, 1988). Both the general cultural preference for personal business ownership over employment, and the unwillingness to trust non-family subordinates on the part of employers, limit the scope and length of employer–employee commitments in the Chinese family business.

With regard to task structure and control, the importance of personal relationships and authority in CFBs means that formal specification of roles and positions is less important than in most Western societies. Equally, jobs and skills are not rigidly defined and separated by formal procedures, but are fairly broad and flexible. In the large Taiwanese firm studied by Silin (1976), roles were fluidly defined, many managers held multiple positions and their responsibilities were liable to be changed suddenly at the behest of the owner. Similarly, many managers in Taiwanese business groups hold a considerable number of posts and are rarely restricted to a single specialized role (Hamilton and Kao, 1990). Overall, then, role and authority specialization are low in these firms.

The strong commitment to patriarchal relationships in the workplace, and in society as a whole, means that superior–subordinate relations are quite remote and distant, particularly those between the owner-manager and employees (Redding, 1990; Silin, 1976). Similarly, as in Korea, paternalism implies a lack of confidence in the abilities and commitment of staff, so that close supervision of work performance is a feature of Taiwanese firms, as is considerable personal discretion in how authority is exercised, especially at the top of the enterprise.

The characteristics of private Taiwanese businesses are summarized in Box 9.5.

Box 9.5   Characteristics of the post-war Taiwanese business system

The nature of economic agents

1   Specialized organizations combined with diversified family-owned businesses.

2   Considerable changes in family business activities.

3   Strong owner involvement in, and control of, management.

4   Profitability and growth important; opportunistic diversification in family businesses; risks managed through limiting commitments and high degree of flexibility.

Market organization

1   Low vertical co-ordination.

2   Low horizontal collaboration except in personally linked partnerships and business groups.

Work co-ordination and control

1   High degree of centralization.

2   Low employer–manual worker interdependence and commitment beyond family-like personal attachments.

3   High manager–manual worker distance and owning family–manager separation.

4   Low task and role specialization except for female semi-skilled workers.

5   Specialized division of labour for unskilled and semi-skilled manual workers; flexibility expected of skilled and non-manual workers.

9.7   Overall comparisons

As Box 9.6 shows, many of the characteristics of the business systems in Japan, Korea and Taiwan vary quite sharply, as well as being distinct from those of Anglo-American business systems as summarized in Box 9.2. In particular, the Japanese business system differs from those of Korea and Taiwan in a number of dimensions. The latter differ most significantly in the nature of dominant firms, while sharing many characteristics in the work co-ordination and control area. The distinctiveness of the Japanese

Box 9.6 *Summary of characteristics of post-war East-Asian and Anglo-American business systems*

Characteristics	Business system			
	Japan	Korea	Taiwan	Anglo-American
The nature of economic agents				
1 Diversity of activities	limited	high	low except for opportunistic diversification	high
2 Rate of change of activities	low	high	considerable	considerable
3 Owner involvement and control	low	high	high	low
4 Risk and growth strategies	risk-sharing with partners	diversification and state support	flexibility, opportunism	diversification, growth through acquisition as well as organically
Market organization				
1 Extent of vertical co-ordination	high	low	low	low
2 Extent of horizontal co-operation between firms	high	low	low except for personal connections	low
Work co-ordination and control				
1 Centralization of decision making and control	low in practice	high	high	medium
2 Extent and scope of employer–employee interdependence and commitment	high	low	low	low
3 Manager–worker distance and differentiation	limited	high	high	medium
4 Work-group task discretion	considerable	low	limited	limited
5 Specialization of tasks, roles and skills	low	low except for non-skilled	low	high

system results partly from its pre-industrial legacy and the associated pattern of industrialization, and partly from the institutional changes made during the US occupation of 1945–52. Many of the common characteristics found in Korea and Taiwan similarly stem from particular features of pre-industrial China and Korea, together with the consequences of Japanese colonial rule over Korea and Taiwan during the first half of the twentieth century and the authoritarian states that directed industrialization in both economies (Whitley, 1992a).

9.8   Changes in East-Asian business systems: globalization and institutional developments

In the past decade or so, a number of significant changes have occurred in the Asia-Pacific which could modify some of these characteristics of East-Asian business systems. Three are especially important. First, the inter-dependence of national economies and firms has grown dramatically as Japanese, and then Korean and Taiwanese, outward investment to other economies, particularly China, increased in the 1980s and 1990s. Second, as these economies have industrialized and developed, their complexity and internal differentiation have increased considerably and growth rates, particularly in Japan, have levelled off. Third, domestic institutions, especially political systems, have changed and this has affected state–business relations. After a brief discussion of the first of these three, this section considers the impact of these phenomena on the Japanese, Korean and Taiwanese business systems.

International economic interdependencies

The recent and current increase in intra-regional trade and investment in the Asia-Pacific is a major component of what many observers see as the globalization of economic activity at the end of the twentieth century. Not only has trade between industrialized economies grown considerably, but more of it is being managed within corporate boundaries and co-ordinated across national borders. As national firms internationalize their operations, we might expect them to become more detached from domestic institutions and agencies, especially the state, and develop more 'international' charactcristics which thcn modify domcstic busincss systcms. In this vicw, the relatively homogenous and distinctive business systems of Japan, Korea and Taiwan should change towards more standardized forms of economic organization.

However, it is important to note that this growth in outward investment from these three economies has not been matched by a correspondingly large inflow of foreign direct investment, or of large firms seeking to raise the bulk of their new investment from international capital markets. Thus, the impact of foreign firms and external ways of organizing economic activities on Japan, Korea and Taiwan has been much less than the impact of firms from these three countries on the other economies of the Asia-Pacific. Indeed, the reproduction of many aspects of inter-firm relations by Japanese companies in foreign locations, as well as some labour management practices, suggests that internationalization here means more the externalization and generalization of Japanese ways of doing business to other societies than the transformation of their domestic economies by foreign patterns of economic organization. Similarly, the restructuring of 'global commodity chains' (Gereffi, 1996; see also Whitley, 1996) has not yet resulted in major changes to the nature and organization of economic agents in Korea and Taiwan (see also Chapter 14).

Additionally, the increasing complexity of domestic economies, and slowing of their growth rates, might be expected to modify the ability of the state to manage economic development and, in particular, to direct the activities of large companies. In the cases of Korea and Taiwan, the role of the state in the economy may become more like the post-war Japanese co-ordinating agency than the more directive and authoritarian agency of most of the post-war period. This tendency is likely to be enhanced by the recent democratization and liberalization of the state in these countries, although the geo-political context and the traditionally high prestige of the state in these societies will limit the reduction of the state's role in managing economic and social development. Insofar as the state continues to become more democratic and open to political competition in Korea and Taiwan, business dependence on the state will probably decline (Kim, 1991), but this does not mean that state–business relations are becoming more Anglo-American. The state remains very powerful in these societies, and firms are unlikely to be able to ignore state policies or agents in their strategic choices.

Changes in Japan

Despite the growth in Japan of foreign portfolio investment and, in some cases, direct foreign acquisition of substantial share holdings in Japanese firms, the extensive networks of reciprocal share holdings and broad business relationships between banks, trust companies, insurance companies and inter-market group members remain important features of the Japanese economy, and share ownership between firms is more often an expression of long-term business commitments than a narrowly focused financial connection. Moreover, substantial foreign share ownership does not confer control, and senior managers continue to enjoy high levels of autonomy from beneficial owners and are not subject to a market for corporate control. Despite low capital gains and dividend payouts in the recession, insurance companies and other large shareholders do not seem to have required radical changes in financial policies or managerial personnel.

Equally, the growth of outward foreign direct investment (FDI) does not seem to have greatly weakened inter-firm ties within Japan. While the inter-market inheritors of the *zaibatsu* may have declined in significance relative to the vertically quasi-integrated *keiretsu* as new industries have developed (see Chapter 6), and the role of the general trading companies has changed to include third party transactions, the overall importance of business groups and particularistic, obligational links between firms does not appear to have declined (Gerlach, 1992; Sako, 1992; Westney, 1996). As large companies have relocated some of their plants to China and elsewhere in the Asia-Pacific, many suppliers have followed to maintain established ties. The comparatively long recession in the 1990s and rise of the yen since 1985 have likewise encouraged considerable restructuring of many large firms and relocation of many plants to China and elsewhere. Most of the labour surplus resulting from the 1980s expansion and its reverse has, however, been managed by established procedures such as 'lending' staff to subsidiaries and sub-contractors, reducing bonus payments and 'temporary' workers, encouraging early retirements, ceasing graduate recruitment and changing jobs rather than engaging in widespread compulsory redundancies. Long-term interdependencies between large employers and their core workforce seem to have survived the early 1990s, and established patterns of work co-ordination and control also do not appear to have changed greatly (Koike, 1994). Given the systemic nature of the post-war Japanese business system, and the limited degree of institutional change that has occurred in the past 20 or so years, this is perhaps not too surprising.

Overall, then, the diversity of institutional contexts of Japanese FDI, the dominant position of many firms in their sectors, often on a worldwide basis, continued commitment to, and dependence on, the Japanese economy and institutions, together with incremental and limited institutional change in Japan, have limited the extent of change in the nature of firms and markets there. A few characteristics of the post-war Japanese business system have been modified, such as the close interdependence between main banks and their major clients and the co-ordination role of the *sogo shosha*. But as successful firms became cash rich and integrated forward into distribution and marketing, substantial changes of the key dimensions discussed above have *not* occurred. Furthermore, they are unlikely to as long as leading firms remain tied to the Japanese economy and its institutions – assuming these latter do not change radically – and to regional economies that they can dominate. Incremental change seems much more probable than discontinuous shifts in firm type and priorities, and certainly a move to Anglo-American forms of economic organization is most unlikely given the limited influence of international capital markets in Japan, the low rate of US and UK FDI into Japan and the success of many Japanese firms in exporting many aspects of their form of capitalism.

Changes in Korea

In the case of Korea, both the extent of internationalization of the *chaebol* activities and of foreign influence on the Korean economy are less than in Japan. However, the move to a civilian presidential regime, greater toleration of opposition political parties and independent trade unions, as well as growing international pressure against overt state financial support of the *chaebol* and bureaucratic regulation of economic activities, represent considerable changes in the institutional context of the Korean business system which are likely to affect the ways in which the *chaebol* develop. As Woo (1991) and Kim (1989) among others have noted, the largest *chaebol* are not so dependent on the state as they were in the 1960s and 1970s, and manifestations of disobedience of state decisions and wishes have become more noticeable in the 1990s, particularly concerning entry into sectors such as cars, petrochemicals and steel and the divestment of owner control. Economic growth, educational expansion and the decline of demographic growth have also resulted in the increase of an educated middle class and a reluctance of many workers to undertake dirty and dangerous jobs at low wages.

The relative liberalization of state direction of the economy and the development of some political competition and of genuine labour representation, together with its greater complexity, seem likely to encourage some decentralization of control within the *chaebol*, as well as the development of horizontal links between them, as the degree of vertical dependence on the state, and the associated overwhelming dominance of political risk, declines. Insofar as diversification was a response to this dependence, it may also decline, as of course the state has requested. However, since overall size remains a crucial feature of *chaebol* success and power, and their growing ability to generate cash reduces their dependence on the state-governed banks, it seems unlikely that they will dispose of substantial subsidiaries, particularly if they think their rivals will acquire them. Relatedly, the strong emphasis on owner control – rather than passive portfolio management – on the part of the owning families in Korea (Janelli, 1993), seems likely to limit internal decentralization, at least as long as trust in formal procedures and institutions remains low.

The rapid expansion of overseas facilities and attempts to compete more on the basis of advanced technologies and innovative products may, of course, encourage less directive and personal managerial practices as organizational complexity grows. However, the *chaebol* remain highly dependent on their home economy and institutions so that the influence of foreign investments remains limited. Additionally, they too are investing quite heavily in China and other parts of the Asia-Pacific, so that they are not dependent on a single type of foreign location with its possibly sharply different institutional context. So far there seems little indication that family owners are willing to hand over the reins of power to 'professional' managers, despite some restructuring of top management and the reduction in size of the chairman's secretariat in some *chaebol*. Similarly, the extent of risk sharing between *chaebol* in new developments remains limited, despite state encouragement in some cases, as does their development of long-term commitments to smaller suppliers and small and medium sized enterprises in general.

Perhaps the most likely area of change in the Korean business system concerns labour management and work structure. Both institutional changes and the increasing complexity of operations and tasks might be expected to encourage some *chaebol* to develop 'Japanese' forms of labour relations and flexibility – as Amsden (1989) claims to have found at the Pohang Iron and Steel Company. As labour markets tighten and workers' skills become more important in improving products and productivity, eliciting commitment from at least the core manual workforce to contribute to corporate goals and use their initiative in a positive manner could gain priority over earlier managerial objectives (You, 1994). Investment in training and internal career ladders for manual workers can thus be expected to grow, as can the use of bonuses and 'fringe' benefits to retain skilled staff. Whether authoritarian supervision practices and tight control over task performance will change dramatically, given recent Korean history and the continued military threat from the North, remains questionable, but outright repression seems less likely to be effective as a labour management strategy.

An important factor affecting the development of new employment policies and supervisory practices is the role of the unions. In particular, the relative strength of independent unions, and whether they are organized on an enterprise, sector or national basis, will obviously influence owners' and managers' investments in the 'white collarization' of manual workers. The highly political nature of union organization and competition in Korea, especially the state insistence on a company-union structure and unwillingness to recognize the independent Korea Confederation of Trade Unions, suggests that Japanese levels of employer–employee interdependence and commitment are unlikely to become institutionalized in the near future. As long as the major employers rely on the state to manage labour disputes and labour organizations are political as well as bargaining entities, together with the continuing distrust between employers and employees resulting from authoritarian management practices and *chaebol* ties to the military-backed regime, it is difficult to see how radically new forms of labour management are going to develop in Korea.

A further constraint on the incorporation of the male manual workforce into full membership of the corporate 'family' is the traditional disdain of manual labour in Korea and the high prestige of, and returns to, formal education, especially in non-technical subjects (Amsden, 1989; Michell, 1988). The labour force remains highly stratified by the formal educational system and manual skills in manufacturing continue to be regarded as less valuable than white-collar skills certified by higher education institutions. As Cho puts it, 'the wide wage differentials between production and clerical types of work do not necessarily reflect differences in their respective productivity' (1994, pp.93–4; see also You, 1994). Since 1987–89, despite the substantial increases in production workers' real wages and some narrowing of differentials, there seems little evidence that these distinctions and prestige rankings have changed significantly in Korea, and so the establishment of Japanese forms of employment commitment to manual workers remains difficult there. Indeed, the intensification of the relocation of many *chaebol* production facilities to China and other cheap labour sites after the strikes and sit-ins of the late 1980s suggests that large employers in Korea find it easier to search for new workers than to implement quite different ways of managing current ones (Wilkinson, 1994, pp.106–7).

Overall, then, the owner-controlled *chaebol* remain quite strongly tied to the Korean economy and the state, despite their growing overseas investment, strong cash flow and the weakening of the state's control over the economy as it has become more complex and political liberalization has grown. The highly diversified, centralized and risk-taking nature of the *chaebol* does not appear to have been greatly modified over the past decade, although some changes in managerial structures and practices have occurred in some of them. Despite government exhortations to support small and medium sized enterprises (SMEs), some policies to assist them, and periodic efforts to restrict the growth and range of activities of the *chaebol*, the Korean economy remains dominated by the *chaebol*, who continue to behave in the 1990s as they did before (Cho, 1994; You, 1994). Significant changes to the Korean business system, then, have not yet taken place, and probably would require much more radical changes in the role of the state than have occurred so far.

Changes in Taiwan

In the case of Taiwan, the democratization of the state and the election of a native Taiwanese as President, coupled with the extensive outflow of investment to China and ASEAN countries, might be thought to reduce the differentiation of Kuomintang (KMT) controlled upstream enterprises from Taiwanese CFBs in export industries and, perhaps, encourage a move away from original equipment manufacturing strategies to more integrated manufacturing and marketing organizations. As the mainlander–Taiwanese divide reduces, and the state becomes more responsive to Taiwanese economic interests, the growth of more Taiwanese firms into large companies with state assistance, especially in research and development activities, could be anticipated, especially if the banking system is reformed and encouraged to invest in smaller firms. Relatedly, the internationalization of operations and investment in distribution and marketing channels in North America and Europe by some CFBs can be seen as leading to the development of more integrated organizations which, perhaps, are becoming less personally controlled by owning families. The liberalization of labour legislation and some loosening of KMT control over unions (Wilkinson, 1994) might also herald less autocratic management practices and greater tolerance of worker autonomy and bargaining rights. Increases in wage rates and tight labour markets could also encourage paternalist employers to develop labour retention and development strategies to upgrade skills and products.

As in Korea, though, the relocation of many plants overseas and some investment in downstream activities have been insufficient to 'internationalize' most Taiwanese companies in the sense of transferring their key activities and personnel out of Taiwan, and have not been accompanied by major foreign investment in the domestic economy – as distinct from the export processing zones. Similarly, although some firms such as Acer and Mitac have developed brand names and tried to move away from a concentration on own equipment manufacture (OEM) activities, their success has been mixed and their impact certainly not as marked as the Korean *chaebol* in North America and Europe. While state support for Taiwanese owned firms has increased in the 1980s and 1990s, especially in electronics (Wade, 1990), the state and the KMT still seem to dominate the heavy industry sectors of the economy, and firms employing less than ten people, including the self-employed, still employed 51.6 per cent of all employees in 1990 (Wilkinson, 1994, p.139). In contrast, those with over 500 employees accounted for 3.9 per cent of all employees then, although this figure rose to 9.5 per cent for manufacturing firms. There appears to be little evidence of a substantial Taiwanese *Mittelstand* (the medium sized company sector in Germany) becoming established, at least up to the early 1990s.

Similarly, the high degree of organizational specialization and considerable ownership diversification in the larger CFBs and business groups seem to have continued into the 1990s in Taiwan. The importance of entrepreneurial familism (Wong, 1988), and its associated low level of trust between owners and non-family employees – or employees with whom family-like relationships have not been established – remains considerable and discourages organizational integration of complementary economic activities. Relatedly, strong owner control, close supervision of work processes and a reliance on authoritarian paternalism as the prevalent way of managing labour relations seem to continue as distinctive features of Taiwanese enterprises which have encouraged the outflow of capital to China and elsewhere as Taiwanese workers became more expensive and demanding (Wilkinson, 1994, pp.142–3). As in Korea, many CFBs in Taiwan have preferred to export their dominant management style and work control practices to locations where constraints are less onerous than to develop new ways of managing. Additionally, when they have established manufacturing operations in Europe and North America, anecdotal evidence suggests they have been much less successful than Japanese firms, partly because of difficulties in adjusting to different managerial and workforce expectations.

Overall, then, the political changes in Taiwan and the increasing internationalization of some CFBs' operations do not yet appear to have been so substantial as to modify radically established patterns of management and development. Even where owner-managers have been educated abroad – as many Taiwanese engineers have been – and state support for industrial development has been considerable, as in the electronics and information technology industries, prevalent ways of managing risks and growth, and the labour force, remain dominant, and the traditional characteristics of CFBs continue to be reproduced in most Taiwanese firms (Deyo, 1989; Wilkinson, 1994). They seem unlikely to change significantly unless the nature of the Taiwanese family alters and the business environment becomes more formally regulated, such that owner-managers develop more trust in formal institutions and processes, as well as in long-term investment in key employees. While political risks in Taiwan have diminished, risks in both product and labour markets remain high for most firms, and risk-sharing institutions are only weakly developed. The pursuit of flexibility is likely therefore to remain a priority for most Taiwanese enterprises.

Conclusion

In sum, then, international and domestic changes in firms' environments have not resulted in significant alterations in the nature of these East-Asian business systems, and seem unlikely to do so without more radical transformations of their domestic institutions and agencies. Because of the distinctive nature of these institutions, incremental changes in firms and markets in Japan, Korea and Taiwan are most unlikely to result in them resembling Anglo-American ones, and so East Asia will continue to exhibit distinctive, but highly competitive, forms of economic organization which challenge Anglo-American ones.

References

Abegglen, J.C. and Stalk, G. (1985) *Kaisha, The Japanese Corporation*, New York, Basic Books.

Amsden, A.H. (1989) *Asia's Next Giant*, Oxford, Oxford University Press.

Aoki, M. (1988) *Information, Incentives, and Bargaining in the Japanese Economy*, Cambridge, Cambridge University Press.

Bae, K. (1987) *Automobile Workers in Korea*, Seoul, Seoul National University Press.

Chandler, A.D. (1990) *Scale and Scope*, Cambridge, MA, Harvard University Press.

Cho, S. (1994) *The Dynamics of Korean Economic Development*, Washington DC, Institute for International Economics.

Chung, K.H., Lee, H.C. and Okumura, A. (1988) 'The managerial practices of Korean, American and Japanese firms', *Journal of East and West Studies*, vol.17, pp.45–74.

Clark, R. (1979) *The Japanese Company*, New Haven, CT, Yale University Press.

Cusumano, M.A. (1985) *The Japanese Automobile Industry: Technology and Management at Nissan and Toyota*, Cambridge, MA, Harvard University Press.

Deyo, F.C. (1989) *Beneath the Miracle: Labour Subordination in the New Asian Industrialism*, Berkeley, University of California Press.

Dore, R.P. (1973) *British Factory – Japanese Factory*, London, Allen and Unwin.

Dore, R.P. (1986) *Flexible Rigidities*, Stanford, CA, Stanford University Press.

Fields, K.J. (1995) *Enterprise and the State in Korea and Taiwan*, Ithaca, NY, Cornell University Press.

Friedman, D. (1988) *The Misunderstood Miracle*, Ithaca, NY, Cornell University Press.

Gates, H. (1987) *Chinese Working Class Lives: Getting By in Taiwan*, Ithaca, NY, Cornell University Press.

Gereffi, G. (1996) 'Commodity chains and regional divisions of labour in East Asia', *Journal of Asian Business*, vol.12, pp.75–112.

Gerlach, M. (1992) *Alliance Capitalism*, Berkeley, CA, University of California.

Greenhalgh, S. (1984) 'Networks and their nodes: urban society in Taiwan', *The China Quarterly*, vol.99, pp.529–52.

Hamilton, G. and Biggart, N.W. (1988) 'Market, culture and authority: a comparative analysis of management and organization in the Far East', *American Journal of Sociology*, vol.94, supplement, pp.552–94.

Hamilton, G. and Kao, C.S. (1990) 'The institutional foundation of Chinese business: the family firm in Taiwan', *Comparative Social Research,* vol.12, pp.95–112.

Hollingsworth, R. (1991) 'The logic of co-ordinating American manufacturing sectors' in Campbell, J.L. *et al.* (eds) *Governance of the American Economy*, Cambridge, Cambridge University Press.

Janelli, R.L. (1993) *Making Capitalism: The Social and Cultural Construction of a South Korean Conglomerate*, Stanford, CA, Stanford University Press.

Kagono, T., Alonaka, I., Sakakibara, K. and Okumara, A. (1985) *Strategic vs. Evolutionary Management*, Amsterdam, North Holland.

Kao, C-S. (1991) 'Personal trust in the large businesses in Taiwan' in G. Hamilton (ed.) *Business Networks and Economic Development in East and Southeast Asia*, Centre of Asian Studies, University of Hong Kong.

Kim, C.S. (1992) *The Culture of Korean Industry*, Tucson, University of Arizona Press.

Kim, E.M. (1989) 'From dominance to symbiosis: state and *chaebol* in Korea', *Pacific Focus*, vol.3, pp.105–21.

Kim, E.M. (1991) 'The industrial organization and growth of the Korean *chaebol*' in Hamilton, G. (ed.) *Business Networks and Economic Development in East and Southeast Asia*, Centre of Asian Studies, University of Hong Kong.

Koike, K. (1987) 'Human resource development and labour–management relations' in Yamamura, K. and Yasuba, Y. (eds) *The Political Economy of Japan, Volume I*, Stanford, CA, Stanford University Press.

Koike, K. (1994) 'Learning and incentive systems in Japanese industry' in Aoki, M. and Dore, R. (eds) *The Japanese Firm*, Oxford, Oxford University Press.

Lincoln, J.R. and Kalleberg, A.L. (1990) *Culture, Control and Commitment*, Cambridge, Cambridge University Press.

Michell, T. (1988) *From a Developing to a Newly Industrialized Country: The Republic of Korea, 1961–82*, Geneva, International Labour Organization.

Odagiri, H. (1992) *Growth through Competition, Competition through Growth*, Oxford, Oxford University Press.

Orru, M., Biggart, N.W. and Hamilton, G. (1991) 'Organizational isomorphism in East Asia' in Powell, W.W. and DiMaggio, P.J. (eds) *The New Institutionalism in Organizational Analysis*, Chicago, IL, University of Chicago Press.

Redding, S.G. (1990) *The Spirit of Chinese Capitalism*, Berlin, de Gruyter.

Sako, M. (1992) *Prices, Quality and Trust*, Cambridge, Cambridge University Press.

Silin, R.H. (1976) *Leadership and Values: The Organization of Large Scale Taiwanese Enterprises*, Cambridge, MA, Harvard University Press.

Wade, R. (1990) *Governing the Market*, Princeton, NJ, Princeton University Press.

Westney, E. (1996) 'The Japanese business system: key features and prospects for changes', *Journal of Asian Business*, vol.12, pp.21–50.

Whitley, R. (1992a) *Business Systems in East Asia: Firms, Markets and Societies,* London, Sage.

Whitley, R. (ed.) (1992b) *European Business Systems: Firms and Markets in their National Contexts*, London, Sage.

Whitley, R. (1996) 'Business systems and global commodity chains: competing or complementary forms of economic organization?', *Competition and Change*, vol.1, pp.411–25.

Wilkinson, B. (1994) *Labour and Industry in the Asia-Pacific*, Berlin, de Gruyter.

Wong, S-L. (1988) 'The applicability of Asian family values to other sociocultural settings' in Berger, P.L. and Hsiao, H-H.M. (eds) *In Search of an East Asian Development Model*, New Brunswick, NJ, Transaction Books.

Woo, Yung-En (1991) *Race to the Swift*, New York, Columbia University Press.

You, Jong-il (1994) 'Labour institutions and economic development in the Republic of Korea' in Rodgers, G. (ed.) *Workers, Institutions and Economic Growth in Asia*, Geneva, International Labour Organization.

Zeile, W. (1991) 'Industrial policy and organizational efficiency: the Korean *chaebol* examined' in Hamilton, G. (ed.) *Business Networks and Economic Development in East and Southeast Asia*, Centre of Asian Studies, University of Hong Kong.

CHAPTER 10

Technological systems, innovation and transfers

Brendan Barker and Akira Goto

10.1 Introduction

Throughout the Asia-Pacific region technology is seen as the driving force behind national economic competitiveness. Led by the USA and Japan and more recently by Taiwan, South Korea, and Singapore – countries in the region have invested heavily to enhance their scientific and technological (S&T) capability. In this chapter we first look at the relationship between technology and economic growth (see also Chapter 3). We argue that the technological capability of the Asia-Pacific region countries has been enhanced both by public sector policies designed to promote S&T, and as a result of the activities of firms undertaking research and development (R&D) and technology acquisition in pursuit of their own competitive goals.

We introduce the concept of a *national system of innovation* which has proved useful in comparing the key characteristics of the systems of national institutions and policies supporting technology development and innovation in different countries. In our analysis of these systems we make a distinction between Asian-Pacific systems (i.e. Japan, the NIEs and the ASEAN countries) the Euro-Pacific systems (i.e. the USA, Australia, Mexico, etc.), and China as a special case.

In the following section we look at flows of technology and knowledge between countries in the region which leads us on to discuss the emergence of a regional system of innovation. In the final section, we briefly look at the relationship between the Pacific region and the global economy.

10.2 Technology and economic growth

The major part of technological progress today occurs as a result of the intense *research and development* (R&D) activity undertaken by industry. Most of this effort is guided by market needs. R&D has two facets; one is to create new knowledge, the other is to create *technological capability* which is of critical importance when firms try to learn technology developed elsewhere.

As the product of R&D is knowledge, there is an inherent problem of *externality*.

Box 10.1 Externality

Externality refers to the way that the activity of one economic agent has effects on another that should not, or cannot, be ignored by the first. The most important of these in market systems is when the 'external effects' of the actions do not pass through the price system and register as a market transaction. There are two major types of externality: negative and positive.

A *negative externality* arises when one action has negative effects on other agents, though the agent that causes these *negative costs* does not have to pay for the damage done. As an example we can point to the way that pollution arising from car exhaust fumes affects pedestrians, but the car driver is not responsible for the added 'cost' incurred by those pedestrians.

A *positive externality* arises when the activity has external affects which produce a benefit to others, but when the agent responsible for those benefits cannot gain financial reward for them. This is the case with R&D activity and technological development. These can produce *spillover benefits* to society at large, which are not taken into account as compensation to that company or agent that produces the benefit. Sometimes this is expressed as an *external social benefit* which is more than the purely *private benefits* accruing to the firm.

While it takes a large amount of time and money to create new knowledge, it can easily be transmitted and copied at little extra cost. In one sense, it is socially desirable that the new knowledge, once created, is used as widely as possible. However, if individual firms are unable to *appropriate* (gain the benefit of) the fruits of their costly R&D, they will have less incentive to invest in R&D. The intellectual property system (e.g. patents) is designed to solve this problem by providing some protection to innovators.

Even with such protection, there are many ways for technology to 'spill-over'. Firms and countries can 'reverse engineer' advanced products (dismantling a competitors' products to learn about the technology embodied in them); they can send their own researchers and engineers to other countries or invite foreign researchers from other countries; they can subscribe to journals or attend conferences; they can learn through licensing agreements; they can learn from the plants established by developed country companies in their countries, etc. Most of these activities are informal and not reflected in R&D and technology trade statistics, which cover only a small part of innovative activity.

The inherent externality of technological knowledge makes it a very difficult 'good' to trade. Usually, the best way for a firm to profit from its superior technology is to manufacture and sell a product (or to employ a process) using that technology. For this reason, the successful exploitation of an innovation requires investment in complementary assets, such as a manufacturing facility or sales network, in addition to the initial investment in the R&D itself. It follows that a stable and innovation-friendly macroeconomic environment is a necessary condition for successful innovation to both occur and be exploited.

With this theoretical framework in mind, we now look at the issues surrounding technological progress and economic growth in the Asia-Pacific region. First, East Asian countries have been, and remain, among the most rapidly growing in the world. The reasons for this extraordinary growth have been the subject of much study and often heated debate (see Chapters 3, 4 and 6 in particular). A reasonable conclusion would appear to be that growth in the region has been driven both by increased inputs (e.g. larger, more highly skilled workforces, greater capital investment) and by the increasing use of new technology which has allowed those inputs to be used more effectively (Chapter 3). The relative importance of these sources of growth may differ among countries and over time.

The second issue relates to the question of who are the major players in this process of technological progress and economic growth. Again, there are two camps. The first contends that the leading role was played by government. The second asserts that market mechanism and competition drove technological and economic development. Once again, these two are not substitutes (Chapter 6). The market mechanism functions in the institutional, social, political and cultural context of any country. In most North-East Asian countries the government played a major role by establishing the institutional framework (such as property rights) and a healthy macro environment (low inflation and government deficits, and a reasonable exchange rate) that allowed innovative activities to be rewarded. More directly, governments also played an important role in defining and implementing industrial policy – particularly with regard to promoting technology-intensive industries. The success of such policies in supporting economic growth has been questioned (we return to this later).

The third issue relates to the nature of technology mentioned above. In spite of attempts to protect new technology by patenting etc., it is still relatively easily transferred. Economic studies indicate the significance of such *R&D spillovers*. Coe, Helpman and Hoffmaister have shown that an addition of US$100 to either the US or Japanese domestic R&D stock raises total GDP in the 77 developing countries as a group by almost US$25 (Coe, Helpman and Hoffmaister, 1995).

Latecomer firms and countries have an advantage in that they can learn and use technology already developed elsewhere. We have already noted that there are many ways in which this learning can occur. For countries that are latecomers to industrialization, learning by borrowing and improving on technologies already developed by firms in more advanced economies has proved to be the most important path to rapid economic growth (Amsden, 1989). To learn and become capable of using advanced technology, the receiving country has to have the capability to do so. In the East Asian countries, well developed education systems and a degree of openness were the background to their capability to learn (Chapter 2).

These characteristics have often been absent in developing countries in other regions and are one reason for the difficulty in replicating the East Asian success story.

It is not surprising therefore that developed countries prefer strong intellectual protection while developing countries prefer a less stringent regime. In recent years this has been a source of friction between developed and developing countries in the region (the disputes in the early 1990s between the USA and China over intellectual property rights being a case in point).

10.3 National systems of innovation

The rate and direction of technical change both shapes and is shaped by the institutional and policy environment in a country. Different national technological and institutional environments have been investigated in an effort to understand why technological change appears to occur more rapidly and efficiently in some countries than in others. One fruitful avenue of research recognizes that innovation takes place in 'systems' of public and private institutions and the linkages between those institutions.

It is through such systems that new knowledge is generated and, together with existing knowledge, comes to be applied. This perspective led to the concept of a *national system of innovation* (NSI) (Freeman, 1988; Lundvall, 1992; Nelson, 1994). A 'national system of innovation' consists of those *organizations, institutions and linkages in a specific country which generate, diffuse and apply scientific and technological knowledge*. The NSI concept begins with an assumption that national competitive performance depends on the technological capabilities of a nation's firms. The ability of these firms to innovate depends on their own capabilities and on their interactions with various external sources of knowledge, facilities and financing. Countries which facilitate these linkages are more likely to flourish than those which do not. (This NSI concept to some extent parallels the concept of a national business system discussed in Chapter 9.)

The NSI concept is not without its critics: indeed, the use of the terms 'national', 'innovation' and 'system' have all been questioned. Nelson addresses these concerns in a review of the seminal 1994 study on NSI he co-ordinated (Nelson, 1996). He accepts that, on the one hand the concept of 'national' may be too broad and on the other too limited. Many innovation systems appear to be *sectorally specific* with different patterns of interaction between sectors in a national context. At the same time many of these innovation systems spill over national boundaries reflecting the fact that scientific and technological activity is increasingly international in its creation and dissemination – in part because of the role of multinational corporations and in part because of the growing importance of international collaborative links between researchers (Chapter 8). Nevertheless, there remain significant differences in the way each country achieves innovation and there is enough commonality across sectors within a country to make the national focus a reasonable one. Furthermore, it is still at the national level that science and technology policy is primarily defined and implemented.

Nelson also addresses definitional problems with the terms 'innovation' and 'system'. Innovation is often taken to mean the first to do something. In the NSI context the term is usually used in a much broader sense to 'encompass the processes by which firms master and set into practice product designs and manufacturing processes that are *new to them*'. Thus innovation in this context is taken to mean both the creation of new knowledge and the exploitation of existing knowledge from other sources inside and outside of the country. Similarly, the term 'system' is used in a more general sense than when it is taken to mean something that is consciously designed and built. In the context of a NSI, the concept is used to refer to the set of institutions whose interactions determine the innovative performance of national firms – including the educational system, the attitudes of firms, the form of the financial system, role of governmental organizations. In this context that is no presumption that the system has been consciously designed or even that it works effectively or coherently.

Comparative studies have attempted to identify structural differences between NSI that promote or hamper innovation in different countries. Work, such as the 1994 Nelson study mentioned above, attempts to describe, analyse and compare the key processes and institutional actors involved – industry, university, government, etc. identifying the similarities and differences of these national systems, and the extent to which such patterns can explain the variation of national economic performance.

In most economies the private sector is the main source of technology development and transfer (see Table 10.1, column 3). The public sector however, plays an important role in monitoring, and participating with, the private sector. Governments support innovation directly, by conducting and paying for R&D, and indirectly, through measures that encourage R&D and commercialization by private firms. National systems of innovation are distinguished in part by the mix of these policies at a given point in time, and in part by persisting patterns of industrial and institutional structures and relationships that form the context for particular cases of innovation and set limits to the policies governments can pursue in the short and medium terms. Each country's technological progress is conditioned by the institutional settings and past historical developments of the country, and these factors are affected by the pattern of innovation of the country at the same time. In other words, technology and institution co-evolve over time and form a unique national innovation system.

National innovation systems can be categorized in several different ways. For convenience we divide systems in the Asia-Pacific region up into those nations with a European heritage (e.g. the USA, Australia, New Zealand); Japan and the NIEs (South Korea, Taiwan, Singapore, Hong Kong); and the remaining 'ASEAN' countries (Brunei, Thailand, Malaysia,

Indonesia, the Philippines and Vietnam) and China. Several caveats are in order regarding this classification. Despite some similarities, there exist significant differences between the countries within each of these categories. The European Asia-Pacific grouping for instance includes some of the richest countries in the world as well as some of the poorest, some of these countries have political and legal traditions rooted in England and France, others a blend of Spanish and indigenous civilizations. Similarly, in spite of much talk of 'shared Asian values', differences between the NIEs and Japan and between the NIEs themselves are no less apparent. This diversity is also true of the ASEAN countries – particularly Vietnam which still maintains a communist government. China is in a class of its own – both because of its size and its unique features.

'European' Asia-Pacific nations

In the category of European Asia-Pacific nations we include the USA, Canada, Australia and New Zealand – together, more problematically, with the Pacific Central and South American countries such as Mexico and Chile. Typically these countries each have a strong, higher education system and a well developed market economy. Traditionally these countries have looked towards Europe for cultural, scientific, and economic links. However, with the growth of East Asia as a major economic region they have become increasingly integrated with the rest of the Asia-Pacific region. All European Asia-Pacific countries are fostering closer S&T and industry ties with the rest of the Asia-Pacific.

Of the European Asia-Pacific countries, the USA is unique in several respects. The sheer size of its economy and R&D expenditure (see Table 10.1) are unparalleled. Large military and medical sectors have driven the development of technologically advanced products. Much research activity is centred on the higher education sector which has also been a particularly successful incubator of highly innovative research oriented firms. This success in commercializing academic research has been supported by an effective venture capital sector which encourages start-up firms. However, US industry has not always been successful in exploiting this strong research base.

In common with the USA, Canada, Australia and New Zealand also have strong basic research traditions. However, in recent years there has also been a growing feeling that high public investment in science has not produced an adequate return in terms of enhanced national competitiveness. New Zealand, in particular, has responded with a comprehensive restructuring of public sector research to foster greater competitiveness and has prioritized its relatively small resource base towards research on agriculture based manufacturing. There have been similar (although less radical) changes in the structure of the Australian science and technology system in an attempt to make both academic and public sector research more competitive and targeted towards commercial outcomes whilst at the same time building business participation in R&D.

Table 10.1 R&D statistics for selected countries in the Pacific region (year?)

	R&D expenditure (million ECU)	R&D as % of GDP (1992)	% R&D Expenditure by Sector of Performance			Number of scientists and engineers (1993)	Share of world scientific papers (1981–84)	Share of US patents (1993)	High technology trade (million ECU)	
			Business	H.Education	Government				Imports (1992)	Exports (1992)
USA	112,503 (1993)	2.67	69.6	15.8	10.8	887,600	34.6	50.1	192,248	172,066
Canada	5,658 (1993)	1.45	55.0	26.0	17.0	66,502	4.5	2.2	49,029	41,360
Mexico	776 (1989)	0.31	52.6	14.4	11.6	8,595	0.3	0.1	17,850	7,209
Chile	434 (1992)	0.78	12.0	44.6	42.4	5,956	0.2	0.0	3,143	285
Australia	2,811 (1990)	1.56	44.2	26.9	27.6	78,538	2.1	0.4	14,361	2,565
New Zealand	280 (1992)	0.98	28.0	31.0	41.0	NA	0.4	0.0	3,231	387
Japan	44,237 (1993)	2.92	66.0	20.1	9.3	753,870	7.3	24.2	37,269	180,778
South Korea	5,176 (1991)	2.33	71.5	7.2	4.4	90,328	0.2	0.9	22,857	22,760
Taiwan	2,331 (1992)	1.82	52.6	14.4	11.6	33,179	0.4	1.4	NA	NA
Singapore	401 (1993)	1.12	62.0	15.8	22.2	9,725	0.1	0.0	26,387	27,139
Hong Kong	NA	0.08	47.6	19.6	32.7	NA	0.2	0.1	36,711	8,282
Malaysia	73 (1989)	0.37	45.8	9.0	46.0	NA	0.1	0.0	15,731[1]	11,095[1]
Thailand	342 (1991)	0.16	5.0	20.2	69.6	NA	0.1	0.0	13,492	5,420[1]
The Philippines	110 (1984)	0.21	21.8	14.7	58.8	5,344	0.0	0.0	3,907	1,408
Indonesia	980 (1993)	0.26	13.0	4.0	81.0	66,668	0.0	0.0	8,566	1,296
China	16,917 (1993)	0.6	22.7	17.7	49.9	418,500	0.9	0.1	29,158	12,064

Notes: [1] = 1991

NA = Not available

Sources: Turpin and Spence (1996 various pages); *European Report on Science and Technology Indicators 1994*, EUR 15897 ZN NSF; *Human Resources for Science and Technology: The Asian Region*, NSF93–303

Central and South American countries face many problems as they attempt to emulate the rapid growth seen in East Asia. With the recent exception of Chile these countries have not been able to create a supportive macroeconomic environment, have little or no active technology policy, have little money to invest in R&D and lack the comprehensive policies for human capital development, all of which were characteristics of the development policies adopted by the East Asian NIEs during the 1950s and 1960s.

'Asian' Asia-Pacific nations

Japan experienced a very high rate of economic growth in the 1950s and 1960s followed by the NIEs (South Korea, Taiwan, Singapore, and Hong Kong) in the 1970s and 1980s. A very active private sector and, except for Hong Kong, active government policy to promote the private sector were the twin engines of this rapid growth. The East Asian-Pacific nations were particularly successful in learning, adapting and exploiting the advanced technology of the developed countries. This effective learning process was supported by the national emphasis on education in these countries. Learning was a prerequisite for firms in these countries to compete effectively in their domestic and export markets.

The governments in these countries maintained a basically healthy macroeconomic policy, i.e. low rate of inflation, low government deficit, and realistic exchange rate, which created an environment favourable for economic growth (Chapters 2 and 4). The governments also used industrial policy to promote specific targeted industries such as steel, auto, and electronics employing such means as protecting the domestic market, providing finance on favourable terms, providing subsidies and other financial incentives, and giving assistance to domestic firms to acquire technology from foreign firms. At the same time, the savings rate in these countries rose rapidly along with the high economic growth, which in turn allowed investment in new advanced plant and equipment (Chapter 3).

The effectiveness of the industrial policy followed by these countries during their development phase remains an open and hotly debated question. It is true that most of the targeted industries grew rapidly and became very competitive in world markets. However, there were also industries which became internationally successful without government help, such as the manufacture of VCRs and facsimile machines in Japan. There are also other industries which, in spite of massive government support have failed to become internationally competitive. For instance, Japan's aircraft manufacturing industry has been a future 'key industry' for more than two decades, with little to show for high levels of public investment. Similarly, the World Bank contends that South Korea's promotion of 'heavy and chemical industries' in the 1970s was associated with a substantial cost to the economy as a whole and wasted precious resources that could have been better used elsewhere (Chapter 6). Nevertheless it remains true that economies in the region were remarkably successful in creating the conditions for rapid and sustained growth. In many ways the emphasis on R&D and technological development in those countries was driven by strategic reasons. The governments wanted to secure their *economic* health as a bulwark against military and possibly economic competition from mainly Communist powers.

Japan is the dominant science and technology power in East Asia (see Table 10.1). The nation has traditionally depended on its industrial sector to take the leading role in R&D, while the university sector has played less of a role in generating new knowledge than is the case in the USA. Nevertheless, Japanese universities played a significant (although often overlooked) role in aiding industry to acquire and exploit new technology. The university sector in Japan continues to be an important source of high quality talent and links into both the national and international scientific communities. Now that Japan has caught up with, and in many areas of technology surpassed, the other industrialized nations, there is a recognition that Japan must focus more on the creation of new fundamental knowledge. In the 1990s attention was being paid to significantly upgrading the research infrastructure and quality of research carried out in the universities and national research institutes.

Like Japan, South Korea also has a strongly industry-based science infrastructure: half of the approximately 1,000 research institutions in the country are in private industry and half of these are heavily concentrated in the ten largest *chaebol* (industrial conglomerates), particularly within the electronics and chemical industries (Table 10.1). Like Japan before it, a traditional reliance on reverse engineering of imported technologies is now being replaced by more indigenous knowledge creation – with an increasing emphasis on more fundamental long-term research.

Central to current innovation strategies in both Japan and South Korea is the internationalization of the R&D base. South Korean industry is now following similar internationalizing strategies to that in Japan in establishing laboratories in the West. Domestic and international co-operative R&D ventures in both countries are being encouraged.

Compared to the breadth of technological development supported in Japan and South Korea, Taiwan and Singapore have been successful in particular niches. Although, for strategic reasons, Taiwan has a number of large, state-owned industries which are not internationally competitive, it also has a very dynamic sector of small and medium-sized companies which act primarily as suppliers to US and Japanese multinational electronics companies. A different strategy is being followed by the Singaporean government which has given particular encouragement to multinational corporations to locate their higher value-added activities in Singapore.

The ASEAN countries

In the 1980s, Japan and South Korea started to actively invest overseas – to be joined subsequently in these investments by the largely ethnic Chinese entrepreneurs of Hong Kong, Singapore and Taiwan who brought much needed technology and management expertise (see next section). The major destination of this foreign direct investment was other parts of East Asia such as the ASEAN countries and China where wage levels were lower and markets expanding rapidly as the economies grew. This investment supported domestic activities designed to enhance the indigenous knowledge base.

For instance, although Malaysia had a well established public research institute base, this was primarily oriented towards agriculture – a legacy of the prior British colonial administration. A current priority is to strengthen institutional capacity and to enhancing industry–public sector linkages. Industry is seen as the source of future growth in national R&D activity. Similarly, Thailand places a high priority in further stimulating growth in private sector R&D involvement as well as in expanding international S&T collaboration as a way of strengthening national capability. Strong support is being given to generic technologies – microelectronics, information technology and biotechnology.

Human resource development is a high priority in both Malaysia and Thailand. Similarly, both the Philippines and Indonesia recognize the importance of education and training if they are to effectively capture international flows of technical and economic capital. However, in the Philippines, where the culture is more Westernized through prior American influence and literacy rates are very high, the brain drain is a significant problem. The Philippines planned to produce an additional 3,000 scientists and engineers by 1998, while at the same time strengthening and upgrading the S&T infrastructure.

Indonesia is still at a comparatively early stage of technological transformation of the economy. Nearly three quarters of total manufacturing output is in industries featuring products with a low-technology intensity. Consequently, small scale industry and the informal sector are prioritized for support. In parallel however, development of sophisticated technological capabilities within 'strategic' industries such as aeronautics, energy and electronics, is being supported as a means to 'pull' the economy out of its developing country status.

Finally, although Vietnam joined ASEAN in 1995, it has a political system that is very different from, and is at a stage of development that is well behind, that of the other ASEAN countries.

China

China is unique in several respects. First and foremost the country is huge. Thus while the proportion of scientists and engineers to the rest of the working population is relatively low, the absolute number is large (Table 10.1). In addition, although per capita GDP is low, a well developed technological infrastructure has been created to underpin an advanced military sector. Because of this technologically sophisticated sector, the absorptive capacity of the country is high in a way which is not true for other countries at a comparable developmental stage.

To sustain growth China must address a number of critical problems. Decentralization will liberate the wealth-creating potential of those provinces favourably located on the Asia-Pacific seaboard. However, this has led to large disparities in wealth which is causing significant tensions between regions in China and the central government. The continued move toward market-based institutions will require reform of the financial sector and state enterprises – which increasingly act as a major drag on the rest of the economy. The recent handover of Hong Kong has created yet more pressures.

Convergence in systems

In recent years there has been growing convergence between countries in the region. For instance, many aspects of Japanese manufacturing systems are becoming globalized (e.g. 'just in time' inventory control, total quality management, extensive subcontracting and more besides). These tend to embody a particular process technology. At the same time many traditional Japanese practices are breaking down in the face of global competition – for instance, lifetime employment. The East Asian-Pacific countries – particularly the more advanced ones – are beginning to place greater emphasis on supporting more fundamental research. At the same time, a number of the European Asia-Pacific countries have begun to prioritize their research in terms of national requirements in a way that has been explicitly modelled on what is believed to happen in the East Asian-Pacific countries.

A major reason for this convergence is the increasing regionalization of innovation systems. National systems of innovation are embedded within the international economy, linked with one another through flows of capital and labour, goods and services (e.g. high technology equipment, consultancy), information and knowledge (e.g. collaborative scientific research) (see Chapters 8 and 14). The R&D process itself is becoming more internationalized. Large multinationals are finding it to their advantage to undertake various aspects of the innovation process in different countries. Furthermore, the costs and risks of undertaking large, expensive R&D projects are increasingly beyond the scope of individual enterprises, leading to a range of international collaborative links between different organizations.

In a later section we look at how these regional systems of innovation are developing. First we examine the flows of technology in the region which are underpinning the emergence of these systems.

10.4 Technology flows

A triangular relationship of technology transfer exists among the USA, Japan, and the Asian NIEs and ASEAN countries (see also Chapter 2). The USA has created various types of new scientific and technological knowledge, which has been diffused to other countries including Japan, the Asian NIEs, and ASEAN countries. Japan and the East Asian countries